MINDS, MACHINES AND EVOLUTION

Minds, machines and evolution

Philosophical studies

edited by Christopher Hookway

Lecturer in Philosophy
University of Birmingham

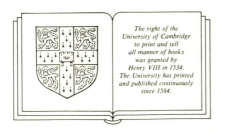

CAMBRIDGE UNIVERSITY PRESS

CAMBRIDGE

LONDON   NEW YORK   NEW ROCHELLE

MELBOURNE   SYDNEY

Published by the Press Syndicate of the University of Cambridge
The Pitt Building, Trumpington Street, Cambridge CB2 1RP
32 East 57th Street, New York, NY 10022, USA
P.O. Box 85, Oakleigh, Victoria 3166, Australia

© Cambridge University Press 1984

First published 1984

Printed in Great Britain at the University Press, Cambridge

Library of Congress catalogue card number: 84-11321

ISBN 0 521 26547 9

British Library Cataloguing in Publication Data
Minds, machines and evolution
1. Intellect   2. Genetic psychology
I. Hookway, Christopher
153.9   BF431
ISBN 0 521 26547 9

CE

Contents

Contributors

Margaret Boden is Professor of Philosophy and Psychology at the University of Sussex.

Daniel Dennett is Professor of Philosophy at Tufts University.

Christopher Hookway is lecturer in Philosophy at the University of Birmingham

David Hull is Distinguished Professor in the Department of Philosophy of the University of Wisconsin – Milwaukee.

John Maynard Smith is Dean of the School of Biology at the University of Sussex.

Elliott Sober is a member of the Department of Philosophy of the University of Wisconsin – Madison.

Neil Tennant is Professor of Philosophy at the University of Stirling.

Yorick Wilks is Professor in the Department of Language and Linguistics at the University of Essex.

Introduction

Since the publication of the *Origin of Species* in 1859, it has been recognized that the theory of evolution through natural selection has massive implications for our understanding of the properties and capacities of human beings. From the nineteenth-century Social Darwinists to modern defenders of sociobiology, thinkers have hailed a new science of man based upon a naturalistic view of *homo sapiens* as an animal subject to evolution through processes of this kind. The hope has been that such a theory could account for the full range of human mental and intellectual characteristics. Since natural selection allowed for naturalistic explanations of, for example, goal-directed patterns of behaviour in animals which were more complex than anything that could be accommodated by earlier naturalistic or physicalist doctrines, it was natural to hope that human behaviour, although much more complex than that of animals, could be explained in the same general fashion; we can understand the mind by seeing it as the product of evolution. Thought and consciousness are not irreducibly mental phenomena which inevitably escape the net of physical or biological explanation, but are rather determined by complex biological and physical processes. This might involve the claim that the most perspicuous vocabulary for describing and explaining mental phenomena is explicitly drawn from evolutionary biology. But it can also be captured in a less reductionist claim: a description of a mental capacity is unsatisfactory if it cannot be shown how a capacity of that kind could have evolved through natural selection. Either way, the view places a substantial constraint upon our understanding of *homo sapiens*, and, at the same time, holds out the hope of an exciting new source of scientific knowledge of mind and its place in nature. Consequently there is now a substantial literature that explores the evolutionary origins of particular human capacities, and attempts to pin down more precisely just how our capacities differ from those of animals – for example by showing that ethological models adequate for the study of animal behaviour may not be sufficiently sophisticated for explaining human behaviour. Such studies are important even for those who do not share the naturalistic perspective which informs many – but not all – of them. If someone supposes that there is an irreducible residue of the mental which cannot be accounted for in naturalistic terms, information about what *can* be explained in virtue of the fact that we are organisms that have developed through natural selection is required if we are to come to an informed clarification of just what that residue is.

Since the 1950s, philosophical speculation about the mind had been largely guided by a different, although related, naturalistic model – that of the computer. We naturally talk of computers reasoning and remembering, of the tasks and calculations that they perform, and it is clear that they can be brought to simulate a wide variety of human intellectual accomplishments. In cognitive psychology and Artificial Intelligence, there has been the assumption that computer models of our capacities provide illuminating descriptions or analyses of those capacities. Since the robot or computer is 'just a machine' this too supports a naturalist or physicalist view – if a machine can simulate our mental activity, then our mental activity cannot be taken to show that we are more than very complicated physical objects. This development is complementary to that produced by the theory of natural selection. Traits and capacities are selected for because of their functions, because of the way their effects contribute to the ability of the organism to survive and reproduce and to nurture its young. Accounts of states and capacities provided within Artificial Intelligence similarly allude to the function of the states and capacities – they show how they enable the agent to utilize available resources to solve particular problems. The close relations between the two models are discussed in the early chapters of Dennett's *Content and Consciousness* (Dennett 1969); and it emerges again in his paper in this volume, when he argues that the claim of a computer simulation to explain how we perform a task must be rejected if it can be shown that the practice of performing the task in that way could not be the product of natural selection.

The papers in this volume are concerned with problems that arise within the kinds of approaches to the understanding of behaviour that I have just outlined. Some deal with general issues about the sorts of explanations that are provided when we make use of the theory of natural selection or the techniques of Artificial Intelligence. Others deal with the application of such models to the explanation of animal and human behaviour, with a particular stress upon the problems raised by consciousness and on what can be learned about the differing capacities of animals and people.

My own paper is more purely philosophical than the others, but it deals in general terms with some aspects of the issue of naturalism. It is particularly concerned with the role of naturalistic models of human cognitive capacities in logic and epistemology, by contrasting the views of two American 'pragmatist' philosophers, both of whom attach importance to science, evolutionary biology and psychology. The first of these, Charles S. Peirce, insisted that epistemology was wholly prior to the natural sciences and should make use of no material drawn from their investigation. The second, W. V. O. Quine, holds that the role of traditional epistemology has been usurped by evolutionary biology and psychology. The paper explores the differing conceptions of truth and rationality which ground the two approaches.

The remaining papers deal more directly with philosophical issues in biology and Artificial Intelligence. The first two of these explore the character of explanation through natural selection. David Hull argues that species, the subjects of evolutionary change, should not be viewed as natural kinds or classes, but rather as historical individuals – individuals which exist in space and time and change or evolve through time. It is a consequence of this that there are no universal laws which apply to all and only the members of a particular species. When we explain the behaviour of a species by reference to natural selection, he urges, what we do should not be assimilated to explanations in the physical sciences employing the familiar covering law model. Rather, these explanations resemble those produced by historians. Moreover, since there cannot be a science which articulates laws governing the behaviour of all members of a single species, Hull's view has consequences for our understanding of the human and social sciences. General laws may have a role in explaining human behaviour, but, if a science is understood as involving a body of laws, there cannot be a distinctively human science. Freud's theories, for example, must be viewed as part of an historical description of the species *homo sapiens*, and not as an attempt to construct universal laws governing the human psyche.

There has recently been extensive debate about the unit of selection – whether traits become widespread only when they benefit individual organisms, or whether they may be selected for because they benefit a larger group; a third influential view is that traits are selected for because they benefit individual genes. Elliott Sober attempts to expose some errors which are present in many of the arguments for group selection or genic selection. He is chiefly concerned to insist that selection is a causal process, and that fitness is a real disposition, so that the issue of at what level selection occurs concerns the causal processes that it involves. From the fact that natural selection leads to the spread of a particular gene in the population, it does not follow that the gene was 'selected *for*'. Examining metaphors and arguments employed by the defenders of genic selection, he shows that they fail to see the consequences of this point.

John Maynard Smith describes two important ideas in recent work on the social behaviour of animals: kin selection and evolutionary game theory. The former considers how a gene may spread in a population because it benefits those related to the animal that has it, even where it reduces the individual fitness of the animal itself. Evolutionary game theory considers how phenotypes evolve when their fitness depends crucially upon the kinds of responses made by others, and applies techniques drawn from ordinary game theory to study this. Maynard Smith displays some of the applications of these ideas, and uses them to indicate some of the differences between the capacities of animals and people – there are game theoretic solutions to problems available to people which are not available to animals.

Neil Tennant's paper provides a wide ranging speculation on the evolutionary origin of language. In the first part of his paper, he considers what differentiates human language from simpler forms of animal 'communication', and attempts to link the evolution of recursive syntactic structure to the capacity for complex higher-order communicative intentions: it is because we can have a reflexive understanding of our communicative activity that we can come to use structured communicative systems. The second part of the paper draws from an examination of experiments on chimp language the conclusion that 'recursively structured language' is 'a unique accomplishment of our species', and considers some different explanations of this result.

The remaining papers are primarily concerned with Artificial Intelligence. Yorick Wilks introduces a number of concepts from computer science which, he suggests, might be used to formulate an account of some of the most familiar features of consciousness and self-consciousness, such as privacy and the unity of consciousness. He uses this discussion as the basis for a critical discussion of the accounts of consciousness and self-consciousness offered by other philosophers interested in Artificial Intelligence. One of the philosophers whose views are discussed by Wilks is Daniel Dennett, the author of the next paper, 'Cognitive Wheels'. He provides a philosophical discussion of the problem that researchers in Artificial Intelligence refer to as the 'frame problem' – roughly, the problem of how we are able to engage so efficiently in fallible *ceteris paribus* reasoning. Having introduced philosophers to what he thinks is an issue of general epistemological interest that has emerged from research in Artificial Intelligence, Dennett surveys some of the responses to it found in the literature, and draws the general moral that Artificial Intelligence has a tendency to rely upon proposals that are 'profoundly unbiological', that could not have emerged through natural selection.

The final paper, by Margaret Boden, brings together the themes of Artificial Intelligence and the understanding of animal behaviour; she investigates how the cognitive models employed in AI can be used to help us to understand the perceptual capacities of animals. Explaining a variety of recently developed ideas in the field, she discusses the issue of when a computer simulation of a form of behaviour can be taken to illuminate the cognitive processes going on within the organism whose behaviour is being studied, and she defends the view that AI can help us to understand the phenomenological character of experience.

The papers derive from a series of conferences held by the Thyssen Philosophy Group in 1981–2, financed through grants from the Fritz Thyssen Stiftung. On behalf of the group, I should like to express our thanks to the Fritz Thyssen Stiftung and to its director, Professor Dr Rudolf Kerscher, for their support.

Christopher Hookway

REFERENCE

Dennett, D.C. 1969, *Content and Consciousness*, London.

Naturalism, fallibilism and evolutionary epistemology

CHRISTOPHER HOOKWAY

In response to the failure of a number of attempts to provide foundations for certain knowledge of empirical facts, many epistemologists have tried to defend various forms of fallibilism. They hold that we may, with justification, be certain of beliefs which, we admit, risk falsification, or that we may be justified in holding beliefs although there are none of which we are certain. In all cases, a central theme is that the failure of the project of providing foundations for knowledge does not warrant scepticism. Along with this has often gone a general rejection of the idea of a First Philosophy, more secure than, or prior to, the sciences, and an acceptance of the naturalistic doctrine that a philosophical account of knowledge should be permitted to use empirical information drawn from the sciences. A more indirect borrowing from the sciences has been the use of evolutionary models, derived from the theory of natural selection, to describe or explain how fallible knowledge can grow. Various aspects of these topics will be considered in this paper, which falls into three parts. In the first, I discuss the relations between fallibilism and naturalism by examining the opposition to naturalism of the pragmatist, C. S. Peirce, and the way that he reconciles this with his fallibilism. The second section examines the claims of Quine to have 'naturalized epistemology', and the third offers some brief critical remarks on the evolutionary epistemology of Donald Campbell.

I. FALLIBILISM AND NATURALISM

The denial of naturalism carries with it the recognition of the possibility of an epistemology which is prior to all of the special sciences, and which can make no use of general or particular facts about nature. There are questions about knowledge which may, or must, be answered using limited resources, although there is disagreement about what the available resources are. For instance, if it is supposed that some of our perceptual judgements have a form of intrinsic credibility, and if a set of canons of rationality can be justified without recourse to the special sciences – they are analytic, self-evident, or a conventionally adopted linguistic framework – then it may be possible to trace the credibility of all rational beliefs to that possessed by this foundation. If a reductive programme of this kind is possible, we may be tempted to provide a rational reconstruction of our knowledge which shows how the credibility of derived claims can be traced to that of the foundation. The epistemological importance of such an exercise is evident, as is the fact that care would have to be taken to avoid circularity, to ensure that we did not make the credibility of a claim to knowledge depend upon beliefs that were not in the foundation. This suggests, perhaps, that the need for a prior epistemology depends, not on the character of the general questions which epistemology starts from, but rather from the kinds of solutions which, in this case, are offered – namely reductive ones. If we are sceptical that an evidential base with intrinsic credibility and a isolatable and justifiable conception of rationality can be found, then we might try to tackle the same problems non-reductively, in which case anti-naturalist scruples seem out of place. This suspicion is supported by the remarks of many fallibilist and pragmatist philosophers about scepticism. It is only if we are in the grip of a mistaken conception of truth that the mere possibility of a belief being mistaken carries with it the threat of scepticism; it is an indication that the sceptic's conception of truth is not ours that his arguments do not prompt an epistemic crisis. There are many things that we are certain of and, although it might be useful to *try* to doubt these certainties, we should not pretend to doubt what we do not doubt in our hearts. Consequently, unless we are convinced of the possibility of a reductive account of knowledge, let us not tie our hands by refusing to make use of facts that we know to be true. This style of argument is frequently found in Peirce's writings, so we should expect him to make use of materials from psychology and biology in his writings on knowledge.[1] However, perhaps the most distinctive feature of his philosophical system, dictating its somewhat Gothic structure, is, from his earliest work, a total repudiation of naturalism, and a defence of epistemology ('Grammar' and 'Logic') as a prior philosophy. In this section, I want to examine how this 'contrite fallibilist' rejected naturalism with a view to seeing more clearly the bearing of naturalistic matters on philosophical questions about knowledge.

The opposition to naturalism shows in his 'classifications of the sciences': mathematics, the only subject needing no foundation, grounds phenomenology, which in turn grounds the general theory of value which issues in logic and epistemology.[2] Finally comes metaphysics which provides a bridge between logic and the special sciences. He was only clear about the

---

[1] Such arguments can be found in the first of Peirce's reviews of Berkeley's philosophy in Peirce (1931–58) at vol. 8, para, 7ff. Henceforth, references of the form N.m will be to paragraph m of volume N of the Collected Papers. Similar arguments are in 'Consequences of Four Incapacities' (5.264–5).

[2] A selection of writings on this topic are in vol. 1 of Peirce (1931–58).

classification as he worked through the foundations of his pragmatism and metaphysics in the 1890s, but it represents the systematization of a set of views that he had been groping towards since the 1860s. It is reflected in two themes that he stressed then, in work reported in the influential set of three papers appearing in the *Journal of Speculative Philosophy* in the late 1860s.[3] The material in these papers is prefigured in several sets of lectures delivered in Cambridge, Mass., from 1865 on. The first of the themes I want to mention – a resolute opposition to the psychologism of Mill and others – is stressed at the beginning of each series of lectures. He groups himself with Hamilton, Boole, Herbart, etc. in holding that logic does not depend upon psychology – it studies the 'products of reasoning' (terms, propositions, arguments) directly, and employs an objective notion of validity defined in terms of an objective notion of truth. Believing, at that time, that the source of psychologism was the idea that no objective treatment of the logic of ampliative inference was possible – together with the desire for a logic which treats all forms of inference in a systematic fashion – he set out to provide an appropriate definition of truth, and of validity, and thus to offer a systematic objective foundation for logic. Of course, this does not rule out the use of naturalistic facts so long as an objective notion of validity is employed – the validity of inductive inference could turn on features of the context in which it is carried out, or the perceptual apparatus of the reasoner. (Peirce remarks that unless logic deals with a fact of psychology it is a mathematical game! But he secures the connection by subordinating psychology to logic. In ascribing psychological states to people we rationalize their behaviour, employing the standards of rationality explained by logic (see 5.266–82).)

The second theme that interests me is implicit in the opening paragraphs of the third of the published papers, 'Grounds of Validity of the Laws of Logic'.[4] Concerned specifically with the issue why there is no circularity involved in a justification of deduction which employs deductive reasoning, he contrasts explaining the validity of a form of inference – for which purpose we can use any of our knowledge – with persuading someone of the correctness of a rule – which requires that we avoid circularity. Our deductive practice *needs* no such justificatory shoring up and cannot be revised by rational argument, hence there is no circularity in deploying it in the explanation. As his work developed, he became increasingly clear that our means for discovering the truth about reality stood in need of a *persuasive* justification.

[3] 'Questions Concerning Certain Faculties Claimed for Man', 'Consequences of Four Incapacities', and 'Grounds of Validity of the Laws of Logic: Further Consequences of Four Incapacities'. All are in vol. 5 of Peirce (1931–58).

[4] 5.318. The discussion is a little more complex than as described in the text and is elaborated in Hookway 1985.

Of course, that epistemology faces problems of persuasive justification does not, by itself, entail that no use can be made of empirical beliefs. Demands for persuasive justification arise in contexts where an agent is faced with a choice. The context determines what materials we can use in justifying a choice and the standards to which appeal will be made. Circularity results only if information is used in justifying the choice which is available only if the choice is resolved in one way rather than another. Use of naturalistic information is wholly disallowed only if there can be some settlable choice of cognitive methods where all of our naturalistic information is available only if we resolve the choice in one of the possible ways. This appears to involve a form of transcendental standpoint. Why does Peirce think that we are faced with such a choice? How can his robust commonsensical fallibilism be reconciled with his recognizing such a demand for justification?

The reconciliation lies in Peirce's view of 'science' and its relation to common sense. He sometimes speaks of the scientific method as one of the possible methods of responding to doubt, sometimes as a 'way of life', but he always seems to see it as optional though supremely rational. It represents a way of life, it seems, that has only really become possible in the nineteenth century, although Kepler may have approximated it. A philosophical conservative, he would have sympathized with the view of his father, a defender of natural theology, that the life of science could be understood as a sacred duty. The scientific method is not identified as a set of methodological rules or strategies. Rather, to adopt the method involves accepting that there is a 'reality', which is as it is independently of what anyone may think of it, but which suitably organized inquiry is fated to discover eventually; around the early 1870s Peirce speaks of reality as the final cause of inquiry. The life of science involves dedicating one's life to the discovery of the nature of reality. In 1878–9, Peirce published a six-part work in the *Popular Science Monthly*, entitled *Illustrations of the Logic of Science*. In the first part of this, 'Fixation of Belief', he outlines the project of grounding logical rules in the 'presupposition' of scientific inquiry – that there is a discoverable reality – and in subsequent papers attempts to do just that.[5] Adopting the 'method of science' involves resolving to use whatever rules can be justified by reference to the hypothesis of reality.

The suggestion that the concept of reality, or truth, is optional is not immediately compelling. And plainly Peirce does not deny that we have some common sense grasp of it; but he holds that taking it seriously transforms the character of inquiry. Ordinary inquiry is directed at the efficient settlement of belief, so that error or ignorance will not interfere

---

[5] Compare 5.369 with (e.g.) 2.693.

4

with our practical concerns.[6] Forming the intention to adopt beliefs only when they correspond to reality postpones the settlement of belief: we are forced to adopt rules which, while they are guaranteed to reveal reality to us in the long run, are not guaranteed to do so in the short run. The inquirer does not believe current scientific results, but simply looks upon them as the current stage on the route to a final description of reality.[7] (He may believe them qua practical man, but not qua scientist.) The individual sees himself as contributing to an indefinite process of inquiry by an unlimited community of inquirers, and he may well not believe that he will be around to see inquiry converge on the truth (5.589, 2.652ff.). Inquiry has no bearing on the practical concerns of life, and science should not be valued for any (unscientific) practical applications that may be made of its current resting places (1.616ff.). Yet this life of contributing to the progress towards knowledge of reality is rational, is a – perhaps the – form of human flourishing. The conflicts and inconsistencies present in our commonsense and other more primitive concepts of inquiry are resolved in a procedure which exhibited a harmony between presumption, aim, and method; it can be pursued in a totally self-conscious, reflective, self-controlled and rational fashion. If we accept Peirce's characterization of science, we must acknowledge a discontinuity between ordinary commonsense procedures of inquiry, which all settle belief in the short run, and the life of science, although, of course, the latter may affect the former. The inquirer is distanced from current results, and sees himself, not as finding things out but as contributing to the cognitive progress of a wider community.

The tasks of Peirce's philosophical epistemology become clearer now. He seeks to provide a substantive characterization of the concept of reality which will enable him to do two things: first, to show how certain rules and procedures are logically correct, how employment of them will suffice to guide us towards knowledge of reality; secondly, to show how it can be rational for a self-controlled agent to seek to contribute to knowledge of reality. I do not intend to say much about how he proposes to do this, or about the background in nineteenth-century intellectual history which accounts for his finding the picture attractive. That it would be out of place to use scientific discoveries in the course of the investigation ought to be clear: if science is optional, it would be improper to use results deriving from that science in justifying it; and, if scientific results are held, tentatively, at arm's length anyway, they are not *certain beliefs* that would be appropriate

6 'The Fixation of Belief', 5.358ff.
7 '... belief is the willingness to risk a great deal upon a proposition. But this belief is no concern of science, which has nothing at stake on any temporal venture but is in pursuit of eternal verities (not resemblances to truth) and looks upon this pursuit, not as the work of one man's life, but as that of generation after generation indefinitely' (5.589); 'pure science has nothing to do with belief' (7.606).

for philosophical argument. Philosophy, although observational, rests upon observations which are open to all – denied only through slips, ignored only because of their obviousness. It rests upon 'acritical' observations and inferences, which are not subject to self-control nor guided by an understanding of the concept of reality. Agreement on philosophical issues does not risk endless postponement, as does agreement in the special sciences.[8]

The justifications of procedures of inquiry are of two distinct kinds. For Peirce, statistical sampling is the fundamental kind of ampliative inference, and for this he derives its 'validity' from his understanding of reality – its repeated use will take us to the truth in the long run.[9] Other methodological issues cannot be solved in this straightforward fashion: reality is not wholly determinate, so there are statements with the property that no long-run agreement on their truth or falsity can be expected, so when are we justified in continuing inquiry into a question which may, for all we know, have no answer? And, since there is no limit to the number of hypotheses that can fit a given body of data, what reason have we to suppose that *we* are capable of producing, and finding plausible, an hypothesis that is on the right lines? With respect to the second of these issues, Peirce holds that it is rational to suppose that there is, in any particular case, an affinity between our sense of plausibility and the nature of reality. This supposition has the form of a 'regulative hope' – both are adopted on the same basis that a card player bases his play on the hope of an improbable distribution of the cards if no other possible distribution gives him any chance of winning at all.[10] But this takes out a philosophical loan that must be repaid in the post-philosophical sciences which explain the affinity in question. Here naturalism seems to slip back in, at least in the attempt to *explain* how knowledge is possible for us. In fact, Peirce's explanation is metaphysical, resting on his panpsychist objective idealism: he rejects the use of natural selection in the explanation because the fact that a faculty was necessary for the commonsense inquiries which facilitate survival and reproduction is no guarantee that it will help us to describe reality. Science has no survival value, and we have to rely upon our sense of plausibility in areas remote from the vital concerns of everyday practice (7.219; Hardwick 1977: 20).

I shall now draw some general morals from this sketch of the structure of

---

[8] Hence much of this philosophical energy, in later life, was devoted to finding a proof of pragmatism which would make it obvious to all – from 'High Metaphysicians' to 'Nominalists'.

[9] The best source for Peirce's views on grounding induction is probably 'The Doctrine of Necessity Examined' (6.35–65).

[10] Cf. 2.113, and Peirce (1976: IV.19): 'The true presuppositions of logic are merely *hopes*; and as such when we consider their consequences collectively, we cannot condemn scepticism as to how far they may be borne out by facts.'

Peirce's philosophical thought. It is useful to distinguish two elements in his view of knowledge and its philosophical elucidation. First, there is a demand for a clear and complete self-consciousness about what we are doing when we form beliefs about the world – a philosophical account of knowledge provides a perspicuous account of knowledge which means that we pursue inquiries knowing what we are doing, knowing why it is rational to proceed as we do, and understanding how we can obtain knowledge. The second element is the picture of serious inquiry as optional, and as something from the results of which the inquirer is distanced. It is plausible to see the first point as spelling out the root problem for a philosophical account of knowledge, and the second as linked to Peirce's anti-naturalism. Whether the view of science led Peirce to look for a prior epistemology, or whether the desire for, or availability of, a prior epistemology led him to think of inquiry as he did, are questions I shall not pursue here. The conception of serious inquiry as optional is required, it seems, if the demand that inquiry be made self-conscious and rational is to call for justification rather than explanation. And, as yet, we have seen no reason to suppose that the need for explanation calls for a prior epistemology. In the next section, I pursue this point by looking at Quine's programme for naturalizing epistemology.

2. NATURALIZED EPISTEMOLOGY

Quine appears to hold that, since, regrettably, the project of providing a reconstruction of human knowledge which traces the credibility of all justified beliefs to the operations of canons of rationality upon intrinsically credible perceptual beliefs has failed, the only remaining motivation for avoiding the use of naturalistic materials in epistemology is an unwarranted desire that our knowledge be shown to be certain. For the fallibilist, epistemology 'or something like it, simply falls into place as a chapter of psychology and hence of natural science', it 'goes on, though in a new setting, and a clarified status'. It is notable that he does not see himself abandoning epistemology, but as continuing it, doing it better than it previously had been done. It studies a human subject who

is accorded a certain experimentally controlled input – certain patterns of irradiation in assorted frequencies, for instance – and in the fullness of time the subject delivers as output a description of the three dimensional external world and its history. The relation between the meager input and the torrential output is a relation that we are prompted to study for somewhat the same reasons that always prompted epistemology; namely, in order to see how evidence relates to theory, and in what ways one's theory of nature transcends any available evidence. (Quine 1969b: 82–3)

7

Transcendental reflection is not required for dealing with what Quine takes to be the traditional concerns of epistemology. It is useful, tentatively, to distinguish two elements in Quine's thinking here: his commitment to naturalism and rejection of the need for epistemology to exercise 'scruples about circularity'; and his list of acceptable sciences, which excludes all of the social and human sciences, cognitive psychology, etc. It is not obvious that the grounds for his naturalism would evaporate if he took seriously a wider variety of forms of discourse. I want to take seriously the suggestion that the sort of inquiry that Quine has in mind could be the heir to traditional epistemology – although I shall not restrict the concerns of the latter to studying the relation of evidence to theory. I shall, therefore, pursue two issues. First, can Quine be forced to acknowledge that questions arise which demand transcendental reflection – does his resistance to such issues flow naturally from his philosophy, or does it require a stubborn closing of the mind? Secondly, can a naturalized epistemology provide the perspicuous self-conscious understanding of inquiry which we saw, in the last section, to lie behind some traditional theorizing – can he cope with normative issues and questions of justification? His refusal to take seriously the possibility of a confirmation theory, for example, can easily lead one to believe that he is closing his eyes to important normative issues.

Notoriously, positivists such as Carnap enunciated a principle of meaningfulness which banned transcendental reflection, but which could only be justified by the sort of argument which it debarred. Wittgenstein, early and late, constantly strained with the temptation to discuss what could not be discussed. One reading of Quine is that his practice conforms to the Wittgensteinian teaching: only questions that can be resolved arise for him. If the reflective clarity about knowledge that we desire can be obtained, it can be obtained naturalistically. His 'robust realism' results from the fact that he cannot attain the standpoint of transcendental reflection from which he can notice what we take to be idealist tendencies in his work. If he could adopt that standpoint, he might describe himself as an empirical realist but a transcendental idealist; but, since he cannot adopt that standpoint, he is just a 'realist'. The 'idealism' shows in his verificationism, and in the indeterminacy of translation, but it never reaches a formulation. Of course, this is a one-sided and distorting reading, but it provides a perspective from which some central Quinean themes hang together.

Peirce's first philosophy requires that we can formulate substantive conceptions of truth and reference without recourse to the special sciences. Employing those conceptions, we can ask how we can know that we have succeeded in referring to anything, and how we can know that we have come up with an accurate description of what we have referred to. Unless we can think about truth and reference from the standpoint of transcendental reflection – unless we have substantive conceptions of those notions – the questions we raise are not intelligible. For Quine, our substantive conceptions do not have this independence of the special sciences. When we raise questions about truth and reality, we carry with us presumptions derived from the special sciences, and thus cannot achieve transcendental reflection. As is well brought out in a recent paper, the views of Carnap's which Quine opposed involved the claim that conventionally adopted analytic linguistic frameworks provided criteria of reality, which set up the standards according to which any question that might arise was settlable (Ricketts 1982). By denying that we could empirically identify the linguistic framework employed by other agents (or, indeed by ourselves), Quine challenged the claim that we can have a substantive prior conception of truth which can be used to formulate questions for transcendental reflection.

But let us look directly at Quine's discussions of transcendental arguments and transcendental reflection. In a recent paper, Stroud argues that Quine can be forced to acknowledge questions which cannot be answered by his naturalized epistemology (Stroud 1981). Stroud grants that if we want to know how a third person can know the nature of reality, we might carry out a psychological investigation of his methods of information processing, and then compare the results of his reasoning with known facts. Naturalistic epistemology may suffice. The problems arise when we shift to the first person, asking how *we* come to have knowledge of the world, and asking how we are justified in dismissing the possibility that reality is wholly other than we take it to be. When faced with these questions, he urges, we must bracket our 'scientific beliefs', and naturalistic epistemology will be of no use. We do not have a conception of how reality is with which to compare our opinions. Quine's response is instructive, although it may at first seem dismissive.

[Stroud] demurs at our projecting ourselves into the subject's place, since we no longer have the independent facts to compare with. My answer is that this projection must be seen not transcendentally, but as a routine matter of analogies and causal hypotheses within our scientific theory … [In] keeping with my naturalism I am reasoning within the overall scientific system rather than somehow above or beyond it … Transcendental argument, or what purports to be first philosophy, tends generally to take on rather this status of immanent epistemology insofar as I succeed in making sense of it. (Quine 1981: 474–5)

I can speculate about how I know about reality, but no bracketing of current empirical certainties is required.

Before asking what feature of Quine's position is supposed to make this response possible, we should note Quine's response to familiar sceptical arguments, for example, those that rest upon evidence for perceptual error and illusion, and upon empirical evidence of delusion. He acknowledges the 'Humean predicament'; both induction and the hypothetico-deductive method are fallible, so that any of the beliefs which result from them could turn out to be in error. He also grants that a sceptic might 'use science to repudiate science'; our entire theory of external objects might be over-thrown.

Experience might, tomorrow, take a turn that would justify the skeptic's doubts about external objects. Our success in predicting observations might fall off sharply, and concomitantly with this we might begin to be somewhat successful in basing predictions on dreams and reveries. At this point we might reasonably doubt our theory of nature in even its broadest outlines. But our doubts would still be immanent and of a piece with the scientific endeavour. (Quine 1981: 475)

Quine's response to someone who believes that there is evidence to warrant this extreme measure is that the sceptic is 'overreacting', manifesting bizarre or deviant patterns of entrenchment of beliefs, different standards of plausibility and evidence. There is no evidence that he thinks they can be argued out of their scepticism, but, since they have convinced neither him nor us, this is no cause for concern. We might try to explain their eccentric trait.

What is at issue in calling this use of the sceptical argument 'scientific'? The intended contrast is between repudiating science because we cannot understand how to bring it into harmony with an antecedently given substantive conception of reality, and rejecting our most general scientific theories because they are constantly surprised by experience. Quite what it would be like to give up material bodies I shall not consider. However, what is behind Quine's refusal to admit a prior substantive concept of reality – a corollary of his rejection of the *a priori* – is that our broadest conception of reality is derived from science; 'science identifies and describes reality' and without science we have no way to think or talk about it at all. Raising questions about whether we are able to know the nature of reality carries with it the scientific baggage involved in our substantive conception of truth. Once we attain the transcendental standpoint, we have ceased to carry with us the substantive concept of truth required to raise epistemological questions. Thus Quine can make use of psychological facts to inform someone such as Stroud that all we look for in inquiry is accurate prediction and control of 'triggerings of our sensory receptors', and can show no interest in further sceptical possibilities.

As is clear from 'Facts of the Matter', (Quine 1977), Quine's substantive conception of reality is taken primarily from physics. Physicalism is adopted as a regulative principle because physical objects provide the most familiar examples of 'things'; Physics is permitted to provide our standards of reality or thinghood. It is because motives, intentions and historical events lack the kind of clear robust reality displayed by electrons, fields and quarks that Quine spurns the intentional; the indeterminacy of translation shows up, not a special character of a distinctive form of discourse, but the extent to which the realm of the intentional fails to meet standards of reality set by physics and physical objects. We may here respond that Quine is overreacting. His general point may survive even if we do not share his preferences for physics, or even science. This is that we do not have an *a priori* conception of reality which allows for a range of possible universes, empirical inquiry determining just which of those possibilities is realized. Rather, science (and maybe even social science and other forms of discourse, such as that embodied in ordinary talk of mind and morality) is the source of the substantive conceptions of reality which must be referred to in discussions of the possibility of knowledge. We cannot, as Peirce would hope, hold science at arm's length and attempt to justify its procedures – unless, that is, we can frame an *a priori* conception of reality of the sort Peirce offers.

We should now turn to the second question that I raised, whether Quinean epistemology is, in fact, sufficiently continuous with traditional Epistemology to provide the self-consciousness about his practice desired by the reflective inquirer (see Putnam 1982). Will it enable him to justify all that needs to be justified, and to explain the remaining features of his practice? Once the aims of inquiry are specified in psychological terms, there is no obstacle to empirical investigations of efficient or possible means to achieving those ends. If the 'ultimate aim' is specified as the securing of predictive control over the future run of experience, then either this can be justified as providing a means to achieving further practical ends, or, if it stands in no need of justification, it may be possible to explain why people have it without the explanation undermining its appeal. We may ask for an explanation of how our perceptual apparatus is a reliable source of information about reality, or how our instinctive judgements of plausibility or similarity can be useful in forming hypotheses or making inductions. Psychological explanations may be to the point here, or speculations about the evolutionary history of the faculties in question. It will be recalled that Peirce made no use of natural selection for similar purposes, and the difference between the projects of the two epistemologists will be clarified if we note why Quine can do so. That our perceptual apparatus is reliable and our abductive sense is sound do not, for the Quinean position, need arguing; we have ample evidence that they have guided us to the truth on many occasions. We simply want to understand how they do so. In that case, there is no reason to expect a general form of explanation linking our cognitive faculties to the truth, explaining the reliability of our natural abductive sense. If natural selection is employed in the explanations, we do not need a general linking of natural selection to the discovery of truth. Rather, we can characterize particular features of our perceptual apparatus (which we know to be the source of their reliability) and ask for an explanation of those features. Elements of the abductive sense may be instinctive, and the result of selection, others the product of training: selection may explain both the innate quality space and the flexibility which, we know, make possible the training which explains our current (reliable) sense of plausibility (Quine 1969c). So far as I can see, even a partisan of naturalistic epistemology is not committed to finding general characterizations or explanations of justification or reliability. It is an empirical issue whether such general reductive explanations are available, and hence whether general notions of justification have any application. This becomes clearer when Quine's scientism is relaxed to the extent of recognizing the autonomy of forms of discourse – for instance, concerning moral or cognitive justification – which are plainly not 'scientific', let alone acceptable to a Quinean 'physicalist'. Self-conscious clarity about our epistemic methods, in that case, would require a perspicuous representation of the characteristics of the forms of discourse in question. This does not prevent our wanting such reflective self-understanding also to involve understanding how our faculties can, in particular cases, lead us to the truth about an empirical subject matter; and naturalistic information has its place in meeting this demand.

So understood, Quine is unsympathetic to the Peircean doctrine that we hold our scientific 'opinions' at arm's length: at least some of our scientific beliefs must be fully accepted. In fact, we may both be surprised that Peirce held that the scientific inquirer distanced himself from all scientific results, and suspect that Quine would grant that this attitude is appropriate for a range of them. Peirce could probably allow the same: his position rests upon the belief that there is a logical guarantee that induction will take us to the truth in the long run, but that our confidence in the short-run efficacy of the method is simply an 'acritical' commonsense certainty which may be susceptible to scientific explanation. Trusting induction in the short run cannot receive a philosophical justification. However, there is a question about what a naturalized epistemology can offer by way of an explanation or justification of the contributions to knowledge that we make by contributing to an ongoing process of inquiry: we want to know, in such cases, not how we have arrived at the truth, but how what we do can be understood as contributing to the fact that someone else (or perhaps ourselves) can arrive at the truth at some time in the future. In the next section, I offer some brief and critical remarks about a recent attempt to provide a general descriptive account of how knowledge develops which would say something to that issue.

3. EVOLUTIONARY EPISTEMOLOGY

The application of evolutionary ideas to the study of knowledge has recently been urged by a number of people, but I shall only discuss Campbell's evolutionary epistemology (Campbell 1974). I shall concentrate upon the claim that there is a fruitful analogy between the development of species through natural selection and the growth of knowledge. There are other elements in Campbell's thought: he seems to think that the most perspicuous model of the mind to employ in understanding human knowledge sees the mind as embodying a structured hierarchy of functionally characterized capacities, each of which works in a way analogous to natural selection; and he defends his view as part of a (reductive) explanation of how the capacities comprising human rationality have evolved. Underlying the analogy is the thought that natural selection can itself be understood as a process whereby information is selected and transmitted, it applies a simple logical model to a natural phenomenon. More important, natural selection provides a model of how there can be change towards a kind of fit or harmony, towards structured complexity, which is neither planned nor the result of goal-directed activity. Variations occur within a population, explicable as genetic mutations or the results of mixing of genetic material. Variations which are not suited to their niche tend not to survive to reproduce, and the characters of those that are successful are transmitted genetically to their offspring. Traits which are advantageous tend to survive and spread in the population, those which are not, do not. Neither in the production of variations nor in the elimination of disadvantageous variations is there any reference to an 'end' of producing 'fit' or successful species: the probability of variations occurring, or of a particular variation occurring, is independent of the need for change to produce a better 'fit' between organism and environment, or of that variation being successful. The general claim that such a variation is disadvantageous has no role in the explanation of the fact that the individual displaying it fails to reproduce; selection does not involve 'criteria' which refer to the endpoint of the process.

The application of this picture to the growth of knowledge seems straightforward. Thagard expresses it neatly:

Evolutionary epistemology notices that variation, selection and transmission are also features of the growth of scientific knowledge. Scientists generate theories, hypotheses, and concepts; only a few of *variations* are judged to be advances over existing views, and they are *selected*; the selected theories and concepts are transmitted to other scientists through journals, textbooks, and other pedagogic measures. (Thagard 1980)

In keeping with the analogy, Campbell holds that the variations are 'blind' – that we come up with a particular hypothesis is not determined by our current experience, is independent of whether the hypothesis is in fact going to prove true or successful, and is not a correction of previous unsuccessful hypotheses. Similarly, he must hold that theories are eliminated due to the clash of experience (for example), but not using criteria that are understood in terms of, or justified with reference to, the aims of inquiry. Unless such points are maintained, the analogy becomes so strained that little that is distinctive about natural selection remains. However, in that case, it does seem that the theory is straightforwardly false. In proposing hypotheses, people are guided by knowledge of past failures, by analogies with theories that have been successful in handling related subject matters; Peirce's 'affinity' between mind and nature is an allusion to something which is required to explain the speed of the growth of knowledge; and testing theories is an intentional activity which appeals to general cognitive aims – to describe reality, anticipate experience, solve problems, produce elegant and simple formalisms, etc. Thagard's excellent hatchet job spells out many more points of disanalogy.

If we allow that the analogy does not provide a useful general descriptive or explanatory account of the growth of knowledge, we may be surprised that it was found plausible at all. Presumably it is an overreaction to a number of points that we have noted: that no logical guarantee of the soundness of our abductive sense can be provided; that our substantive conception of reality or of the aim of inquiry may itself be revisable; that while experience might lead us to abandon a theory with some confidence, proper acceptance should be postponed to the long run – true theories are survivors. It may reflect the thought that although we do not aim at the 'truth' – i.e. our immediate aims are for simple solutions to empirical problems – nevertheless, the truth is what we end up with. Thus, even if inquiry is a goal-directed activity, the goals in terms of which it is directed do not represent a substantive conception of the 'end' to which the process tends. But, while these points may be reasonable, and some of them may be true, this attempt to embed them in a general theory or schema seems unhelpful. Looking backwards over the history of inquiry, from the security of our current views, we may see evidence of the cunning of reason bringing us gradually closer to the approximately true, but from that perspective we can offer descriptions and explanations of what was going on which show, for instance, that hypothesis selection was not 'blind'. Looking forward, and viewing ourselves as contributing to the development of provisionally held theories, it seems to offer no more than the hope that we might make a contribution even if we do not really understand what, how, or to what. As a theory, it has little to contribute to our reflective self-understanding of ourselves as agents of inquiry.

REFERENCES

Campbell, D. C. 1974. 'Evolutionary Epistemology', in *The Philosophy of Karl Popper*, ed. P. A. Schilpp. La Salle, Illinois.

French, P. *et al.* (eds) 1981. *Midwest Studies in Philosophy* VI. Minneapolis.

Hardwick, C. S. 1977. (ed.) *Semiotic and Significs: Correspondence of C. S. Peirce and Victoria Lady Welby*. Bloomington.

Hookway, C. J. 1985. *Peirce*. London.

Peirce, C. S. 1931–58. *Collected Papers*, ed. C. Hartshorne, P. Weiss, and A. Burks. Cambridge, Mass.

Peirce, C. S. 1976. *The New Elements of Mathematics*, ed. C. Eisele. The Hague.

Putnam, H. 1982. 'Why Reason Cannot be Naturalized', *Synthèse* 52, 3–23.

Quine, W. V. 1969a. *Ontological Relativity and Other Essays*. New York.

Quine, W. V. 1969b. 'Epistemology Naturalized', in Quine 1969a: 69–90.

Quine, W. V. 1969c. 'Natural Kinds', in Quine 1969a: 114–38.

Quine, W. V. 1977. 'Facts of the Matter', in *American Philosophy*, ed. R. Shahan and K. Merrill, 176–96. Norman, Oklahoma.

Quine, W. V. 1981. 'Reply to Stroud', in French *et al.* 1981: 473–6.

Ricketts, T. 1982. 'Rationality, Translation and Naturalized Epistemology', *Journal of Philosophy* 79, 117–36.

Stroud, B. 1981. 'The Significance of Naturalized Epistemology', in French *et al.* 1981: 455–72.

Thagard, P. 1980. 'Against Evolutionary Epistemology', *PSA* 1980, ed. P. D. Asquith and R. N. Giere, 187–96. East Lansing, Mich.

Historical entities and historical narratives

DAVID L. HULL

Human history remains so recalcitrantly idiographic because it is the story of a single species – it represents the vicissitudes of an individual (Ghiselin 1974) of unparalleled flexibility. What general theory could encompass it? (Gould 1980: 116)

INTRODUCTION

Why do historical narratives seem to be more explanatory than the traditional covering-law model of scientific explanation can justify? Why do genuine scientific laws continue to elude the sciences of 'man?' The answers to both of these questions hinge on certain distinctions that are so basic to our way of conceptualizing the world in which we live that they deserve to be termed 'metaphysical'. Science has developed under the assumption that certain regularities in nature are spatio-temporally unrestricted. They are extrapolatable to all places and at any time that the conditions are right. Laws of nature are supposed to encapsulate these regularities. On this view, our formulations of laws of nature may change through time as our understanding improves, but the regularities themselves do not change. In order for laws to be spatio-temporally unrestricted, any class that functions in a law must itself be spatio-temporally unrestricted. As a terminological convenience, I term these classes 'natural kinds'. Natural kinds do not function in the natural regularities themselves. Their exemplifications or instantiations do that. Of the various sorts of entities that instantiate natural kinds, one of the most important is historical entities. Historical entities are spatio-temporally localized particulars that develop continuously through time while staying internally cohesive. Historical entities may undergo total turnover of their constituent elements just so long as they do so gradually and remain sufficiently cohesive in the process.

As I have defined them, neither natural kinds nor historical entities exhaust the metaphysical categories to which they belong. Many classes do not function in laws of nature, and many sorts of spatio-temporally unrestricted entities besides natural kinds do. For example, 'planets larger than the Earth' and 'albinic organisms' are spatio-temporally unrestricted. Although Earth is spatio-temporally localized, the classes defined in terms of it need not be. Although all albinic organisms may be limited to Earth, they need not be. But neither class functions in any law of nature, nor appears to be the sort of class that holds out any promise of ever functioning in such a law. Similarly, substance terms such as 'gold' function in scientific laws, and one might wish not to treat such terms as class terms.

Others might prefer to draw their metaphysical categories differently. For example, one might prefer to interpret historical entities as spatio-temporally localized classes. On this interpretation, an organism, instead of being an historical entity, would be a class of cells descended from one or more initial germ cells (Gasking 1961). My only objection to this way of construing things is that it makes the category 'individual' all but empty. Everything save possibly bare particulars gets lumped into a single metaphysical category – classes. But regardless of whether one treats historical entities as a peculiar sort of spatio-temporally localized class or as a typical sort of individual, historical entities can be treated as spatio-temporally unrestricted only on pain of contradiction. The core distinction is between those notions that are extrapolatable and those that are not.

One might complain that the category 'spatio-temporally unrestricted class' is empty. According to one standard theory of cosmogony (Weinberg 1977), the universe may be finite. Hence, all classes, no matter how they are defined, will in point of fact have a finite extension (Kitts & Kitts 1979). If so, then the distinction under discussion can be redrawn to distinguish between those classes that are defined in terms of a spatio-temporal relation to a spatio-temporal focus and those that are not but happen to be spatio-temporally localized and restricted because the universe at large happens to have these characteristics.

Finally, one might object that too many obstacles stand in the way of treating natural laws as universal truths. Instead they are singular statements of fact describing a relationship between universal properties and magnitudes (Dretske 1977). I have no objection to this way of putting things, just so long as the distinction is retained between those statements that warrant extrapolation from those that do not. Both Bode's law and Kepler's laws appeared to apply to the solar planets known at the time when they were first enunciated. Bode's laws turned out not to be extrapolatable to all solar planets, let alone all planets in general. If Kepler's laws had been applicable only to the solar planets, they would still have been true and important but not laws of nature. The term 'law' has such an honorific connotation that a strong tendency exists to term everything that is scientifically important a 'law'. I think that this tendency should be resisted. Historical entities are important, but from this it does not follow that a statement describing an historical entity is a law of nature.

In this paper, I do not argue for the metaphysical categories which I use. Instead I show the consequences that these traditional distinctions have for our treatment of historical explanations and for those theories that deal necessarily with a single species such as *Homo sapiens*. Historical explanations can be divided into at least two types – integrative explanations and narrative explanations (Goudge 1961, Hull 1981). Integrative explanations show how a part fits into a more inclusive whole and how this organization is maintained through time. As such, integrative explanations are more general than functional explanations. Functional explanations are integrative explanations of systems in which elements can be said to have a 'function' in the sense of a positive function. But not all organized wholes are functional systems. Narrative explanations trace the course of development of historical entities – the sequences of events in which they participate. The explanatory import of historical narratives derives from the continuity and cohesiveness of historical entities as central subjects, not deductions from laws of nature (Hull 1975). Laws do play a role in historical explanations but not as premises in covering-law explanations. Instead they determine which entities have the characteristics necessary to function as historical entities in natural processes. In this sense, historical entities are theory-dependent.

In this paper I treat organisms as paradigm historical entities. Hence, they can function as central subjects in historical narratives. A description of Napoleon's career is a paradigm example of an historical narrative. But organisms also exist related in lineages. A description of the Tudors also counts as an historical narrative. Elsewhere, Ghiselin (1974) and I (Hull 1976, 1978) have argued that biological species in general are best construed as historical entities, not as they have been traditionally interpreted as natural kinds. If so, then *Homo sapiens* is an historical entity. As such it need have no essence, no nature. Hence, any system based on human nature is in trouble. More than this, any empirical claim that is limited necessarily to *Homo sapiens* may well be true, but it cannot possibly be a law of nature. Even if all swans were white, the claim that all swans are white would no more be a law of nature than the claim that Richard Nixon erased the famous eighteen minutes on the White House tapes. I emphasize, however, that something's being a description does not automatically make it non-important. Instead of construing all sorts of non-extrapolatable statements as laws so that they can share in the importance of laws, I retain the conventional metaphysical distinctions and extend the value usually attributed to laws to certain non-laws.

THE GREAT CHAIN OF BEING

One of the most fundamental themata in Western thought has been the Great Chain of Being (Lovejoy 1936). Although the metaphysical systems in which this conception functioned varied tremendously and interpretations of these systems vary even more widely, certain characteristics of the beings related in the great chain are fairly standard. For most workers, the Great Chain of Being was a totally atemporal ordering of eternal, immutable, discrete natural kinds. According to these systems of thought, if the species horse is a genuine natural kind, it must be eternal, immutable and discrete. Particular exemplifications of natural kinds are quite another matter. For certain workers, these exemplifications were held to be just as eternal, immutable and discrete as natural kinds; for others not. Although I cannot discuss all possible permutations of these characteristics for natural kinds and for their exemplifications, I do sketch two representative combinations: (1) both natural kinds and individuals having all three of these characteristics, and (2) natural kinds having all three characteristics while individuals lack all three. Plato and possibly early Wittgenstein may have held the first view; Aristotle the second view. I say 'may' because scholars differ with each other endlessly on almost every particular of every philosophical system ever put forth. This fact says something either about the ambiguity of philosophical systems or about the creativity of historians of philosophy, or possibly both.

In its most extreme form, the claim that natural kinds are eternal entails that both natural kinds and their exemplifications exist throughout all time. Like God, they always were and always will be. Quite obviously the commonsense exemplifications of ordinary natural kinds are not eternal. One might plausibly have claimed at one time that the species horse is eternal but not Bucephalus. Individual horses quite obviously are born and die. But in most metaphysical systems, only the most fundamental kinds and their exemplifications are held to be eternal. Ordinary objects are made up of some sort of absolute simples, and only these simples and their properties are really eternal. For example, if the absolute simples are cubes, then straight edge is a natural kind of the most basic sort. As such, it is eternal. But cubes can be arranged in a variety of shapes. Only a few of these combinations may exist at any one time, but at least their potentiality is built into the make-up of the absolute simples. In this sense, these derivative shapes are also eternal.

Comparable observations hold for immutability and discreteness. One complex individual might be transmuted into another merely by rearranging its constituent cubes. These derivative natural kinds might even exist in a variety of intersecting, near continua. But one simple cannot be transmuted into another. A cube cannot be transmuted into a tetrahedron. Nor can the boundaries between these simples be fuzzy. The natural kind 'straight edge' is absolutely distinct from the natural kind 'plane surface', and one absolute simple is sharply distinguishable from all other absolute simples.

Not all metaphysical systems are so other-worldly. On one common reading of Aristotle, ordinary individuals like Bucephalus exemplify ordinary natural kinds like horse. The species horse is eternal because at all times horses exist – not the same horses throughout all time but some horses or other. Individual horses come and go, and once an individual is gone, numerically this same individual cannot come into existence again. The preceding claim has nothing to do with empirical possibilities – cloning, organ transplants, and the like – but concerns the metaphysical notion of an individual. As long as one holds that individuals are severally eternal, one need not deal with the problem of the re-emergence of individuals. The three commonest criteria for this distinction are retention of constituent matter, essence, and continuity of development. According to present-day understanding, organisms can undergo a total turnover of the stuff of which they are made during the course of their existence – perhaps several times over. That we continue to consider an organism a single individual in the face of a total change in material substance indicates that we do not individuate organisms in terms of retention of their constituent material.

Essence and individuality are more closely connected. Organisms undergo ontogenetic development, sometimes metamorphizing in a series of stages that differ quite markedly in gross appearance. A caterpillar and a moth do not look very similar to each other. One alternative with respect to the connection between essence and individuality is that if an individual can undergo such changes, then the states must not have been essential. Because a single individual can be transformed from a caterpillar into a moth, these are stages in the life cycle of a single individual. Its essence must include all such stages. Another alternative is to allow that an individual can change its essence while remaining the same individual. Thus, a sample of lead might be transmutable into a sample of gold while remaining the same sample.

Opinions differ with respect to the role of retention of material substance and essence in the individuation of individuals. Less variation in opinion exists with respect to continuity of development. If individuals can develop at all in a particular metaphysical system, they must do so continuously. An organism undergoing its life cycle remains numerically the same individual because these changes, no matter how drastic, are continuous. If an organism were to disintegrate into its constituent atoms and then a new organism reassembled using these same atoms, it would still be a new organism, perhaps an organism of the same kind but not the same individual organism. Once again, these observations do not concern physical possibility but the way in which individuals are individuated. A horse identical in every respect to Bucephalus save location in time and space might arise, perhaps by cloning. It would count as a horse but not as Bucephalus. As organisms are commonly conceived, their essence is in their origin.

Philosophers have discussed the alternative of individuating individuals in terms of their origins and continuous development thereafter and have generated all sorts of puzzles. What if Alexander the Great had been conceived one second earlier or a minute later? Would he still count as the same individual? What if he had been conceived on the floor instead of in bed? What if his father actually had not been Philip II of Macedon but a God, as Alexander's mother Olympias claimed? I think such contrary-to-fact questions are inappropriate for individuals. All that matters in the individuation of individuals is what *does* happen, not what *might* have happened but did not. For example, two drops of mercury are just a fraction of an inch apart on a flat surface. Are they two drops or one? The obvious answer is two. 'But what if the surface had been jiggled, or a needle drawn through one drop to the other, or a host of other possibilities?' If none of these contingencies occurred, then the two drops of mercury remain two drops; if not, not. In the individuation of individuals, unrealized potentials do not count. In order for the opposite alternative to be warranted, some means other than intuitions must be provided for making the relevant decisions, and none has been forthcoming (for further discussion, see Mackie 1974, Wiggins 1980).

The claim that natural kinds are eternal even though their exemplifications are temporary can be made to seem more plausible by considering a more realistic example. According to present-day conceptions, the physical elements are defined by their atomic number. Any atom with atomic number 79 is an atom of gold. The distribution of gold atoms in the universe changes through time. Certain atoms of gold get transmuted into atoms of some other element. They remain the same atoms in the process if the change is minor, like the loss of a single neutron and electron. They are new atoms if the process is accomplished by the total dissolution of the atoms involved and the reassembly of new atoms. During the early history of the universe, no gold existed at all. It is possible that at some date in the future, all gold atoms will have been destroyed. However, throughout all this change, gold as a natural kind remains unchanged in the sense that a slot for it remains in the periodic table. The natural kind gold is built into the make-up of the universe. Contrary-to-fact conditionals are warranted with respect to such natural kinds.

Although natural kinds are immutable, it does not follow that individuals cannot change from one natural kind to another, although they might well lose their individuality in the process. Alchemists were, unbeknownst to them, attempting to contravene the laws of chemistry in attempting to transmute baser metals into gold by chemical means. They were not contravening any metaphysical principles. Similarly, well into the modern period, naturalists thought that members of one species could on rare occasions give rise to members of another species (Zirkle 1959). However, such occurrences did not threaten the immutability of species. Allowing that natural kinds themselves change through time nullifies the entire purpose of natural kinds. In order for change to be comprehensible, so it seemed, something must remain unchanged. One might reshape a piece of wire from a circular shape to a square shape, but in doing so, one would not be squaring a circle, nor would circularity be evolving into squareness. The whole point of natural kinds is to remain unchanged in the face of change.

Finally, natural kinds were treated traditionally as being discrete. Sharpness of boundaries in conceptual space was intimately connected to the reality of the distinctions being made. The only boundaries that counted as real boundaries were those that are absolutely sharp. At the verbal level, this means that the names of natural kinds must be definable in terms of traits that universally covary, that is, in terms of properties that are severally necessary and jointly sufficient for membership. On this view the Great Chain of Being is a compact series of discrete natural kinds, not a literal continuum. Many borderline cases might exist in the exemplifications of these natural kinds, but in the face of all these borderline cases, the natural kinds themselves remain discrete.

Naturalists long before Darwin were aware of the extensive variability present in the living world. They even studied this variation, but the goal of these studies was to see through the variation to the discrete natural kinds. Aristotle repeatedly emphasized that organisms form continuous series (*Hist. An.* VIII.1, 588b). But he can easily be interpreted as claiming that organisms form compact series of discrete natural kinds. These series are 'continuous' in the sense that no gaps exist between natural kinds; only sharp boundaries. More recently Lennox (1980) has reminded us that, for Aristotle, species are a matter of 'the more and the less'. Only kinds at a much higher level are actually discrete. If so, then the preceding observations must be moved up to these higher levels (for a fuller discussion, see Hull 1982a).

Although philosophers before Wittgenstein argued that not all class names need be defined by means of universally covarying traits – statistical covariation is good enough – he was the first to popularize the view. One weakness of treating certain notions as 'cluster concepts' is that too often

23

the elements of a cluster are not presented explicitly and the weights for each of the elements stated. Another is the likelihood that the cluster does not reflect an objective state of affairs in the world but only our own ignorance and confusion. On more careful study, statistical variation can at least sometimes be reduced to universal covariation. The names of biological species have been the chief example of cluster concepts that do not exhibit either of the preceding weaknesses. If species evolve gradually, then no matter what traits are used to define them, these traits will covary only statistically. And taxonomists set out in exhaustive detail the variation of the traits they use in their classifications (Hull 1965).

The contrast between traditional definitions and cluster concepts does not seem very drastic on the face of it, but its metaphysical implications are basic. If definitions are supposed to capture the essence of a group, then the essences of the classes defined statistically are not discrete but gradate imperceptibly into one another, an admission that transfers the imperfections of the empirical world into our very conceptions (Hull 1982a). Wittgenstein's suggestion is more drastic than it might first appear.

TEMPORALIZING THE GREAT CHAIN OF BEING

Prior to Darwin, naturalists did many things to the Great Chain of Being. They broke it up into separate embranchements, they dissolved the conceptual boundaries between species, they arranged species in interlocking circles and trees, but one thing that they did not do was to temporalize the Great Chain of Being. In order to explain and to justify at least partially this non-standard claim, I examine in this section the views of three scientists – Lamarck, Lyell and Darwin. Lamarck believed that species evolve, but his conception of evolution did not challenge the immutability of species. Early on Lyell believed that species come into existence and pass away but not by means of one species evolving into another. For early Lyell, species are eternal, immutable and discrete. Not until Darwin did anyone argue that species lack *all* the basic characteristics of natural kinds. Strangely enough, however, Darwin did not conclude thereby that species are not natural kinds. The failure to take this final step has plagued our understanding of the evolutionary process and the nature of natural kinds ever since.

Lamarck (1809) treated organisms but not species as genuine children of time. Even though species 'evolve' for Lamarck, they remain eternal and immutable. According to Lamarck, very simple organisms are generated spontaneously at the bottom of several 'trees of life'. These simple organisms are impelled through successive generations up their respective tree by an innate urge to increased perfection. The environment they happen to confront determines which branch of the tree they take. However, in the midst of all this change, the species themselves remain unchanged. The organization of these trees of life is eternal and immutable. All the species that make up his several trees of life are equally extant. The simple organisms at the base of a tree are just as alive and well as those at the termini of its branches. Organisms proceed up their tree through successive generations, but their places are immediately taken by organisms following them up the Great Escalator of Being. On Lamarck's system, no species can become permanently extinct. Perhaps some world-wide calamity might kill off all the members of a particular species. It does not matter. Once the appropriate environment comes into existence again and the right organisms confront this environment, the extinguished species would become exemplified again.

For Lamarck, however, species are not discrete. Not only do organisms change gradually through successive generations from one species to the next, but also the boundaries between species are amorphous. The *order* of species in a tree is not arbitrary; the place where one chooses to draw the dividing line between successive species is, however, totally arbitrary. Lamarck, accordingly, concludes that species are not real. Notice, even though species are eternal and immutable, just because they are not discrete, Lamarck denies them reality. The lack of only one of the traditional defining characteristics of natural kinds is sufficient for Lamarck to deny species reality.[1]

Comparable remarks hold with respect to the early views of Charles Lyell. Lyell (1832) maintained that species go extinct as the conditions for their existence deteriorate but they re-emerge by some unknown natural process if and when the appropriate conditions reappear. For example, in the 4th edition of his the *Antiquity of Man* (1873: 440), Lyell makes the following observation about his own earlier views:

[1] In the following quotation, Vrba (1980: 82) indicates that these same distinctions are equally operative today in discussions of the reality of species:

> The question of the reality of species is central to the debate. The requirement of specific discreteness in time basically amounts only to the condition that the beginning and end of a species should be recognizable (at least theoretically) evolutionary events. One possible contribution towards specific discreteness would be constancy of species-specific characters; that is, characters would change only during speciation events and which remain unique attributes of a species throughout its duration. (If such species-specific characters exist, they may of course not be expressed in the gross morphology, let alone in fossils, but rather elsewhere in the phenotype.) However, such constancy of characters is obviously not the only hypothesis that can be advanced under an assumption of real, discrete species. Even if no characters remain constant, differences in evolutionary rates may demarcate species' origins from durations. Finally, if the origins and durations of species were distinguished by neither the quality nor the quantity of evolutionary change, one could argue that a species is discrete simply because it has a distinct beginning (the splitting event from an ancestral species) and a distinct end (terminal or phyletic extinction).

The only point on which I doubted was, whether the force [that produces new species] might not be intermittent instead of being, as Lamarck supposed, in ceaseless operation. Might not the births of new species, like the deaths of old ones, be sudden? Might they not still escape our observation?

Lyell believed that species could re-emerge but not by members of one species becoming members of another species as Lamarck supposed. Nor did Lyell think that species could be ordered through time according to their appearance in any simple progression. He argued against nearly everyone else at the time for a roughly steady-state universe.

Darwin held quite a different view of species and their production. In the *Origin* (1859: 313), he remarks, 'When a species has once disappeared from the face of the earth, we have every reason to believe that the same identical form never reappears.' The differences between Lyell and Darwin over the nature of species can be seen with reasonable clarity in the following exchange between the two men soon after the appearance of the *Origin*. In a letter to Darwin, Lyell (Wilson 1970: 475) poses a problem about the evolution of the class Mammalia, but it applies equally to all taxa:

I wish you could give me the slightest reason why it [Mammalia] should not begin more than once in more than one place. I incline to think it has not, but why? According to the principle of selection, why when once in any quarter of the globe, at any one period, the step in advance has been taken, are the inferior types elsewhere to be checked, & not to presume to work up into any Gnus [genus] of corresponding grade & class?

The question is a good one. Why cannot a taxon evolve more than once? This question can be treated either as empirical in nature or metaphysical. In his response to Lyell, initially Darwin (1899: ii.134) treats the issue as if it were empirical:

I have a very decided opinion that all mammals must have descended from a *single* parent. Reflect on the multitude of details, very many of them of extremely little importance to their habits (as the number of bones in the head, &c. &c.). Now this large amount of similarity I must look at as certainly due to inheritance from a common stock. I am aware that some cases occur in which a similar or nearly similar organ has been acquired by independent acts of natural selection. But in most of such cases of these apparently so closely similar organs, some important homological difference may be detected.

Darwin is arguing that perhaps all the functional characteristics that mammals share might arise in independent creations under similar conditions but not all the non-functional characteristics that they share. Any need can be met in a wide variety of ways. The many peculiarities in the way that all mammals meet certain needs cannot be explained in terms of common environmental factors in their origins, only in terms of common descent. But in a footnote, Darwin (1899: ii.136) adds the following consideration:

N.B. – I know of no rodents on oceanic islands (except my Galapagos mouse, which *may* have been introduced by man) keeping down the development of other classes. Still *much* more weight I should attribute to there being now, neither in islands nor elsewhere, any known animals of a grade of organization intermediate between mammals, fish, reptiles, &c., whence a new mammal could be developed. If every vertebrate were destroyed throughout the world, except our *now well-established reptiles*, millions of ages might elapse before reptiles could become highly developed on a scale equal to mammals: and, on the principle of inheritance, they would make some quite *new class*, and not mammals; though possibly more intellectual! I have not an idea that you will care for this letter, so speculative.

According to Darwin, the vast majority of species that have ever existed are extinct. In his tree of life, only the terminal twigs are extant. More than this, in the preceding quotation at least, Darwin treats species as if their essence is in their origin. Mammalia evolved from species of reptile long since extinct. Assume that the current representatives of the class Mammalia were to die off. The claim that the evolution of new species of organisms identical in every respect to present-day mammals is unlikely in the extreme is empirical. Too many highly contingent states of affairs would have to occur in precisely the right order. But, the claim that on the 'principle of inheritance', this new group would not count as Mammalia but 'quite a *new class*' is a metaphysical claim about how such classes are to be individuated. I cannot begin to claim that Darwin saw the issues as clearly as I have presented them here or that he held such a view consistently. To the contrary, he constantly changed his mind about the nature of species (Sulloway 1969, Kottler 1978). His vacillation is easy to understand. Without entirely realizing it, he had run up against one of the basic themata of his own and previous ages – the nature of natural kinds.

According to traditional notions of natural kinds, natural kinds are eternal, immutable and discrete. One of the paradigm examples of natural kinds throughout the history of Western thought has been biological species. According to Darwin, species lack *all* the traditional characteristics of natural kinds. They are temporary, mutable and fuzzy. Several alternatives present themselves at this juncture. First, one can simply reject Darwin's notion of evolving species. Regardless of anything Darwin and subsequent biologists might think, biological species are eternal, immutable and discrete. Each species is characterized by a set of 'underlying traits'. Any organism that exhibits an appropriate set of traits belongs to that species regardless of all else. If an organism were to arise somehow identical in every respect save origin to an extinct species of pterodactyl, it would belong to this species. As unlikely as it might seem, the dodo may one day live again (Kitts & Kitts 1979, Caplan 1980, 1981).

On the preceding interpretation, the Great Chain of Being remains as atemporal as ever. Only its exemplifications are in point of fact temporal beings. Although most species that have ever existed currently have no representatives, some day in the future they might become re-exemplified as Lyell supposed. The only thing that stands in the way of such events is contingent improbability. My main objection to this way of construing things is that on this view species cannot evolve by natural selection. In order for variations to build up differentially in a species, species must be construed as lineages, not a spatio-temporally unrestricted classes (Hull 1976, 1978). Of course, just because Darwin entitled his book the *Origin of Species*, it does not follow that all later workers are stuck with species as the units of evolution. Perhaps species as taxonomists recognize them are not the things that evolve. As a result, two quite distinct notions co-exist in biology: species as spatio-temporally unrestricted classes and species as evolving lineages. My only complaint about this way of putting the situation is that species in the first sense play no role whatsoever in any biological theory. They are classes but *not* natural kinds.

Second, one can acknowledge that species lack all the traditional characteristics of natural kinds but insist that nevertheless they are natural kinds. Just because most workers throughout recorded history treated natural kinds in a particular way, it does not follow that we must perpetuate their errors. Species are spatio-temporally restricted classes like the members of the Supreme Court of the United States and all the nuts and bolts in my car. One problem with this alternative is that once again species are being viewed as precisely the sorts of classes that cannot function in scientific laws. One has succeeded in keeping species classes at the cost of making them scientifically unimportant. Natural kinds have been reduced to mere classes. More than that, most individuals have been transmuted in the process into mere classes.

For several years now I have been urging a third alternative: conceptualizing species as historical entities. Although species lack all the traditional characteristics of natural kinds, they possess all the traditional characteristics of historical entities. They develop continuously through time. On the punctuated equilibrium model of speciation, the beginnings and endings of species are reasonably sharp and species never undergo a complete changeover in their characteristics while remaining one of the same species (Eldredge & Gould 1972, Eldredge & Cracraft 1980). To the extent that phyletic evolution can occur, the opposite is the case: the boundaries between chronospecies are not sharp and a lineage can undergo total change. Whether one acknowledges new species in this process is a moot question. On any view of speciation, however, species undergo regular, total replacements of their constituent organisms. The important feature of species as historical entities is the retention of internal cohesiveness as they undergo continuous development. Although the empirical difficulties in applying such a conception of species are formidable, a growing number of the most theoretically sophisticated biologists have come to see the point of treating species as ordinary historical entities rather than as highly bizarre natural kinds. Whether one views this transition as a 'demotion' depends on the value one places on natural kinds over historical entities.

One final modification must be made in the species concept if species are to be treated as historical entities. Previously I noted that in the individuation of historical entities, unrealized potentialities do not count. Rivers, corporations and species can both split and merge. Any river might split into two. Any two rivers in reasonably close proximity might merge into a single river. A particular river is not treated as indefinitely many rivers because potentially it might split, nor are all rivers in close proximity considered a single river because they might merge. The same can be said for corporations and species. However, the most important definition of 'species', the species category, includes reference to potential interbreeding. According to Mayr's (1942: 120) classic definition, 'Species are groups of actually or potentially interbreeding natural populations, which are reproductively isolated from other such groups.' On this definition, two populations that remain forever distinct can still belong throughout this time to the same species if the only things preventing them from exchanging genes are geographical and/or ecological barriers.

Two common objections have been raised to Mayr's biological species definition: one, that it is not operational, and two, that it entails that asexual organisms do not form species. The obvious reply to the first objection is that theoretical terms are never totally operational and could not perform their appropriate roles if they were (Hull 1968). The second objection is not so easily met. In the last analysis, however, one must admit that perhaps not all organisms form species (as evolutionary units), just as not all organisms form hives or colonies (Hull 1980).

For the purposes of this paper, the important feature of Mayr's definition is his reference to potential interbreeding. If unrealized potentialities are relevant in the individuation of species, then species cannot be historical entities. Happily this particular problem is no longer a problem. In more recent statements of his biological definition of 'species', Mayr (1969: 26) has eliminated reference to 'potential interbreeding', not because of operational considerations, but because everything that needs to be said can be said in terms of 'reproductive isolation'. In his more recent work, Mayr (1978: 52) has explicitly adopted the position on the ontological status of species set out in this paper:

Uniquely different individuals are organized into interbreeding populations and into species. All the members are 'parts' of the species, since they are derived from and contribute to a single gene pool. The population or species as a whole is itself the 'individual' that undergoes evolution; it is not a class with members.

HISTORICAL ENTITIES AS CENTRAL SUBJECTS

Philosophers of science are infamous for arguing that the only thing that can count as a genuine scientific explanation is inference (preferably deductive) from laws of nature together with a variety of non-lawlike statements. Although both the laws and the statements of special circumstances are equally *necessary* in such derivations, all the explanatory import is provided by the laws. To the extent that the laws are weak and exception-ridden, the explanation is weak. In the absence of derivation from laws, explanation is impossible. The problem posed by science is that many putative scientific explanations can be construed as covering-law explanations only at the price of extreme artificiality and distortion. Chief among the sorts of non-covering-law explanations that nevertheless seem explanatory is a special sort of historical explanation – historical narratives.

Elsewhere I have argued that the traditional analysis of science need not be modified in order to account for the apparent explanatory power of historical narratives if only one acknowledges the importance of historical entities in natural processes (Hull 1975, 1981b). Traditional scientific laws concern natural processes – the revolution of planets around stars, the relation of temperature and pressure in enclosed gases, the deposition of sediments at the bottoms of lakes, seas and oceans, and the evolution of species. Some of these laws, however, range over historical entities. For example, in order to come up with the laws of celestial mechanics, physicists had to recognize both the appropriate individuals (planets, stars, moons, etc.) and the appropriate characteristics of these individuals (mass, position, velocity, etc.). They then had to organize these characteristics in the correct way.

The discovery of the right characteristics and their interrelations is considered a major achievement in science. The discovery of appropriate individuals can be just as difficult a process, but for some reason it is rarely considered very important. One possible explanation for theoretically significant individuals being taken so much for granted is that, early on in the history of science, commonsense individuals such as stars, lead balls and the like were adequate for scientific purposes. However, as science has proceeded, commonsense individuals have ceased to be adequate and have been replaced by highly theoretical entities. Quarks and baryons are not your ordinary individuals. Neither are species and genes.[2] Another source of the low status of individuals in present-day philosophies of science is the old metaphysical prejudice for entities that are eternal, immutable and discrete over those that are temporary, mutable and fuzzy. Anything that can be explained by reference to a natural kind is really explained. Anything that is explained merely by reference to one of the exemplifications of a natural kind is really not explained at all.

I can see the point of the first conviction but not the second. A particular instance of a regularity can certainly be explained by reference to this regularity, but there is more to nature than the sorts of regularities enshrined in laws of nature. Events can be organized in two ways, according to the processes that produce them and in sequences determined by the continued existence of historical entities. Covering-law explanations are appropriate for the former; narrative explanations for the latter. For example, organisms are theoretically significant entities in the evolutionary process. They are one of the major foci of the interactions that make replication differential (Hull 1978). The justification for treating organisms as theoretically significant depends on this reference. However, organisms can be identified and followed through time in relative isolation from such theoretical considerations. The same can be said for species as evolving lineages. Species evolve through a process of mutation, replication and selective retention. Their development through time can be traced, however, in the midst of ignorance about the actual processes that produced them. The tracing of historical entities through time is largely a matter of historical reconstruction, not inference from laws of nature.

It comes as a surprise to most people that evolutionary theory plays a relatively minor role in paleontology (Raup 1981). Most of the issues over which evolutionary biologists disagree have little in the way of implications for phylogenetic reconstructions. About all that matters is that evolution be a process of modification through descent. The only fact about the evolutionary process that could influence paleontology is the size of speciation events. If speciation is a gradual affair or occurs in relatively small steps (Eldredge and Gould 1972), then in principle phylogenetic reconstructions can be made continuous. In practice, of course, there will always be such large gaps in the fossil record that these gaps will hide all but the most saltative of changes. But, excepting for such considerations, the fossil record is compatible with all current versions of

---

[2] Ordinary discourse does not always lend itself easily to making certain distinctions. Quarks are a typical natural kind, but particular instances of a quark are not typical individuals. Comparable observations hold for baryons, species and genes.

evolutionary theory. As a result, evolutionary theory is not much help in reconstructing phylogenetic sequences.

In general, the phylogenetic trees and historical narratives (scenarios) that evolutionary biologists construct are none too dependable. Too much of the data that paleontologists need to justify both their trees and their scenarios (Tattersall and Eldredge 1977) are either missing or ambiguous. for this reason, Gould (1976) terms paleontological historical narratives 'just so stories'. He cannot mean the term to be too derogatory, however, because he himself has spent much of his professional career producing such just so stories (see also Patterson 1980). Physicists seem to be in a much stronger position. Paleontologists have difficulty in producing warranted reconstructions of events that took place only a few million years ago. Physicists claim that they can tell us in great detail what happened during the *first three minutes* in the formation of the universe (Weinberg 1977). This asymmetry can be explained by reference to the respective theories. The story that physicists tell of the events that took place in the beginning is not a matter of historical reconstruction but theoretical inference. Given current physical theories and the existence of red-shifted 'fossil radiation' left over from the big bang, physicists can date the beginning of the universe.

In covering-law explanations an event is inferred from one or more process laws and statements of particular circumstances. In historical reconstructions – Goudge's (1961) integrative explanations – historical entities are inferred on the basis of historical records. One can recognize Napoleon as an historical entity and trace his existence through time on the basis of the traces he left without a very extensive understanding of the processes governing human history. We had better be able to, because we are painfully ignorant of these processes. We can do the same for continents, societies and other historical entities. To the extent that an historical entity can be recognized, an historical narrative can be constructed of the events in which this historical entity participated. The events mentioned and the sequence in which they are presented cannot be justified by any laws of nature. In most cases, these laws are either totally unknown or else of little help in constructing the historical narrative. For example, Napoleon invaded Russia. No one can deduce Napoleon's invasion of Russia from any laws of nature. We can, nevertheless, know that he did and include this event in the historical narrative that chronicles his career.

In a sense historical narratives are easy to come by. We can present them even though we are largely ignorant of the laws governing the relevant processes. In another sense they come very dear. They must be produced by the laborious process of uncovering historical records of past events. To make matters worse, each historical narrative must be undertaken anew.

When one understands the processes governing Mars' path around the sun, one can reason quite easily to the path other planets will take. Once one has a good understanding of Napoleon's career, one is partway down the road to tracing the careers of other people who interacted with Napoleon, but they must be traced on their own. They are not instances of a natural kind. There are as many historical narratives as there are historical entities. The task is endless. Another reason that scientists seem to value covering-law explanations more than historical narratives is that the former are in principle reducible to inferences from a very few basic principles while for the latter, though possibly finite in number, the number is so large that we know in advance that we can produce narrative explanations for only a tiny fraction of all the historical entities that ever existed. Discovering a new law of nature is a much more momentous occasion than discovering a new historical entity and tracing its course. Darwin is famous for his theory of evolution, not the numerous new species he discovered on his voyage.

The contrast between explaining something by reference to the continuing existence of an historical entity and explaining it by derivation from a law of nature can be seen in the following example. 'Why aren't the mammals indigenous to Australia eutherians? All the environmental conditions were perfect for the establishment of such highly advanced mammals.' The answer is that eutherians evolved elsewhere and failed to make their way to Australia. From what we know of the processes governing the survival and reproduction of higher animals, we can conclude that eutherian mammals would have rapidly established themselves had they invaded Australia. That they did not succeed in finding their way to Australia is hardly a law of nature, but it is part of the historical narrative for eutherian mammals.

Advocates of covering-law models would naturally respond that the putative 'two' sorts of explanation are one. What I have termed historical narratives would merely be put into the statements of particular circumstances. The point I wish to emphasize is that sometimes the laws in covering-law models are sufficiently strong to warrant the inference to the occurrence of a particular event with little aid from the statements of particular circumstances. They are genuinely covering-law explanations (Sober 1983). But sometimes the laws are so ineffectual that the statements of particular circumstances carry the explanatory burden. In Australia, small kangaroos fill the ecological niche filled in most other areas of the world by large rodents because of the contingencies surrounding the population of Australia. Such explanations are better termed 'particular circumstances explanations', than covering-law explanations.

For those permanently wedded to the covering-law model of scientific explanation, nothing but derivation from a law of nature will count as an explanation. Regardless of whether one wants to term the reconstruction of historical entities and the chronicling of their trajectories through time 'explanations', these activities are important parts of science. Such activities might even be construable as potential covering-law explanations. The only things missing are the laws. It may well be true that part of the psychological satisfaction imparted by historical explanations involving historical entities stems from the assumed though unknown laws governing the processes. However, I think that most of it derives from the continuity provided by historical entities in the absence of very extensive understanding of the processes governing the career of the historical entity. This psychological satisfaction may be spurious, but I do not think so.

HISTORICAL ENTITIES AND THE SCIENCES OF MAN

Nothing strikes a biologist as being so peculiar as the obsessive attention paid by certain scientists to one species out of millions. From a variety of perspectives, particular species are especially interesting – a species of bacteria that can live just on sulfur, a species of nematode in which the male lives as a parasite in the pharynx of the female, and on and on. But I suspect that scientists would look askance at the declaration of the science of aardvarkology devoted to the study of the African aardvark. When the species in question is *Homo sapiens*, nary an eyebrow is lifted. Paleontologists reconstruct the phylogenetic development of past species. A certain brand of anthropology devotes itself to the 'recent' development of a single species. Although most paleontologists limit themselves to only a sub-portion of the phylogenetic tree, few would be content to study the recent phylogenetic development of a single species unless that species happens to be our own.

Our interest in ourselves is certainly understandable, but the erection of entire sciences, academic departments, etc., around the study of ourselves seems a bit excessive. But a problem more serious than anthropocentrism confronts the sciences of 'man'. As long as biologists viewed *Homo sapiens* as a natural kind, the search for human nature and the laws governing human beings qua human beings made perfectly good sense, as much sense as looking for the essence of gold and the laws governing its behavior. As it turns out, there are only about a hundred or so physical elements while species come in the millions. Physicists can afford to spend considerable time studying each of the elements. Biologists are in the unhappy predicament of species going extinct faster than they can study them. They are also reconciled to finding only 'statistical' laws for species. Perhaps all gold under certain conditions is malleable, but no matter the conditions, the covariation of traits descriptive of particular species both at any one time and through time tends to be only statistical. Most North American crows

(*Corvus brachyrhynchos*) are black, but not all, and not everything that is black is a North American crow. Similarly, no blood type, skin color, hair texture, sex, or eye color is universally distributed among all human beings today, let alone throughout the duration of *Homo sapiens*. Perhaps genotypes are in some sense 'unitary', but this unity does not result from genetic homogeneity. The evidence for extensive intraspecific heterogeneity is overwhelming (Wills 1981).

The most common objection introduced at this point is that all the members of a sexual species at least do have something in common which is at the same time unique to them – the ability to breed with one another. The two obvious replies to this objection are that the father of the biological species concept has dropped 'potential interbreeding' from his more recent formulation of this definition and, more importantly, than the biological definition is of the term 'species', not the names of particular species. As Mayr (1978) has pointed out, even though particular species are historical entities, the species category is not. If species are the things that evolve, then the species category (as distinct from particular taxa) is a natural kind. Just as the term 'planet' can denote a natural kind even though 'Mars' does not, the term 'species' can denote a natural kind even though '*Cygnus olor*' does not. The only way that a particular species could be defined in terms of interbreeding is by the specification of a particular organism or organisms as a focus for this relation. For example, one might define '*Homo sapiens*' as Adam and Eve and all their descendants. As implausible as these particular foci might be, no matter which people were chosen for this role, the result would be the same: *Homo sapiens* would be an historical entity.

The compulsion to find the eternal, immutable essence of *Cygnus olor* or *Corvus brachyrhynchos* is, to say the least, minimal. Some species are monothetic: one or more characteristics can be found that uniquely denote these species. Others are polythetic. For some reason, however, the desire to find some trait that all human beings possess and no non-humans possess is all but overwhelming. But no matter the trait chosen, either some people do not exhibit it or else members of some other species do. The amount of intellectual wriggling that goes on to make *Homo sapiens* monothetic is dismaying. 'Human beings are essentially X. Any human being who ostensibly lacks X really possesses it at least potentially. So a particular person lacks the genetic information for the formation of thumbs. That person still has a thumb at least potentially. Conversely, the exhibition of X by members of any other species is only apparent. No matter how extensively members of other species seem to communicate with each other, they really do not possess a language. Only human beings use language.'

I find such special pleading intellectually disgusting. But worse still, it seems totally otiose. Some species are monothetic. Why is it so incredibly important that *Homo sapiens* be among this group? The only answer I can think of turns on the metaphysical predilection for traditional natural kinds. *Homo sapiens* must have a nature if this nature is going to function in explanation. However, if the human species has evolved the way that other species have evolved, then it cannot have a traditional 'nature'. It cannot be eternal. It cannot be immutable. It *may* be relatively discrete, especially if it arose the way that Eldredge and Gould (1972) suggest that most species arise – by punctuational means. Although the theoretical justification is not as great, Geertz (1965: 106) has argued forcefully for this same conclusion with respect to a cultural definition of human nature:

The notion that unless a cultural phenomenon is empirically universal it cannot reflect anything about the nature of man is about as logical as the notion that because sickle-cell anemia is, fortunately, not universal it cannot tell us anything about human genetic processes. It is not whether phenomena are empirically common that is critical in science – else why should Becquerel have been so interested in the peculiar behavior of uranium? – but whether they can be made to reveal the enduring natural processes that underly them.

One might argue that the term 'species' is multiply ambiguous the way that 'bark' is. Just as dogs bark and trees are covered in bark, one can bark one's shins and float down a stream in a bark. Ordinary people may well use 'species' in a variety of ways, philosophers in another half-dozen or so ways, and so on. I am in no position to dictate English usage even if I were of a mind to do so, which I am not. Ordinary people can use the term 'species' any way that they see fit – just so long as they do not simultaneously attempt to trade off the evolutionary usage of this term. Nothing precludes a philosopher from defining 'species' in such a way that species cannot evolve, but then it follows that this philosopher is not talking about the same things that evolutionary biologists are talking about when they refer to species.

A more serious objection in this same vein is that biology itself is broken down into sub-disciplines with different goals and methods. Perhaps each of these sub-disciplines requires a different species concept. In one, species may be natural kinds, in another historical entities, in another they are events, and so on. Periodically, systematists have grown exasperated at attempting to discern evolutionary species when species are going extinct faster than we are classifying them. Why not treat species as natural kinds defined by certain differentia? Such taxospecies might on occasion coincide with biospecies, but it would not make any difference whether they did or not. One consequence of this decision is that biological systematics is divorced from evolutionary theory. Philosophers agree with each other about precious little, but one belief that is at least common among philosophers of science is that scientific classifications are scientifically significant only to the extent that they are theoretically committed. Hence, if classifications built up of taxospecies are to be scientifically significant, they must make recourse to some scientific theory, perhaps not evolutionary theory but *some* theory.

Of course, it is always possible that diremptions exist in nature, that different sorts of natural phenomena are totally independent of each other, including phenomena at different levels of analysis. Perhaps my reductive tendencies are showing, but I fail to see the justice of calling entities that are irreducible to each other by the same name. If the species concepts of, say, molecular geneticists and evolutionary biologists are irreducibly different, I think that only confusion can result from using the same term to denote them. I myself prefer to strive for a single, univocal species concept applicable throughout biology. I think that species as historical entities functioning in the evolutionary process is the best candidate for such a univocal species concept. Such an interpretation has its benefits. It also has its costs. If species are interpreted as individuals and no uneliminable references can be made to particular individuals in scientific laws and theories, then no scientific law or theory can be limited *necessarily* to a single species. It may just so happen that a particular theory is exemplifed at the moment by only a single species. It may even be the case that throughout the history of the universe only a single species exemplifies a particular law. The alternative I wish to investigate is those putative theories and laws limited *necessarily* to a single species. If species are individuals, it follows that such theories are at most true descriptive statements, possibly theory-laden, but not themselves laws or theories. They lack the requisite generality and extrapolatability.

Alex Rosenberg has pursued this implication of species being individuals for the social sciences at great length in his *Sociobiology and the Preemption of Social Science* (1980). In this paper I examine only two representative examples – operant conditioning and Freudian theory. The laws of operant conditioning are not limited to human beings. To the extent that they are applicable to all, they are supposed to apply to anything that can be conditioned – planaria, yes; petunias, no. Nor are these laws limited necessarily to organisms that have evolved here on earth. It might be the case that the inhabitants of other planets that seem to pop in so frequently for visits can be conditioned in the same way the pigeons and people can; perhaps not. In order for something to count as a genuine law or theory, it need not apply to everything, just everything that fits a particular description. The only limitation on these descriptions is that they must be spatio-temporally unrestricted.

Because scientists who limit their interest to human beings alone are only now being confronted with the question of the domain of their theories, it is difficult to tell if they intend their theories to be limited necessarily to *Homo sapiens*. The theories of Freud and Piaget appear to be so limited. Many objections have been raised to Freud's theory of human development. At times it seems that, if it is applicable at all, it is applicable only to middle-class Viennese Jews at the turn of the century. Like all scientists, Freud continued to develop his theory throughout his life, and his disciples have changed it even more markedly in the meantime. Hence, it is impossible to talk about some one thing termed 'Freudian theory', but for sake of argument, let us assume that at least one version of Freudian theory exists in which the id, ego and superego are central.

Do all people have ids? The notorious distance between Freud's theoretical apparatus and anything that might be considered a test of his theory need not be belabored here, but that is not what I am asking. Are Freudians committed to all people having ids, even the profoundly retarded? Certainly Freudian therapy cannot be utilized in such cases, but the theory might nevertheless be applicable. The more important question is whether or not anything besides people *could* have an id. Must one be born of human beings, be raised by human beings, be a human being for Freud's theory to apply? I think the answer to this question must be yes. Human females no longer suffer from penis envy, just as hysteria seems to be on the wane, but in a much more fundamental sense, a female carp cannot suffer from this malady. So much of Freud's theory is bound up with the peculiarities of human beings and their culture that, at the very least, it is extremely unlikely that any other being would possess enough of these peculiarities for the theory to apply. All this says is that Freudian theory is highly particularized. It does not entail that it is nothing but a description. Only if the entities to which it applies must be born of human beings does it cease to be a candidate for a genuine scientific theory.

Inherent in Freud's theory is the notion of normal psychological development. Although Freud changed the details about the requisite stages, their order, the things which could impair normal development, etc., he retained the view that such sequences exist, at most one for males and one for females. From what biologists know of the ontogenetic development of other species, Freud's assumption is questionable at best. Species commonly possess the ability to proceed down alternative developmental pathways given the appropriate sequence of conditions. These pathways taken collectively are termed the 'reaction norm' for the species. Certain pathways may be quite common because the requisite environmental conditions are quite common, but all developmental pathways are equally 'normal' in the sense of lying within the reaction norm for the species. For example, a certain sort of marine invertebrate possesses the potential of being either male or female in the larval stage. When it settles to the bottom, it becomes a female if it lands on anything but the proboscis of a member of its own species; otherwise a male. In low concentrations, females prevail; in high concentrations, males become more common.

From a biological perspective, Freud's theory gains little support. But of greater importance, if species can evolve gradually through time, a property widely distributed in a species at one time might become rare and disappear entirely. For example, at one time most moths of a particular species in the industrial areas of England were light brown. Melanic forms were rare. Quite rapidly, the black form became more common. As pollution controls took effect, the brown form began to stage a comeback. Neither color state in and of itself is in any sense biologically more normal than the other. Thus, if the basic psychological make-up of human beings follows the same principles as all other traits, it is possible for some people not to have an id. At one time, ids might be quite common. Later, they might become quite rare or disappear altogether.

The preceding discussion has an air of unreality to it, partly because few of us take Freud's theoretical apparatus all that seriously any more, partly because we are used to treating the human species as a natural kind, and the essences of natural kinds are not supposed to change through time. The id is not a very good candidate for a theoretical entity in science if it is necessarily limited to a particular segment of the phylogenetic tree. Freud's theory does not thereby become nothing. It becomes a description of how a particular system functions for a certain period under particular circumstances. Perhaps some general principles can be derived from studying such systems, but descriptions themselves, as important as they may be, are not scientific theories akin to quantum theory and evolutionary theory. I began this paper with a quotation from Gould (1980: 116) to the effect that human history is 'so recalcitrantly idiographic because it is the story of a single species'. It represents the 'vicissitudes of an individual' of 'unparalleled flexibility'. No description of the vicissitudes of this individual can count as a law of nature. Nevertheless, a general theory might encompass it, not as the particular individual it is, but as an instance of some natural kind, possibly as an example of a cosmopolitan species or a dominant species, but not as *Homo sapiens* qua *Homo sapiens*.

One final comment before I close: in the preceding discussion I have treated '*Homo sapiens*' and 'human beings' as equivalent expressions, when in certain contexts they are not. Nothing exasperates a philosopher more than treating people as if they were biological organisms instead of 'persons'. Conversely, biologists are liable to become a bit impatient with the elusive nature of 'personhood' (for an illustrative example of this conflict see the exchange between Hickman 1981, Boving 1981, Libet 1981, Goodhart 1981, Rooney 1981, and Hefferman 1981).

CONCLUSION

Much of the emphasis in past discussions of historical explanations has been misplaced. Too much time has been spent arguing that all sorts of statements are really laws of nature so that historical explanations can share in the same sort of explanatory force characteristic of covering-law explanations. Terming simple descriptions 'laws' may be a good propaganda device, as effective as terming spinsters 'bachelorettes', but from the point of view of assertive content, nothing has been changed by such maneuvers. Descriptions of the continued existence of historical entities and the sequences of events in which they participate may be theory-laden, but they are hardly laws of nature. It does not follow that explanations in terms of these descriptions have no explanatory force. Philosophers can hardly claim to explain very much by reference to laws of nature in their own activities. They can claim that covering-law explanations are the only genuine sort of explanation only by admitting that they themselves have never explained anything.[3]

REFERENCES

Aristotle. 1910. *Historia Animalium*, trans. D'Arcy Thompson. Oxford.

Boving, B. G. 1981. ' "Human Life" Testimony', *Science* 213,154.

Caplan, A. 1980. 'Have Species Become Déclassé?', *PSA* 1980, ed. P. D. Asquith and R. N. Giere, 71–82. East Lansing, Mich.

Caplan, A. 1981. 'Back to Class: A Note on the Ontology of Species', *Philosophy of Science* 48, 130–40.

Darwin, C. 1859. *The Origin of Species*. London.

Darwin, F. (ed.), 1899. *The Life and Letters of Charles Darwin*. New York.

Dretske, F. I. 1977. 'Laws of Nature', *Philosophy of Science*, 44, 248–68.

Eldredge, N., and J. Cracraft, 1980. *Phylogenetic Patterns and the Evolutionary Process*. New York.

Eldredge, N., and S. J. Gould, 1972. 'Punctuated Equilibria: An Alternative to Phyletic Gradualism', in *Models in Paleobiology*, ed. T. J. M. Schopf, 82–115. San Francisco.

Gasking, D. 1961. 'Clusters', *Australasian Review of Psychology* 38, 1–36.

Geertz, C. 1965. 'The Impact of the Concept of Culture on the Concept of Man', in *New View of the Nature of Man*, ed. J. R. Platt, 93–118. Chicago.

Ghiselin, M. 1974. 'A Radical Solution to the Species Problem', *Systematic Zoology* 23, 536–44.

Goodhart, C. B. 1981. 'Human Life', *Science* 213, 494.

Goudge, T. A. 1961 *The Ascent of Life*. Toronto.

Gould, S. J. 1976. *Ever Since Darwin*. New York.

[3] This paper was written in part under a fellowship from the Guggenheim Foundation. I wish to express appreciation for the suggestions for improving this paper offered by the participants in the September 1981 Thyssen Philosophy Group.

Gould, S. J. 1980 'The Promise of Paleobiology as a Nomothetic, Evolutionary Discipline', *Paleobiology* 6, 96–118.

Hefferman, B. 1981. 'Human Life', *Science* 213, 496.

Hickman, J. C. 1981. ' "Human Life" Testimony', *Science* 213, 154.

Hull, D. L. 1965 'The Effects of Essentialism on Taxonomy', *The British Journal for the Philosophy of Science* 15, 314–26; 16, 1–18.

Hull, D. L. 1968. 'The Operational Imperative – Sense and Nonsense in Operationism', *Systematic Zoology* 17, 438–57.

Hull, D. L. 1975. 'Central Subjects and Historical Narratives', *History and Theory* 14, 253–74.

Hull, D. L. 1976. 'Are Species Really Individuals?', *Systematic Zoology* 25, 174–91.

Hull, D. L. 1978. 'A Matter of Individuality', *Philosophy of Science* 45, 335–60.

Hull, D. L. 1980. 'Individuality and Selection', *Annual Review of Ecology and Systematics* 11, 311–32.

Hull, D. L. 1981. 'Integrating and Narrative Explanations', *Pragmatism and Purpose* ed. L. W. Sumner, J. G. Slater, and F. Wilson. Toronto.

Hull, D. L. 1982a. 'Linné and Natural Kinds', *Proceedings of the Texas Linnaeus Symposium*, ed. J. M. Weinstock, forthcoming.

Hull, D. L. 1982b. 'Hypotheses that Blur and Grow', in *The Estimation of Evolutionary History*, ed. T. Duncan and T. Steussy. New York.

Kitts, D. B., and Kitts, D. J. 1979. 'Biological Species as Natural Kinds', *Philosophy of Science* 46, 613–22.

Kottler, M. J. 1978. 'Charles Darwin's Biological Species Concept and Theory of Geographic Speciation', *Annals of Science* 35, 275–98.

Lamarck, J. B. 1809. *Philosophie zoologique* trans. H. Elliot (1963). New York.

Lennox, J. 1980. 'Aristotle on Genera, Species, and "the More and the Less" ', *Journal of the History of Biology* 13, 321–46.

Libet, B. 1981. ' "Human Life" Testimony', *Science* 213, 154–5.

Lovejoy, A. O. 1936. *The Great Chain of Being*, Cambridge.

Lyell, C. 1832. *Principles of Geology*, 3 vols. London.

Lyell, C. 1873. *The Geological Evidence of the Antiquity of Man*, 4th ed. London.

Mackie, J. L. 1974. '*De* what *Re* is *De Re* Modality?', *Journal of Philosophy* 71, 551–61.

Mayr, E. 1942. *Systematics and the Origin of Species*. New York.

Mayr, E. 1969. *Principles of Systematic Zoology*. New York.

Mayr, E. 1978. 'Evolution', *Scientific American* 239, 47–55.

Patterson, C. 1980. 'Cladistics', *Biologist* 27, 234–40.

Raup, D. M. 1981. 'Evolution and the Fossil Record', *Science* 213, 289.

Rooney, R. P. 1981. 'Human Life', *Science* 213, 494–95.

Rosenberg, A. 1980. *Sociobiology and the Preemption of Social Science*. Baltimore.

Sober, E. 1983. 'Equilibrium Explanation', *Philosophical Studies* 43, 201–10.

Sulloway, F. J. 1969. 'Geographic Isolation in Darwin's Thinking', *Studies in the History of Biology* 3, 23–65.

Tattersall, I., and Eldredge, N. 1977. 'Fact, Theory, and Fantasy in Human Paleontology', *American Scientist* 65, 204–311.

Vrba, E. 1980. 'Evolution, Species and Fossils: How Does Life Evolve?', *South African Journal of Science* 76, 61–84.

Weinberg, S. 1977. *The First Three Minutes*. New York.

Wiggins, D. 1980. *Sameness and Substance*. Cambridge.

Wills, C. 1981. *Genetic Variability*. New York.

Wilson, L. G. (ed.) 1970. *Sir Charles Lyell's Scientific Journals on the Species Question*. New Haven.

Zirkle, C. 1959. 'Species before Darwin', *Proceedings of the American Philosophical Society* 103, 636–44.

Force and disposition in evolutionary theory[1]

ELLIOTT SOBER

I. INTRODUCTION

In the introduction to his book on causality, Patrick Suppes (1970) quotes with amusement an essay by Russell on the concept of cause:

All philosophers, of every school, imagine that causation is one of the fundamental axioms or postulates of science, yet, oddly enough, in advanced sciences such as gravitational astronomy, the word 'cause' never occurs ... The law of causality, I believe, like much that passes muster among philosophers, is a relic of a bygone age, surviving, like the monarchy, only because it is erroneously supposed to do no harm ... No doubt the reason why the old 'law of causality' has so long continued to pervade the books of philosophers is simply that the idea of a function is unfamiliar to most of them, and therefore they seek an unduly simplified statement. There is no question of repetitions of the 'same' cause producing the 'same' effect; it is not in any sameness of causes and effects that the constancy of scientific laws consists, but in sameness of relations. And even 'sameness of relations' is too simple a phrase; 'sameness of differential equations' is the only correct phrase.

'Perhaps the most amusing thing about this passage', says Suppes, '... is that its claim about the use of the word "cause" in physics no longer holds. Contrary to the days when Russell wrote this essay, the words "causality" and "cause" are commonly and widely used by physicists in their most advanced work.'

There is a similar story to be told about the concept of causation in evolutionary theory (ET). In the work of Darwin, and, indeed, in non-mathematical discussion down to the present day, natural selection is conceived of as a causal process. To say that there is selection for a given trait is to say that possessing that trait causes differential reproductive success. But mathematical modelling of evolutionary processes, beginning with the ground-breaking work of Wright, Fisher, and Haldane, and also continuing down to the present day, does not make use of the word 'cause'. The concept of *selection for* a property is replaced by the concept of *selection of*

[1] This paper was written during the tenure of a grant from the John Simon Guggenheim Foundation, which I acknowledge with thanks. I am also grateful to the Museum of Comparative Zoology, Harvard University, for its hospitality during 1980–81.

objects. Roughly, to say that there is selection of objects of a given kind is to say that objects of that kind, on average, are more reproductively successful than objects which are not of that kind. One might imagine Russell surveying the state of the art in ET right now. He might decide that mathematical modelling in population genetics, and to a lesser degree in theoretical ecology, is the entire 'real' content of the subject, and that anything not explicitly formulated in the mathematics is gratuitous marginalia.

It would be a bit high-handed to greet this position with amusement, since it is presupposed by a very influential point of view within ET. Yet criticism, if not derision, is what the idea deserves. I hope to supply a measure of it in what follows.

Causal considerations play a major role in the continuing controversy in ET over the 'units of selection'. Evolution by natural selection will occur in a set of objects if and only if (i) the objects differ from each other, (ii) some are more reproductively successful than others, and (iii) the reproductive success of offspring correlates with the reproductive success of parents (Lewontin 1970). But this abstract characterization of 'heritable variation in fitness' leaves open what 'objects' instantiate the required conditions. Darwin's standard formulation required that the objects be *organisms*. In 1962, V. C. Wynne-Edwards published *Animal Dispersion in Relation to Social Behavior* in which he systematically defended an alternative to this Darwinian position.

If selection is always for and against individual organisms, then it must be a mistake to explain an adaptation by claiming that it is for the good of the group or species in which it is present. Yet, such group-selectionist modes of thinking were not unknown in ET. Wynne-Edwards raised them to the level of consciousness, and argued that the Darwinian model was incapable of accounting for a whole range of adaptations. George C. Williams then published *Adaptation and Natural Selection* (1966) which attacked Wynne-Edwards' deviation from the Darwinian line. But rather than simply returning to the older idea of organismic selection, Williams used his attack on group selection as a forum for articulating a point of view that had been gaining currency ever since evolutionary theory was combined with Mendelian genetics to forge the 'Modern Synthesis'. This is the idea that it is not groups or even organisms that natural selection acts upon, but rather it is the *single gene* which is the unit of selection. This idea was then popularized by Richard Dawkins in his influential book *The Selfish Gene* (1975). One task of this paper will be to clarify the distinction between group, organismic, and genic selection. It will emerge that the idea of a level of selection crucially involves considerations of what properties are *selected for*; i.e., of what the causal mechanisms are that underlie the existence of heritable variation in fitness.

44

Besides showing that causal ideas rear their ugly heads in ET, I want to argue a point of more general philosophical significance. The ideas of *force* and *disposition* have often been attacked by philosophers on the grounds that they make use of the notions of *causal agency* and *causal power*. Just as Russell suggests in the above quotation that to the degree that causal ideas are not just hocus-pocus, they can be reduced to the mathematical idea of function, so philosophers have attempted to isolate what is scientifically respectable about the ideas of force and disposition by 'reducing' these ideas to certain counterfactual relations that obtain among objects. The impetus behind these reductions is usually to show that forces are not 'things' and that dispositions are not 'occult qualities'. Talk of forces and dispositions is simply a way of describing the regularities that objects obey.

I want to challenge the following two reductionist construals of the ideas of force and disposition:

(F)   To say that a set of objects is subject to a given force is merely to say how those objects will behave, if nothing else interferes.

(D)   To say that an object has a disposition to do X is simply to say that the object will do X, if the 'triggering conditions' are satisfied and nothing else interferes.[2]

The idea behind both these principles is to reduce force and disposition to their *ceteris paribus* effects.

These issues about the status of forces and dispositions arise within ET because selection is a force and fitness is a disposition. Mathematical treatments of fitness and selection lend themselves to the reductionist interpretations just mentioned. The fitness value and selection coefficients attaching to an object (a gene, say) are mathematically interderivable. What these numbers represent is how that gene will increase or decrease in frequency in the population, as long as no other evolutionary forces interfere. So talking about there being selection for a gene, or about the fitness of a gene, seems basically to be a way of describing how that object would behave in certain circumstances.

The contrary position which I will defend construes force as a stronger concept than disposition, and disposition as a stronger concept than that of *ceteris paribus* effects. Hypotheses of group, organismic, or genic selection describe the causes of fitness differences between objects. And if 'fitness' is to pick out a real, scientifically respectable property, and not an artifactual

---

[2] The conditionals involved here are to be understood subjunctively, and not as demanding that their antecedents be contrary to fact. Also, since the force and disposition to be considered in what follows – natural selection and fitness – are probabilistic, principles F and D will require reformulation. Rather than the *ceteris paribus* effect following necessarily, it will be a probabilistic consequence of the existence of the force or the possession of the disposition that certain relative frequencies have certain probabilities (in accordance with laws of large numbers).

pseudo-parameter, it must describe the causes of reproductive success, and not just the net changes that are attendant on such success. My case for decoupling selection and fitness will be presented in the context of clarifying the difference between group and organismic selection. My case for decoupling fitness and *ceteris paribus* effects will be developed in the context of clarifying the difference between organismic and genic selection. If selection is a force and fitness is a disposition, then a consequence of the discussion will be a rejection of the reductionist principles F and D.

Before launching into the biology, I want to illustrate these two points by very simple examples drawn from other sciences. The first is from physics. The classical law of gravitation asserts that two objects produce a force between each other (the force due to gravity) which varies inversely as the square of the distance between them, and directly as the product of their masses:

$$F_{\mathrm{g}} = \frac{Gm_1 m_2}{r^2}$$

Similarly, Coulomb's law states that two charged bodies produce a force between each other (the force due to electricity) which also varies inversely as the square distance between them, but directly as the product of their charges:

$$F_{\mathrm{e}} = \frac{q_1 q_2}{r^2}$$

Coulomb's law needs to be understood as allowing for the possibility of *insulation*; two charged bodies will generate that force, only if no insulator prevents this from happening. Let us suppose, just for the sake of the example, that gravitational forces can be insulated against as well.

Imagine that we are observing two objects whose masses and electrical charges are such that

$$\frac{Gm_1 m_2}{r^2}$$

happens to be identical with

$$\frac{-q_1 q_2}{r^2}$$

There is an insulator between the two objects, however. The problem is that we do not know whether it is an electricity insulator, or a gravity insulator. The two objects are generating a gravitational force or an electrical force, but we cannot tell which. It will be impossible to say which of these is the force involved, if all we are permitted to do is watch how the two objects move. On either hypothesis, they will accelerate towards each other in conformity with $F = ma$.

No sceptical doubts ought to tempt us in this case, however, since there are two obvious ways in which we can tell which of the hypotheses is correct. First of all, we know that there is more to a force than its *ceteris paribus* effects. Forces have sources; we know what physical arrangements create various forces, and what physical arrangements serve as insulators. So rather than just focusing on the two objects involved, we might look at the environment. Secondly, we might introduce several more objects into the system and see how they behave. If we introduce objects whose masses and charges are not so conveniently correlated, their behaviour will tell us what force is involved. So either by attending to properties of the actual physical system which we initially failed to take account of, or by considering what would happen in a certain counterfactual situation, we can say whether the motions are due to gravitational or electrical forces. I take it that this example refutes the reductionist principle F.

Turning now to principle D, I have found several examples of psychologists who seem to deny that a certain disposition exists, even though they have no doubts about the truth of the associated subjunctive conditional (see Sober 1982 for details). Consider the psychometricians who think that there is no such thing as general intelligence (see Block & Dworkin 1976, and Gould 1981 for discussion). Their reason appears to be that they suspect that the skills and inclination underlying one ability to learn (say, the ability to do a certain word problem quickly) have nothing much in common with the skills and inclinations underlying another (say, the ability to size up a salesperson quickly). One might, as a mere contrivance, somehow average over these disparate contexts and define a 'general intelligence quotient'. But this would not represent anything real. Notice that as dubious as this 'disposition' appears to be, there can be little doubt that some people learn more quickly than others. The associated subjunctive conditional is not in question.

Dispositions do not exist simply in virtue of certain subjunctive conditionals holding true. Such conditionals are a dime a dozen. A scientifically respectable dispositional property must be a univocal characteristic that underlies all the instances in which the subjunctive conditional displays itself. Possessing the dispositional property is what makes an individual obey the subjunctive conditional in question. The reductionist principle D fails precisely because it neglects this causal idea in the concept of disposition.

Although principles F and D may appear to have little plausibility in these extrabiological contexts, they exercise a considerable influence in ET. F is implicit in any definition of group selection stated just in terms of the fitnesses of the actual organisms and groups involved. Group selection and organismic selection are distinct varieties of causal process, which, in certain special circumstances, may have precisely the same instantaneous effects. Principle D is part and parcel of the point of view defended by Williams and Dawkins in favor of genic selectionism; they hold that even though a gene may have different impacts on the organisms it occurs in, depending on the genetic context it is in, there is nevertheless such a thing as 'the' fitness of the gene.

2. GROUP SELECTION

One of the most important concepts that Williams deploys in the context of his argument against group selection is that of 'artifact'. Time and again, he is concerned to show that traits which provide a group advantage may not be present because of group selection. They may be artifacts of selection processes that have occurred at lower levels of organization. A related idea is that we must not automatically think that group selection occurs whenever one group outsurvives and reproduces another. Again, this difference may simply be the upshot of individual selection occurring within the two groups. This idea of 'artifact' makes clear that the existence of heritable variation in the fitness of groups is not a sufficient condition for group selection, even though it is a sufficient condition for selection (at some level or other) to exist.

We might highlight this point by considering a very simple example, one which I hope will be reminiscent of our earlier discussion of the classical law of gravitation and Coulomb's law. Imagine a set of internally homogeneous populations. In population number 1, all the individuals are 1 foot tall. In population number 2, they are all 2 feet tall, and so on, for ten such populations. Suppose that there is a carrying capacity for the populations; whenever a population reaches a certain number of individuals, it sends out migrants who form their own colony. We will assume, for the sake of simplicity, that there is no migration between groups and that each colony is founded by individuals from the same group. We observe this set of populations for some generations and note that the average size of individuals increases. We also note that the frequency of populations of tall individuals also increases. What are we to conclude is the cause of these changes?

One possibility is that there has been individual selection for height. The fitness of an individual is determined just by his own height. The other possibility is that there has been group selection for groups having greater average height. On this alternative hypothesis, the reproductive success of an individual is independent of its own height and is determined just by the kind of group it is in. Since both these hypotheses are consistent with the observed changes in the ensemble of groups, how might we tell which of them is true?

The two strategies discussed in connection with the physical example might be pressed into service. We could look at the ecological conditions determining these differences in fitness and try to see whether individuals are fit because of their own phenotypes or because of the phenotypes of the groups they are in. We also could intervene in the system by artificially creating populations that are not internally homogeneous and see how those populations and the individuals they contain fare.

The fitness values of the individuals and groups that actually exist fail to tell us whether we have organismic or group selection. For just this reason, principle F cannot be defended by individuals who take seriously the issue over the units of selection. Williams' own idea of selection processes having artifactual consequences at other levels suggests that he too should reject F. But, as we shall see in our discussion of genic selection, Williams presupposes precisely this principle in his defence of the single gene as the unit of selection.

The example just discussed strongly suggests that group selection can be defined as occurring whenever an organism's fitness depends on the kind of group it is in. If 'depends' means 'is influenced by', we have here a characterization of group selection which is much too permissive. It is virtually a truism that an organism's fitness is *always* affected by the other organisms that are in its group (Sober 1980). A stronger formulation suggests itself – namely, that the fitness of each organism depends *just* on the kind of group it is in. Dissimilar organisms may have identical fitnesses, if they are in the same group, and otherwise identical organisms may have different fitnesses, if they are in different groups.

It is essential that we understand 'depends' in a causal, not simply in a computational, way. Even if there is group selection in our example of the internally homogeneous populations, it would still be true that the fitness of each organism can be predicted just from its own height. It will also be true that its fitness can be predicted from the average height of the group it is in. Computational sufficiency is not what is at issue; what matters is causation. If, in the above case, there is selection for tall groups, as opposed to selection for tall individual organisms, then an organism's fitness depends (in the causal sense) on the group phenotype, and on nothing else.

One clarification ought to be noted. Selection for groups having this or that trait may occur simultaneously with other kinds of group selection, with selection processes at other levels, and with other evolutionary processes as well. When group selection for groups having a given characteristic is one among a number of evolutionary forces at work, it is not essential that each individual in a group have the same overall fitness. This would be required only when there is just one force at work. So we might think of the above definition as describing the way in which one component in the overall fitness of organisms is determined.

A related point is that the overall fitness of organisms and of groups do not tell us whether there is group selection at work. Even when identical twins live in different groups and have different fitnesses, we can not tell if this is due to group selection, or to the existence of different sorts of individual selection processes occurring in the different groups. The problem becomes still more difficult when genotypes are represented in one population but not in another. Overall fitness represents a kind of net effect, which can be decomposed in different ways into component forces (*pace* Wimsatt 1980).

Biologists are regularly reminded that fitness is not a unitary property of the organism in itself, but involves the system of relations by which organism and environment are bound together. In the same spirit, biologists rightly feel repelled by the idea that natural selection is a property just of the environment which exists independently of the organism and impinges on the organism in one way or another. This latter idea appears to distinguish natural selection from most familiar physical forces. A gravitational or electromagnetic field can be present in a given locale even when there are no objects present to experience it. But for natural selection, *esse est percipe*. Without variation, there can be no selection.

It is important not to forget the organism when considering the environment's role in evolutionary processes. But the environment ought not to be short-changed either. When we are interested in the *causes* of evolution, the idea of natural selection will allow that a given array of fitness values may have multiple selective explanations. In the above example, selection might either be for tall individuals or for tall groups. In this sense, natural selection exists independently of the fitness values it engenders. However, when we shift our attention from the causes to the *consequences* of evolution, the distinction between selection and fitness may be ignored. Whether group or individual selection is the force at work in the example, it will be true that tall individuals *and* tall groups enjoy differential reproductive success.

It is gratifying to find these biological ideas already enshrined in the ordinary meanings of 'selection for' and 'selection of'. My young son has a toy which takes all the mystery out of this distinction. Plastic discs with circles cut out of them are stacked with spaces in between in a closed cylinder. The top-most disc contains very big holes, and the holes decrease

in size as one moves down from disc to disc. At the top of the cylinder are found balls of different sizes. A good shaking will distribute the balls to their respective levels. The smallest balls end up arrayed at the bottom. The next smallest sized balls settle at the next level up, and so on. It happens that the balls of the same size also happen to have the same color. Shaking sends the black balls to the bottom, the pink ones to the next level up, and so on. The whole cylinder (plus paternally administered shaking) is a selection machine. The device *selects for* small balls (these are the ones which pass to the bottom). It does not *select for* black balls (even though these are the ones which pass to the bottom). But when we ask after a shaking what was selected, it is equally correct to say that the black balls were selected and that the small ones were. 'Selection for' focuses on causes; 'selection of' picks out effects.

3. GENIC SELECTION

Williams provides several empirical reasons for thinking that group selection will rarely have a significant effect on an evolutionary process. These reasons have to do with certain contingent facts about organisms and groups. For example, if it is generally the case that groups found colonies more slowly than organisms reproduce, this fact can be harnessed to argue that group selection will be a relatively 'weak force' in evolution (see Sober 1980 for discussion). The general properties of groups and of organisms cited do not entail that group selection never occurs, or that it never could. Indeed, Williams concedes that at least one persuasive case of group selection has been found in nature. I will describe this example so as to anchor our discussion of group selection to some real biology (thought experiments get one only so far) and so as to set the stage for some issues that arise in connection with Williams' and Dawkins' arguments on behalf of genic selectionism. For a moment, I want to stress that Williams' empirical approach to the units of selection problem is exactly the right one. I take it to be a regulative principle in this area that any *a priori* argument for or against a putative unit must be wrong.

Williams's lone example (see 1966: 117ff. for his discussion) is the evolution of the segregator distorter *t*-allele in the house mouse *Mus musculus*. The hypotheses formulated and confirmed by Lewontin and Dunn (1960) (described in Lewontin 1970) postulate three distinct levels of selection acting simultaneously. The *t*-allele is a great example of a selfish gene. When organisms whose chromosomes come in pairs form sex cells, normally one chromosome from each pair finds its way into a gamete. For heterozygotes – individuals which have different alleles at the same location (locus) on homologous chromosomes – this will mean that half of the gametes have the one gene and half have the other. But the *t*-allele subverts this Mendelian process (see Crow 1979 for discussion). Heterozygote males with the *t*-allele on one chromosome and the normal allele on the other produce about 85% *t*-bearing sperm. The *t*-allele garners for itself greater than its fair share of gametes. Genic selection (or perhaps chromosome selection favoring chromosomes with a *t*-allele) will be a force that leads the frequency of the gene to increase in the population.

However, males which are homozygous for the *t*-allele (i.e., which have a *t*-allele at the relevant locus on both chromosomes) are sterile, and so there is selection against the *t*-allele at this higher level, which for the sake of exposition I shall call the organismic level. Lewontin and Dunn (1960) took both these selective processes into account and formulated a prediction of what the frequency of the *t*-allele should be in nature. Their observations showed that the *t*-allele's real frequency was lower than the predicted value. A third force was required to explain the data.

The third force was group selection. The house mouse lives in small semi-isolated local populations. When all the males in a local population are homozygous for the *t*-allele, the population becomes extinct. Williams refers to this as a 'poisoning effect'. Females in the group will carry copies of the *t*-allele, and so their failure to reproduce will tend to reduce the *t*-allele's frequency.

Notice that in this process, organismic and group selection are in the same direction; both act against the *t*-allele. It is sometimes thought that group selection must be for characteristics that benefit the group at the organism's expense – that is, that group selection must be selection for 'altruism'. This is not true, and the *t*-allele provides an example. Notice also that the evolution of the *t*-allele conforms nicely to our proposed characterization of group selection. Groups all of whose males are homozygous are selected against, and the females in such groups are dragged down, regardless of their own phenotypes.

With this example in mind, I now want to take up another argumentative thread that runs through Williams' book. Besides appealing to empirical facts about the reproduction of organisms and groups, Williams also argues that lower-level selection hypotheses are more parsimonious. I certainly do not wish to suggest that parsimony arguments are 'non-empirical' and always count for nothing (see Sober 1981 for a formulation of Williams' argument which, though different from the one that Williams had in mind, at least makes sense of how parsimony can count as a reason in this context). But it is important to notice that the dialectical ground has shifted somewhat.

Refuting group selection is one thing, and the population genetical arguments Williams makes stand on their own. But, as I mentioned earlier, Williams goes on to defend a positive thesis; his preferred level of organization is the single gene. Now there is a lot more to choose from than just groups and genes; conceivably, one might opt for the whole organism, or for whole chromosomes, or for complexes of genes found at multiple loci, or even for the genotype found at a locus of a pair of homologous chromosomes. But Williams will have none of this; the unit of selection is the 'meiotically dissociated gene'.

Williams realizes that his positive position runs into conflict with some fairly standard ideas within ET. It is commonly remarked that the fitness of a gene depends on its genetic context; it is not the single gene which is selected for and against, but rather a complex of genes at different loci which collectively have effects on the organism's phenotype. Bean-bag genetics fostered the illusion that each phenotypically salient trait is controlled by a single gene. But this naive picture has given way to the idea that there is a many–many relationship between genotype and phenotype. Williams is no lover of bean-bags, and he is well aware of the fact of genetic relativity. However, this does not count against the dictates of genic selectionism:

Obviously it is unrealistic to believe that a gene actually exists in its own world with no complications other than abstract selection coefficients and mutation rates. The unity of the genotype and the functional subordination of the individual genes to each other and to their surroundings would seem at first sight, to invalidate the one-locus model of natural selection. Actually these considerations do not bear on the basic postulates of the theory. No matter how functionally dependent a gene may be, and no matter how complicated its interactions with other genes and environmental factors, it must always be true that a given gene substitution will have an arithmetic mean effect on fitness in any population. One allele can always be regarded as having a certain selection coefficient relative to another at the same locus at any given point in time. Such coefficients are numbers that can be treated algebraically, and conclusions inferred for one locus can be iterated over all loci. Adaptation can thus be attributed to the effect of selection acting independently at each locus. (Williams 1966: 56–7)

Dawkins (1975), in his popularization of this idea, addresses the same question: how can single genes be selected for and against, if genes build organisms only in elaborate collaboration with each other and with the environment? He answers by way of an analogy:

One oarsman on his own cannot win the Oxford and Cambridge boat race. He needs eight colleagues. Each one is a specialist who always sits in a particular part of the boat – bow or stroke or cox, etc. Rowing the boat is a cooperative venture, but some men are nevertheless better at it than others. Suppose a coach has to choose his ideal crew from a pool of candidates, some specializing in the bow position, others specializing as cox, and so on. Suppose that he makes his selection as follows. Every day he puts together three new trial crews, by random shuffling of the candidates, for each position, and he makes the three crews race against each other. After some weeks of this it will start to emerge that the winning boat often tends to contain the same individual men. These are marked up as good oarsmen. Other individuals seem consistently to be found in slower crews, and these are eventually rejected. But even an outstandingly good oarsman might sometimes be a member of a slow crew, either because of the inferiority of the other members, or because of bad luck – say a strong adverse wind. It is only *on average* that the best men tend to be in the winning boat.

The oarsmen are genes. The rivals for each seat in the boat are alleles potentially capable of occupying the same slot along the length of a chromosome. Rowing fast corresponds to building a body which is successful at surviving. The wind is the external environment. The pool of alternative candidates is the gene pool. As far as the survival of any one body is concerned, all its genes are in the same boat. Many a good gene gets into bad company, and finds itself sharing a body with a lethal gene, which kills the body off in childhood. Then the good gene is destroyed along with the rest. But this is only one body, and replicas of the same good gene live on in other bodies which lack the lethal gene. Many copies of good genes are dragged under because they happen to share a body with bad genes, and many perish through other forms of ill luck, say when their body is struck by lightning. But by definition luck, good and bad, strikes at random, and a gene which is consistently on the losing side is not unlucky; it is a bad gene. (Dawkins 1975: 40)

Although Dawkins begins this passage with the announced intention of addressing the issue of context dependence, his skillful metaphor leads him to consider a situation in which oarsmen are good and bad pretty much *in*dependently of context. But later in the book, Dawkins sets himself a harder problem: what would happen if a team's performance were improved by having the members communicate with each other? Suppose that half the coach's candidates spoke only English and half spoke only German:

What will emerge as the overall best crew will be one of the two stable states – pure English or pure German, but not mixed. Superficially it looks as though the coach is selecting whole language groups *as units*. This is not what he is doing. He is selecting individual oarsmen for their apparent ability to win races. It so happens that the tendency for an individual to win races depends on which other individuals are present in the pool of candidates. (Dawkins 1975: 91–2)

Even in the face of such context sensitivity, genic selectionism wins the day.

What these passages from Williams and Dawkins suggest is a certain *representation argument*: if a selection process can be represented in terms of selection coefficients attaching to single genes, then it is reasonable to view it as a case of genic selection. Dawkins, again following Williams, finds this parsimonious.[3] But the problem with this line of thinking is that it proves far too much: *Every selection process can be described in this way.* Even the example of the *t*-allele, which Williams explicitly cites as a real case of group selection, is describable in terms of such selection coefficients. *If alternatives to genic selection are to be* a priori *possible, then the representation argument must be wrong.*

The quotation from Dawkins perhaps indicates where the difficulty lies: we find there a conflation of *selection of* and *selection for*. Given the usual definition of evolution as change in gene frequency, it can hardly fail to be true that if there is evolution by natural selection, then there must be selection of genes. That is, the *effect* of this process must be that some genes increase in frequency. But our earlier discussion should lead us to be wary of inferring that genes are selected for and against from the obvious fact that genes are selected. My son's toy selects black balls, but it does not do this by selecting for black balls. The net result of the coach's selection regimen is that individual oarsmen were selected. But it does not follow just from this that he was selecting for and against individual oarsmen. To take seriously Williams' artifact idea, we were forced to interpret the controversy over the units of selection as one over causation. But the representation argument advanced in favor of genic selection jettisons that very idea. Causation is displaced by computation as the main consideration.

It is useful in this context to illustrate how the position of genic selectionism leads us to 'represent' selection processes. Indeed, it is a fairly

---

[3] Although it appears that Williams and Dawkins think that parsimony favors genic selection because of its role in this representation argument, a parsimony argument for lower-level selection can be given an independent motivation. See Sober 1981 for details.

ELLIOTT SOBER

elementary exercise in population genetics to define selection coefficients
for single genes from selection coefficients attaching to higher-level genetic
units. We will consider a simple model of the phenomenon of heterozygote
superiority, one in which we consider two alleles at one locus and attribute
constant fitnesses (which represent differential viabilities) to the three genotypes. Where p is the frequency of the A allele and q is the frequency of the a
allele in the population, the frequencies of the three genotypes, both before
and after selection, as well as their fitnesses, are represented in the following
table:

	AA	Aa	aa
frequency before selection	p^2	$2pq$	q^2
fitness	w_1	w_2	w_3
frequency after selection	$\dfrac{p^2w_1}{\overline{W}}$	$\dfrac{2pqw_2}{\overline{W}}$	$\dfrac{q^2w_3}{\overline{W}}$

$\overline{W}$ is the average fitness of the population, and has the value
$p^2w_1 + 2pqw_2 + q^2w_3$. Its function in this model is simply to ensure that the
three frequencies after selection add up to 100%.

If the heterozygote is the fittest of the three genotypes, selection will
eliminate neither of the two alleles, but will drive the gene frequencies to a
stable equilibrium $\hat{p}$, which is a function just of the three fitness values (and
is thus independent of the frequencies before selection begins):

$$\hat{p} = \frac{w_2 - w_3}{(w_2 - w_1) + (w_2 - w_3)}$$

To understand what this model says, let me sketch one of its textbook
applications – namely the sickle cell trait in human beings. Individuals who
are homozygous for the sickle cell allele (a) suffer severe anemia, which is
often fatal in childhood. Individuals who are heterozygotes (Aa), however,
suffer no anemia, but enjoy enhanced resistance to malaria. And
individuals who are homozygous for the A allele, have no anemia and no
enhanced resistance. So if the population lives in a malarial region, Aa will
be fitter than AA, and aa will be least fit of all. In this case, the model
predicts that the population will remain polymorphic (neither A nor a will
go to fixation at 100%). But with the eradication of malaria, AA and Aa
become equal in fitness, both being superior to aa, and the model predicts
that the sickle cell allele a ought to disappear. These predictions are born
out by observations of human populations.

Notice that the model we have just described attributes fitness values to
the three genotypes AA, Aa, and aa. No mention was made of the fitness of

56

the two genes A and a. But Williams and Dawkins are entirely correct in their observation that fitness values for genes can always be computed. Let us see how this may be done. The genotypic fitnesses w_1, w_2, and w_3 jointly represent how the frequencies of the three genotypes are modified in the passage from egg to adult. They are a kind of 'tax' imposed by mortality. If we define W_A, the fitness of the A allele, so that it plays the same mathematical role, we will require that $W_A \times$ frequency of A before selection = frequency of A after selection $\times \overline{W}$. Now the frequency of A before selection is p, and its frequency after selection is

$$\frac{w_1 p^2}{\overline{W}} + \frac{w_2 pq}{\overline{W}}$$

This means that the fitness of the A allele is

$$W_A = w_1 p + w_2 q.$$

By parity of reasoning the fitness of a is

$$W_a = w_3 q + w_2 p.$$

Notice that the allelic fitnesses are just weighted averages of the genotypic fitnesses. A consequence of these definitions is that the allelic fitnesse are not constants; there is no fixed mortality associated with the alleles in every generation, the way there is with the genotypes. Rather, the fitnesses of the alleles themselves evolve as a function of their own frequencies.

Both the genotypic model stated initially, and the equations just given in terms of allelic fitnesses, succeed in 'representing' the phenomenon of heterozygote superiority, if all this means is that each correctly traces the trajectory of gene frequencies. But the two models nevertheless have very different consequences when they are asked to answer other questions about the evolutionary process involved. To see why this is so, let us consider what each will say about the population when it is at its equilibrium frequency $\hat{p}$. Let us consider an extreme example – one in which the two homozygotes are lethal, and therefore have fitnesses equal to o. In this case, the equilibrium frequency of the two alleles is 0.5. Before selection, the three genotypes will therefore be represented in proportion ¼, ½, ¼. After selection, this will change to the proportions 0,1,0. When the surviving heterozygotes reproduce (and then themselves die – this is a discrete generations model), the population will then return to its ¼, ½, ¼ configuration. The genotypic frequencies will continue to zig-zag in this way, even though the allelic frequencies remain constant at 0.5.

Why is the population zig-zagging? The obvious answer is that selection favors the heterozygote at the expence of the homozygotes. This is what takes the population from ¼, ½, ¼ to 0,1,0. Then Mendelism takes the population back to ¼, ½, ¼. There is no mystery here, as long as one is willing to talk about genotypic fitnesses. But the genic selectionism of Williams and Dawkins permits no such straightforward answer. At equilibrium, the genic fitnesses are identical, and so there is no selection for or against either allele. If all natural selection is genic selection, then there is no selection when the population is at equilibrium. The zig-zagging must indeed be a puzzle.

This balanced lethal system is indeed a very special case of heterozygote superiority. But as far as the causal structure of selection processes is concerned, the balanced lethal brings out in an especially clear way something that I think is true of all cases of heterozygote superiority, both before and after they reach their gene frequency equilibria. The change in gene frequencies is caused by selection at the level of the genotype. A consequence of the genotypic fitnesses and frequencies at any one moment is that the two alleles have their own momentary fitness values. But these shadows disappear as soon as they are cast, only to be replaced by new numbers reflecting new gene frequencies. Allelic fitnesses are artifacts, not causes. Genes are selected as the population moves towards equilibrium. But there is no selection for genes.

I will not take up the question of whether genic selectionism is ever a plausible view. This is an empirical question, and the conclusions I have drawn from examining a simple constant viability model of one locus with two alleles should not be assumed to characterize what occurs in nature. Still, it is important to note that the form of argument I have pursued is hardly limited to this model. The strategy of averaging is the magic wand of genic selectionism. When selection appears to act on whole chromosomes, or on gene complexes scattered over many chromosomes, or on pairs of organisms (as in fertility selection), the trick of averaging over contexts can be pressed into service (see Sober & Lewontin 1982 for details). The result of this mathematical manipulation is to obtain a number that attaches to a single gene. As mentioned earlier, the same procedure can even be applied to group selection processes. Once we realize the universal applicability of the method, we clearly see its vacuity.

The fitness values assigned to single genes are averagings over disparate biological contexts. Such fitness values resemble the psychological property of 'general intelligence' (at least as it is understood by some psychologists). Indeed, such fitnesses bear an uncanny resemblance to that old philosophical chestnut, the predicate 'grue'. In all these cases, there can be no doubt that the predicate truly applies to some objects but not to others. Yet, there is a failure of existential generalization, as it were. Although my shirt is grue, there is no such thing as the property *grue*. Similarly for general intelligence, and similarly for the fitness of a gene in heterotic systems. If this is right, then we have a further counterexample to the reductionist principle D – the one linking dispositions with their associated subjunctive conditionals. Although there is no such thing as the fitness of a single gene in the example considered, it nevertheless is true that the gene will increase or decrease in frequency, *ceteris paribus*.

4. CONCLUDING REMARKS

I have given a gloss to the example of the internally homogeneous groups discussed in Section 2 which differs from that given to the example of heterozygote superiority, and this calls for comment. Even when the internally homogeneous populations differ in productivity owing just to individual selection, it seems reasonable to grant that each group has a certain disposition. This disposition is a fitness value, and the groups have their different fitness values because of a process of individual selection. Of course, this dispositional property of the group is, in a sense, reducible to the separate dispositions of its parts, but that does not show that there is no such thing as the group disposition. When each of the molecules in a closed chamber of gas collides with the wall of the chamber, we talk of the gas as a whole exerting pressure. The pressure of the gas seems to be a genuine dispositional property, even though it is the upshot of events at the micro-level. Similarly, the productivity of the group in this example is a genuine, though reducible, disposition.

The fitness of a gene in the heterozygote superiority example is another matter. Not only is there no genic selection in this case, it is additionally true that there is no such thing as the fitness of a gene. Both the force *and* the disposition fail to exist. A gene's having a certain fitness in this example is more like an emerald's being grue than it is like a volume of gas's exerting a certain pressure.

We might conceive of natural selection as acting on a system of objects by first making distinctions between those objects. Selection for a trait first of all implies that a distinction is made between objects having the trait and objects lacking it. The upshot of this distinction making is that the objects selected are endowed with a causal power; having the trait in question will cause them to be more reproductively successful. So when we have individual selection for tallness, an individual's being tall will cause it to be more reproductively successful. A consequence of this will be that groups of organisms may differ in *their* properties. In our contrived example, some groups will tend to have higher productivities than others. Now there is no particular reason why those properties of wholes should not turn out to be causally efficacious in their own right.

So selection endows objects with fitness values, and those fitness values go on to cause differential reproductive success. Our example of the internally homogeneous populations is (on one of its versions) a case in which there is group fitness without group selection. In the heterozygote superiority example, however, not only is there no genic selection, but there additionally is no such thing as the fitness of a gene. Selection, in this case, distinguishes some genotypes from others. The mathematical upshot of this is that a gene will have a fitness coefficient whose value changes as the population evolves. But this fleeting shadow, as far as I can see, does not itself succeed in causing anything.

The distinction between these two examples is admittedly a fine one, and the main conclusion of our discussion of the units of selection is, in any case, independent of it. To understand how fitness differences at one level can be artifacts of selection processes occurring at others, we were forced to construe the idea of a unit of selection in terms of the causes of evolution. A consequence of this outlook, however, is to undermine the main argument that defenders of genic selectionism have offered on its behalf. The gene's eye point of view does not, contrary to appearances, cut through the superficiality of higher-level phenomena and get to the bottom of things. Genes are, it is true, among the micro-objects out of which organisms are fashioned. But genic selection coefficients will often simply be the shadows cast by causal processes at higher levels.

REFERENCES

Block, N., and Dworkin, G. 1976. 'IQ, Heritability, and Inequality', in *The IQ Controversy*, ed. N. Block and G. Dworkin, 410–540. New York.

Crow, J. 1979. 'Genes that violate Mendel's Laws', *Scientific American*, 240, 134–46.

Dawkins, R. 1975. *The Selfish Gene*. Oxford.

Gould, S. J. 1981. *The Mismeasure of Man*. New York.

Lewontin, R. 1970. 'The Units of Selection', *Annual Review of Ecology and Systematics* 1, 1–14.

Lewontin, R., and Dunn, L. 1960. 'The Evolutionary Dynamics of a Polymorphism in the House Mouse', *Genetics* 45, 705–22.

Sober, E. 1980. 'Holism, Individualism, and the Units of Selection', in P. Asquith and R. Giere (eds.), *PSA 1980*, vol. 2, Proceedings of the Biennial Meetings of the Philosophy of Science Association, East Lansing, Mich.

Sober, E. 1981. 'The Principle of Parsimony', *British Journal for the Philosophy of Science* 32, 145–56.

Sober, E. 1982. 'Dispositions and Subjunctive Conditionals', *Philosophical Review* 91, 591–6.

Sober, E., and Lewontin, R. 1982. 'Artifact, Cause, and Genic Selection', *Philosophy of Science*, 49, 157–80.

Suppes, P. 1970. *A Probabilistic Theory of Causality*. Amsterdam.

Williams, G. 1966. *Adaptation and Natural Selection.* Princeton.

Wimsatt, W. 1980. 'Reductionistic Research Strategies and their Biases in the Units of Selection Controversy', in *Scientific Discovery*, vol. 2, ed. T. Nickles. Dordrecht.

Wynne-Edwards, V. C. 1962. *Animal Dispersion in Relation to Social Behavior.* Edinburgh.

The evolution of animal intelligence

JOHN MAYNARD SMITH

The last twenty years has seen a major effort, theoretical and observational, to understand the evolution of animal societies. In this essay, I first discuss what level of intelligence is assumed in our theories, and what level is revealed by our observations. I then ask what qualitative differences exist between animal and human societies, and in what ways these differences depend on human intelligence.

The two leading concepts in the analysis of animal societies are kin selection (Hamilton 1964) and evolutionary game theory (Maynard Smith & Price 1973). The central idea of kin selection is that a gene A, causing an animal to be more likely to perform an act X, may increase in frequency in a population even if act X reduces the individual fitness (expected number of offspring) of the animal itself, provided that the act increases the fitness of animals related to the actor. Following Haldane (1932), biologists refer to such acts as 'altruistic'. It may require considerable skill to calculate in just what circumstances particular acts will evolve. This has led some people to commit what may conveniently be called 'Sahlins' fallacy' (Sahlins 1976), and to suppose that the operation of kin selection requires that animals, or people, are able to perform the necessary calculations.

If this were so, kin selection could operate only in species of high intelligence. But it is not so. One of the clearest examples of kin selection occurs in a bacterial plasmid (Maynard Smith 1978); despite misunderstandings of the phrase 'selfish gene', no one supposes that plasmids think. If, for example, members of a particular species have neighbours related to them by $r = 1/13$, say, then an act X which reduces an individual's fitness by 1 unit, and increases that of a neighbour by 14 units, will be favoured by selection. There is no need for the animal to calculate r.

Of course, if an animal *could* distinguish close relatives from distant ones, then selection would favour a gene causing altruistic acts to be directed preferentially towards the former. Can animals do this? Parents certainly care for their own offspring: is there evidence of preferential care for other relatives? There are several possible mechanisms. First, an animal might direct altruistic acts towards individuals with which it had been raised; in most cases this would have the effect of directing the acts towards relatives. Second, an animal might direct altruistic acts towards genetic relatives of those with which it was raised. This is known to happen in bees (Greenberg 1979) and isopods (Linsenmair 1972); it requires surprising powers of discrimination, and some memory. A third possibility is that an animal might be able to recognise its own genetic relatives. There is evidence that Rhesus monkeys in captivity can do this (Wu *et al.* 1980).

Animals do behave differently towards different conspecifics, both in cooperative interactions and in mate selection (Bateson 1980), and the criteria used in discrimination are correlated with actual genetic relationship. There is, however, no reason to suppose that animals have a concept of genetic relationship. In contrast, we do have such a concept. Some anthropologists (notably Dickemann 1979) have interpreted human societies on the assumption that people act so as to maximise their inclusive fitness; i.e. that they behave as predicted by kin selection theory, with the added assumption that individuals know, at least approximately, their degree of relatedness to other members of their society. I know of no very explicit discussion of how this could come about, in evolution or in individual development. The hypothesis appears to be that we have inherited from our animal ancestors the habit of discrimination, but have added an additional criterion, namely the conscious calculation of relatedness, to the criteria of propinquity, and perhaps physical and biochemical similarity, used by animals.

I turn now to evolutionary game theory. I first describe the basic ideas, to bring out the conceptual differences between classical and evolutionary game theory. I then discuss where the boundary may lie between games animals play and those that only people can play.

Imagine two animals fighting over some resource. Two 'pure' strategies are available to them – an aggressive strategy, Hawk (H), and a less risky one, Dove (D). The 'payoff matrix' might then be

	H	D
H	$-2,-2$	$2, 0$
D	$0, 2$	$1, 1.$

In evolutionary game theory, we imagine a population of animals pairing off at random and playing this game. Each animal has a strategy – pure H or pure D, or a 'mixed' strategy, 'play H with probability p and D with probability $1-p$'. After playing each animal reproduces its kind, and dies; the *number* of offspring produced is equal to some initial constants, say $+10$, modified by the payoff received. Thus a Hawk which met a Hawk would produce 8 offspring, and one which met a Dove 12 offspring.

The population will thus evolve, and the relative frequencies of different strategies will change. The payoffs are interpreted as changes in fitness arising from the contest. Evolutionary game theory is concerned with the trajectories of evolutionary change, and in particular in finding an 'Evolutionarily Stable Strategy', or ESS. An ESS is a strategy such that, if all members of a population adopt it, no alternative, 'mutant', strategy can invade the population.

Applying this idea to the Hawk-Dove game, it is clear that H is not an ESS, because a population of Hawks would average -2 per contest, whereas a Dove mutant would average 0. Similarly, Dove is not an ESS. It turns out that the mixed strategy, 'play H with probability $1/3$; play D with probability $2/3$' is the only ESS of the matrix shown. A population of individuals adopting this strategy could not be invaded by any mutant. If only the pure strategists, H and D, were present, the population would evolve to a 'genetically polymorphic' equilibrium consisting of $1/3$ H and $2/3$ D.

Evolutionary game theory is a way of thinking about the evolution of phenotypes when fitnesses are frequency-dependent; i.e. when the best thing to do depends on what others are doing. It does not require that contests be pairwise, and is not confined to fighting behaviour; it has been applied to the evolution of the sex ratio, of dispersal, of growth strategies in plants, and so on.

As I see it, the differences between classical and evolutionary game theory concern two main points: the meaning of a 'payoff', and the contrast between dynamics and rationality, and, arising from this, the meaning of a 'solution'. Both forms of game theory require that the possible outcome for a given player be ranked on a linear scale. In the evolutionary version, the payoffs are changes in fitness; hence, although they may be difficult to measure, they do fall naturally on a linear scale. In the classical version, some difficulty arises in arranging a set of qualitatively different outcomes – e.g. loss of money, reputation, or life – on a single scale. The justification for a scale of 'utility' is that any two outcomes can always be ranked, because an individual must always have a preference between them. I will leave to others how far this solves the difficulty; my point is that no comparable difficulty arises in evolutionary game theory.

More fundamental is the fact that evolutionary game theory is based on a well-defined dynamics – the evolution of the population – and the 'solutions' of the game are the stable stationary points of the dynamics. In contrast, classical game theory supposes rational players, and seeks a solution in terms of how such players would behave. Despite this conceptual difference, however, there is a close similarity between an ESS and a 'Nash equilibrium', which is the central equilibrium concept in classical game theory. In a two-person game, if player 1 adopts strategy A and player

2 adopts B this constitutes a Nash equilibrium if neither player would gain by changing his strategy, so long as his opponent sticks to his. An ESS differs in two respects. First, an ESS of a 'symmetric' game such as the Hawk-Dove game (i.e. a game in which there is no external asymmetry conferring different roles on the two players) requires that both players adopt the same strategy. Thus 'player 1 plays H, player 2 plays D' is a Nash equilibrium of the Hawk-Dove game, but it is not an ESS because, in the symmetric case, there is no way of distinguishing the players. Second, the definition of an ESS contains a criterion for the stability of the equilibriun which is missing from the definition of Nash equilibrium.

Since ESS's arise from a dynamics, there is no assumption of rationality any more than there is in the case of kin selection. However, some games (or, more precisely, some strategies) do require intelligence to play. I now describe three games – the repeated prisoner's dilemma, the queuing game, and the social contract game – which are played both by men and animals, but in which the strategies available to men are more extensive than those available to animals.

An example of the prisoner's dilemma game is as follows:

		Player 2	
		Cooperate (C)	Defect (D)
Player 1	Cooperate (C)	4,4	0,5
	Defect (D)	5,0	2,2

The game is paradoxical for the following reason. No matter what player 2 does, it pays player 1 to defect. It also pays player 2 to defect. So, rationally, both should defect, yet both would be better off if they cooperated.

Not surprisingly, the only ESS of the game is Defect. Suppose, however, that the game was played between the same two opponents ten times. Consider two strategies, Defect and Tit-for-Tat (TFT) – i.e. cooperate in the first game, and subsequently do as your opponent did last time. The payoff matrix then becomes

	D	TFT
D	20	23
TFT	18	40

It is clear that TFT is an ESS; TFT strategists, when playing each other, get the benefits of cooperation. However, Defect is also an ESS. Hence there is a problem of how cooperation could evolve in the first place, although it would be stable once it had evolved. In practice, the early stages probably require the operation of kin selection. Trivers (1971) used essentially this argument to account for the evolution of 'reciprocal altruism', in which animals cooperate only with those that cooperate with them. More recently, Axelrod and Hamilton (1981) have shown (for a slightly altered model) that Tit-for-Tat is stable against any alternative strategy, and not just against Defect.

Trivers imagined that reciprocal altruism would evolve in species capable of recognising individuals and remembering how they behave, and of behaving differently towards different partners. He did not have to suppose that an animal could foresee the consequences of its behaviour; still less did he have to suppose that an animal could imagine what it would do in its partner's place. Packer (1977) has shown that baboons are capable of reciprocal altruism. Baboons have a gesture for soliciting help from others: Packer showed that those individuals which most frequently responded to solicitations from others are also those most likely to receive help when they solicit. Axelrod and Hamilton point out that reciprocal altruism could evolve without the need for individual recognition in a sessile organism; in principle, it could evolve in a plant. Thus, imagine a sessile species in which each individual has only one neighbour. Then the strategy 'cooperate with your neighbour if he cooperates; otherwise defect' would be an ESS, although I have some difficulty in seeing how it would evolve in the first place.

To summarise on the prisoner's dilemma, we must distinguish between sessile and mobile animals. For the former, since they play against only one or a few opponents, there is no need for learning; the genetically-determined strategy 'cooperate with your neighbour if he cooperates; otherwise defect' can be stable. For reciprocal altruism in mobile animals, as demonstrated by Packer in baboons, more is needed. Since each baboon interacts with many others, and since there may be a long delay between action and reciprocation, stability requires that a baboon should recognise individuals, and remember how each has behaved, or, at the very least, associate with each individual a positive or negative sign, depending on how it has behaved. We are not, however, forced to suppose that a baboon reasons, as a man would, that it will pay to be nice to X, because X is likely to reciprocate.

A queue is a sequence of individuals, arranged according to time of arrival, and *not* according to size or strength, such that the first in the queue has prior access to some resource. Wiley (1981) reports that striped wrens form 'age queues', with the oldest male, at the head of the queue, taking over a breeding territory when the incumbent dies; such queues may be commoner than we have thought. The stability problem is clear. If a larger bird is low in the queue, why does it not displace the bird at the head? We do not know the answer, although there are several possibilities.

My reason for mentioning queues, however, is that there are ways in which a human queue might be stabilised which are unlikely to operate among animals. Some possibilities are as follows:

(i)   A man stays in line because he has been taught that it is wrong not to.
(ii)   A man who jumps the queue will acquire a reputation which will damage him in later social contacts.
(iii) A man who attempts to jump the queue will be restrained by the police.
(iv)   Any attempt to jump the queue will be resisted by all other members.

The first three of these possibilities explain stability by events external to the queue itself. If we take reciprocal altruism seriously, method (ii) might conceivably operate in animals, although not in the case of age queues; methods (i) and (iii) could not. Method (iv) is the most interesting. Clearly, collective resistance could stabilise the queue; the problem is why individuals should join in collective resistance. Let us consider animals first. It is conceivable that collective resistance would be individually advantageous. For example, suppose that, in the queue $\alpha - \beta - \gamma$, α is challenged by γ. It might pay β to help α to beat off the challenge, because if he does not the sequence might become $\gamma - \alpha - \beta$, and β has dropped from second to third. (It is harder to see why γ should help α to resist a challenge by β.) If the alternative strategies are 'resist only challenges to oneself', and 'resist any challenge', the latter would be favoured by selection provided that it was usually advantageous. It would not have to be advantageous in every possible case. Thus I can imagine that animal queues are stabilised by collective resistance, without having to suppose that individual animals perform complex calculations. However, there is no evidence that this is what happens.

In human beings, some individuals might perceive that it would be in the general interest if queue-jumping was prevented, particularly if a complete breakdown of the queue made the resource unavailable (if the driver sees a fight at a bus stop, he doesn't stop). If so, they might persuade the queue members to bind themselves to wait in line, and to punish transgressors. Note that this is possible even if there are a minority of individuals (perhaps the strongest person in the queue) who do not benefit. This brings me to my third game, the 'social contract' game.

Suppose that the payoff to all the members of a small group is greater if all cooperate than if all defect. Then the members might agree to cooperate, and to join in punishing any member who defects. Even if the act of punishing was cheap, and of being punished expensive, this would still not be sufficient to guarantee stability, because of the problem of the 'free rider'. Thus a member who cooperated, but did not join in punishing, would be better off than someone who cooperated and did join in punishing. Hence a social contract can ensure stable cooperation only if it reads 'I will cooperate; I will join in punishing any defection; I will treat any member who does not join in punishing as a defector.'

Could an analogous behaviour occur in animals? If, for some specific action X (e.g. jumping an age queue), animals (i) did not do X, (ii) drove out of the group any animal that did X, and (iii) drove out any animal that did not join in driving out an X-doer, then the behaviour would be evolutionarily stable. The difficulty, of course, lies in imagining how such a complex behavioural syndrome, which is stable only when complete, could arise in the first place. This illustrates Elster's (1979) point that natural selection is a hill-climbing process which can only reach local optima, whereas rational behaviour can reach a global optimum. (Elster is, however, wrong in thinking that natural selection cannot reach the mixed ESS of the Hawk-Dove game.)

Despite the difficulty of imagining how a behaviour involving the three components outlined in the last paragraph could arise in the first place, I think it is quite possible that the explanation of stable age queues in animals may be of this kind. A similar mechanism may perhaps account for the fact that some group-living animals drive sick or injured individuals out of the group. To drive out a sick individual is sometimes advantageous, because the sickness may be infectious. If, in the above specification, we replace 'doing X' by 'being different from typical members of the group', we have a mechanism that will explain this behaviour.

The crucial difference between men and animals, then, lies in the nature of the action X which is proscribed by the contract. In animals, X would have to be genetically specified, although it might be specified merely as being different, in any way, from other members of the species. In man, X could be a newly acquired possibility (e.g. human cloning or hang-gliding), perceived by some individuals as being socially undesirable, the perception being communicated to others linguistically. Even language may not be enough to account for the agreement in a social contract not to do X, when X is not genetically specified. Thus, suppose that a member of the group recognises that he or she would be better off if no one did X. Before that member would embark on an attempt to persuade others, he would have to recognise that others might feel about X as he did.

To play the social contract game successfully, therefore, when the prescriptions of the contract are culturally rather than genetically specified, an animal would have to think of others as having motivations similar to its own, so that it could foresee their future behaviour, and it would have to communicate symbolically. The game is therefore useful in illustrating the kinds of strategies animals cannot adopt. However, I do not think it is a particularly appropriate model of human social interactions, for two reasons. First, it treats all members of a social group as having the same set of possible actions. In fact, owners of land or factories can do things non-owners cannot, as can men with weapons compared to those without, or even men as compared to women. Hence social contracts may bind, not all members of a society, but members of some group within society. The problem is to explain how individuals come to identify their interest with that of a specific group, and why different societies tend to divide into groups along different lines, according to economic class, religion, race, etc.

The other weakness of the social contract model lies in its excessively rational and legalistic nature. In practice, I suspect that 'contracts' are arrived at as much by religious and ideological persuasion as by rational discourse, and maintained more by the threat of social ostracism than by legal restraint. The ideological nature of social contracts means that they need not always correspond to individual self-interest. However, they cannot depart too far from it; men can be swayed by beliefs, but not too far. Of course, one group in society may be able to impose its will on another.

Returning to my brief of animal intelligence, animals can and do act as members of a group against other conspecific groups. The groups are usually composed of genetic kin, but not always. The cohesion of the group may be cemented by joint display activities, as in the cacophony of a troop of howler monkeys. However, I would not claim that these displays have any culturally mediated symbolic meaning, as do the myths and rituals which bind human groups. Perhaps the main consequences of the lack of high intelligence in animals is that they are not as good as we are at fooling themselves.

REFERENCES

Axelrod, R., and Hamilton, W. D. 1981. 'The Evolution of Cooperation', *Science* 211, 1390–6.

Bateson, P. 1980. 'Optimal Outbreeding and the Development of Sexual Preferences in Japanese Quail', *Zeitschrift für Tierpsychologie* 53, 231–44.

Dickemann, M. 1979. 'Female Infanticide, Reproductive Strategies, and Social Stratification', in *Evolutionary Biology and Human Social Behaviour*, ed. N. A. Chagnon and W. Irons, 321–67. Duxbury, Mass.

Elster, J. 1979. *Ulysses and the Sirens*, Cambridge.

Greenberg, L. 1979. 'Genetic Component of Bee Odor in Kin Recognition', *Science* 206, 1095–7.

Haldane, J. 1932. *The Causes of Evolution*. London and New York.

Hamilton, W. D. 1964. 'The Genetical Evolution of Social Behaviour', *J. Theoretical Biology* 7, 1–32

Linsenmair, K. E. 1972. 'Die Bedeutung familienspezifischer "Abzeichen" für den Familienzusammenhalt bei der monogamous Wüstenassel Hemilepistus reanmuri Audoin u. Savigny', *Z. Tierpsychol.* 31, 131–62.

Maynard Smith, J. 1978. 'The Evolution of Behaviour', *Scientific American* 239.3, 136-45.

Maynard Smith, J., and Price, G. R. 1973. 'The Logic of Animal Conflict', *Nature* 246, 15–18.

Packer, C. 1977. 'Reciprocal Altruism in *Papio anubis*', *Nature* 265, 441–3.

Sahlins, M. 1976. *The Use and Abuse of Biology*, Ann Arbor, Mich.

Trivers, R. L. 1971. 'The Evolution of Reciprocal Altruism', *Quarterly Review of Biology* 46, 35–57.

Wiley, R. H. 1981. 'Social Structures and Individual Ontogenies: Problems of Description, Mechanism, and Evolution', in *Perspectives in Ethology*, vol. 4, ed. P. P. G. Bateson and P. H. Klopfer, 105–30. New York.

Wu, H. M. H., Holmes, W. G., Medina, S. R., and Sackett, G. P. 1980. 'Kin Preference in Infant *Macaca nemestrina*', *Nature* 285, 225–7.

Intentionality, syntactic structure and the evolution of language[1]

NEIL TENNANT

INTRODUCTION

... imagine a class of beings who were capable of having intentional states like belief, desire and intention but who did not have a language. What more would they require in order to be able to perform linguistic acts? Notice that there is nothing fanciful in the supposition of beings in such a state, since as far as we know the human species once was in that state. Notice also that the question is conceptual and not historical or genetic. I am not asking what additions would need to be made to their brains or how language did evolve in the history of the human race ...

The question needs to be made narrower, because there are all sorts of features of actual languages that are irrelevant for our present discussion. Presumably such beings would need a recursive device capable of generating an infinite number of representations, they would need quantifiers, logical connectives, modal and deontic operators, tenses, color words, etc. The question I am asking is much narrower. What would they need in order to get from having intentional states to performing illocutionary acts?

The first thing that our beings would need to perform illocutionary acts is some means for externalising, for making publicly recognisable to others, the expressions of their intentional states. A being that can do that on purpose, that is a being that does not just express its intentional states but performs acts for the purpose of letting others know its intentional states, already has a primitive form of speech act. (Searle 1979a: 193–4)

I beg my reader's forbearance for beginning my own paper with such a long quotation from another. It happens to mention almost every topic I shall be discussing here. I hope to show that the phenomenon of recursive syntax may bear on the intentional ingredient in human communication. I hope also to say something useful about the structure of primate brains as well as the mechanisms of linguistic evolution, both issues that Searle sets to one

[1] The earliest version of this paper was read to the Epistemics Research Seminar in the University of Edinburgh in 1980. A longer and rougher version was the basis of the Thyssen Group discussion. Its present form owes much to the criticism offered on that occasion. John McDowell challenged the privileged status of what I have here called the first scenario; part of the paper now responds to that challenge. I am grateful to Peter Lamarque, William McGrew and Arnold Chamove for drawing my attention to useful references. Less directly, but no less importantly, this paper is the result of Florian von Schilcher's encouragement to think in evolutionary terms.

side as irrelevant to the conceptual question he is pressing. This paper accordingly falls into two not wholly unconnected parts – one philosophical, the other biological.

Language has obviously evolved. But it has left no fossil record. Deficiency of sufficiently diachronic facts ironically testifies to the tremendous selective advantage language must have conferred upon its users.

Evolutionary theorising is a matter of making inferences to the best explanation. Today such inferences about the origins of language can draw on a vast assemblage of data and hypotheses in neighbouring disciplines. Those who belittle the value of new integrative speculation are, in a phrase of Bennett's, dogmatically defeatist. To be sure, the Linguistic Society of Paris in 1860 banned publication of the theorising about the origins of language then in vogue. But in the century since we have come to understand better the structure of natural language, and have made some conceptual progress in the philosophy of language. We have learned much about our own brains and vocal tracts, and those of our primate cousins. Ethologists have studied many different systems of animal communication. Darwinian theory has been synthesised with modern genetics. We have attended closely to how children learn to speak. In the light of all this, I do not think it premature to put forward an evolutionary scenario for natural language.

I

It is a philosophical commonplace that we cannot learn very much about human language from the singing of birds or the dancing of bees. Systems of animal 'communication' are held to be mere signalling systems, systems for which there is some doubt as to the meaningfulness of the messages contained therein as opposed to their characteristic causal efficacy in evoking or triggering certain responses.

The dance of the bees has a repertoire of wiggles and tilts and speeds. Certain features of their performance are found to be correlated with and hence to convey information about direction and quality and distance of food source. But do the movements 'convey information' to fellow workers in the hive in any more *semantic* a fashion than, say, a bruise on a child's face conveys to his mother the information that he has had a nasty bump?

At first sight, it is unclear what the answer ought to be. The bruise is a direct causal consequence of the bump. Knowledge of human physiology would enable witnesses of the bump to predict the appearance of the bruise. Similarly, detailed knowledge of bee physiology should enable one to predict that the bees' locating a food source will have as a causal consequence (even if only statistically) the subsequent pattern of wiggles and tilts in the hive. For bee dance is inflexible, and can be manipulated genetically (cf. T. Eisner & E. O. Wilson 1977: 241).

So is it just a matter of degree? Can one argue that the bees' dance is as much a causal consequence of this earlier experience as the bruise was of the bump? Compare Armstrong:

> ... utterances of sentences in the communication situation are signs in exactly the same sense of the word 'sign' that black clouds are a sign of rain ... an analysis of linguistic meaning will be given in terms of this basic, black cloud, sense of 'signify'. (1971: 429)

If he is correct, then the 'semantic' status of apine dance, if we suppose the bruise to lack such status, is to be recovered from certain distinctive features of the underlying causal story.

Indeed this is a challenge that even the materialist should be willing to accept. He can begin to analyse the distinctive features of communicative interactions while still using the language of the mentalist. That is, he can attribute beliefs, desires, intentions, and so forth in giving a simpler account of a complex matter. The complexity of the account will increase vastly when replaced by ultimate 'physical' talk, if this indeed be possible. Nevertheless, the complexity imparted by the faithful physicalist version should not blind us to the features that distinguish the causal processes in the bees' brains or whatever from those involved in the swelling after the swipe. The difficulty lies precisely in spelling out what these distinctive features are, and how they are pertinent to the contrast between conveying information on the one hand, and, on the other, being black and blue.

It may turn out that the distinctive features of a causal story associated with semantic content are precisely those that require the language of belief, desire and intention, in order for their isolation to have any point within the overall causal explanation of what happens when the speaker communicates with another. Ironically, too, it could turn out that much less goes on physically when John sees Mary and tells Dick about it, than when John gives Mary a black eye that tells Dick of his blow.

So what is there to linguistic meaning, over and above mere causation? One might offer the following reason why one could regard apine dance as having communicative significance lacking in the case of the bruise; that the dance is a somehow 'arbitrary' or 'rule-governed' causal product of the sighting of food. It is arbitrary in that the rules (consciously followed or not) in accordance with which this behaviour is produced, *could have been otherwise*, while yet serving the same communicative purpose. That is, as a piece of adaptive behaviour, whether wholly instinctual or partly learned, it may very well *now* follow as a causal consequence of the sighting; but that precisely *this* sort of dance should have come to serve this purpose is, in a phylogenetic perspective, quite accidental. Selective pressures for a system of communication of this kind might have produced, through different mutations for new behaviour, a different dance or indeed wholly different behaviour types, serving the same function. In fact, another species of bee that communicates about food sources (*Apis florica*) does so in the same way except in so far as it wiggles in the horizontal rather than the vertical plane, and so can indicate directly the angle of the food source from the sun. *Apis mellifera* (the common bee) has to have a convention as to which angle in the vertical plane corresponds to this latter angle. *Apis mellifera*, if put on a horizontal honeycomb, dances just like *Apis florica*.

This 'conventional' behaviour is described with scare quotes because it is not clear that one would be justified in reading into it the constellation of reciprocal beliefs and intentions that someone like Lewis takes as constitutive of conventional behaviour. The bees' behaviour has developed phylogenetically and of course may now be regarded as a more or less necessary causal consequence of their finding food. The analysis is to hold whether or not the striking similarity between the dances of the two species is the result of their common descent from a dancing ancestral species, or the result of this sort of dance's being an optimal solution to the 'evolutionary problem' of efficient communal food use. With enough genetic mutations at hand, the behaviour could perhaps have evolved independently in each species. This phylogenetic perspective *appears* to separate nicely what is essential in the dance to its being a signal or message of some kind. The dance constitutes a rudimentary system of communication, whether or not it is entirely instinctual, entirely learned or the result of a mixture of the two strategies.

But to see communicative significance as deriving from the phylogenetically arbitrary status of apine dance, as a solution to their coordination problem, is open to a serious objection.[2] This is that the dance might have been the only way, given apine physiology immediately before its evolutionary debut, to solve that problem. If a certain behaviour pattern were, in some suitable sense, phylogenetically necessary, what would justify one in attributing content to it?

Now although in evolutionary terms, given the amounts of genetic variability usually at hand, it is likely that such behaviour has been arbitrary in the required sense (witness *Apis mellifera* v. *Apis florica*), one must concede the conceptual point here. Armstrong even goes as far as asking 'is it not conceivable that the whole of syntax and semantics should have been innate so that all mankind spoke the one, wired-in, nonconventional language?' (1971: 437).

What, then, justifies the attribution of content to exercises of evolved forms of behaviour? A promising line of thought, due to McDowell, is that

2 This objection I owe to David Hull.

all one requires is *transfer of information* simpliciter. This holds regardless of whether the mechanism, behavioural, chemical or otherwise, might have evolved arbitrarily or might have been the only possible one phylogenetically. The natural function of this communicative behaviour, whether wholly instinctual or not, is to impart to fellow creatures 'cognitive stand-ins for the states of affairs they represent'.

... communication is the instilling of information. Consider, first, instinctive communicative behaviour like that of the [bees] ... The function of such behaviour is to furnish information about the environment to [bees] which witness it; here 'function' occurs in something like the sense in which it is the function of the heart, say, to circulate the blood. When what gets transmitted is misinformation, there has been a malfunction of a natural process. A malfunction is as such a defect ... Aims pursued in communicating do not enter the story. There are no such aims since the behaviour is instinctive. But in an account of the (no doubt rudimentary) notion of content which seems undeniably applicable in this case, the natural function of the behavioural repertoire can serve, as it were, instead; it can occupy a position analogous to the position which was supposed to be occupied in an account of the notion of the content of an assertion, by the alleged fact that in making assertions, we aim at truth.

When the communicative process functions properly, sensory confrontation with a piece of communicative behaviour has the same impact on the cognitive state of a perceiver as sensory confrontation with the state of affairs which the behaviour, as we may say, represents; elements of the communicative repertoire serve as epistemic surrogates for represented states of affairs ... elements of such a repertoire represent states of affairs by virtue of standing in for them in a creature's cognitive dealings with the world. (McDowell 1980: 133–4)

Compare now the case of the bruise. Bruising, it is reasonable to suppose, has never served the adaptive function of informing others that the body has been hurt. It is rather the kind of causal concomitant of the blow that has wholly to do with internal processes of tissue regeneration. So far, so good; we have separated bees from bruises. What about us? Is not a belief/intention ingredient essential to the notion of linguistic communication in the human case? Certainly the Gricean analysis would have it so. Grice himself might assimilate apine dance to the category of phenomena that have what he called natural meaning as opposed to the non-natural meaning of expressions of natural language. The question that McDowell is pointing to, however, is whether, in the analysis of human communication, Grice's contribution concerns more what it is to be human than what it is to communicate. Let us for the time being not take a stand on this issue but address ourselves to the whole phenomenon in its strong sense.

Whether a system with finitely many basic signals is a system of communication in the strong sense – that is, a linguistic system – depends on whether the characteristic behaviour within which and against which it is interpreted is complex enough to sustain attributions of higher-order beliefs and intentions to the creatures concerned. If one has to resort to such an intentional framework in order to make sense of the behaviour, in order to explain what the creatures are doing and why, and has so to resort after exhausting all possibilities of more austere, less anthropomorphic frameworks of explanation, then one is on the route to linguistic meanings. Wittgenstein invites one to consider a primitive signalling system as the system of communication of a whole tribe. We can aquiesce in this thought experiment only because we implicitly assume that enough behavioural complexity will be discovered for us to regard tribe members as having beliefs and intentions, even if, *ex hypothesi*, their very simple language does not permit them to express these beliefs and intentions. Provided a tribe member can recognise an intention that he should respond appropriately to a signal in the simple system, we are happy to regard the signal as linguistically meaningful to him, rather than simply causing or triggering certain behaviour – as was the case with the bees.

When radically interpreting the speech of a totally alien tribe (or species), one has to consider all the evidence there is concerning mental states. Their attributions go hand in hand with, and must be adjusted to, our attributions of meaning to utterances. One requires a background of considerable behavioural complexity before one is justified in attributing to any creature beliefs, intentions and so on.[3] Davidson (1975) would even maintain that this requires that they have mastery of a language; that it is wrong even to think in terms of quasi-beliefs or proto-beliefs when trying to explain even quite complex behaviour of languageless creatures. This insistence, however, does not mesh well with an attempted evolutionary account of language, which it is my concern to sketch. It appears unduly insistent on the primacy of certain conceptual connections between cognition and language.

Nevertheless, it is easy to underestimate just how complex behaviour has to be before attributions of attitude and meaning pass methodological muster. Davidson rightly enjoins the radical interpreter to be *nasty* in thinking up as many competing interpretations of observed behaviour as possible. A good example of how nasty one can be is to be had from the

---

[3] There is little force in the objection that we presently have no precise way of measuring or rank ordering degrees of behavioural complexity. The same is true of deductive complexity in mathematics, but every mathematician can intuitively judge that one proof is deeper or more complex than another (or at least there are clear cases where this is so). Advances in cybernetics and our study of the complexity of programmes may one day yield the sort of measure or ordering one seeks. The complexity of a behavioural 'flow chart' might depend on its number of sensory inputs and motor outputs and on how feedback loops are nested, and so on. Alternatively, one might study the logical complexity of the experimental tests that we intuitively require an animal to pass before attributing various intentional states to it.

chimpanzee language experiments. A scholarly audience will forgive this quote from *The Listener*:

The Gardeners first taught Washoe by shaping her hands for each sign. Hands together means – 'more'. When Washoe got close, she was rewarded by getting more of what she wanted. Soon she was using the sign for more of anything – food, rides, and so on – proof that she had grasped the general concept of the word.

Let us be nasty towards Washoe. The word 'more' has its meaning disclosed through combination with terms telling one what it is of which 'more' is in question. No doubt the word as used by infants will occur on its own, without the added term, and adults satisfying the need will work out the missing term from context. But adults respond linguistically too, supplying the missing substantive with the wanted substance. The child in due course in new contexts uses the modifier with substantives, thereby expressing his desires more clearly. The process of learning words, learning their grammatical categories and acquiring them in correct combinations is very much a two-way affair. It involves requests, solicitous enquiries, offerings, forbiddings and factual commentary. But does Washoe use the hand signal, allegedly meaning 'more', in this way? Does she offer more of things to her interlocutors when 'asked', as well as demand things from them? Does she perform several different speech acts with the word, questioning, commanding, wishing, stating? Watching the film of Washoe with Leakey's commentary, the nasty radical interpreter is struck by any number of competing interpretations of Washoe's signing. Why not interpret her as expressing something tantamount to 'I have an unfulfilled desire', or, 'make me feel nice!'? Either of these – quite unconnected with 'more' of anything – would cohere with the facts just as well as the 'more' hypothesis and explain the same range of behaviour. If Washoe has an unfulfilled desire, one can rest assured that the eager and attentive experimenters will gather from context what it is and fulfil it if at all possible. It is not unlikely either that the formation of the desire will be closely linked with current experiences and will therefore probably be fulfilled by providing more of whatever is salient in the context – porridge, or rides in a plastic tub, etc. Likewise the hand sign might mean 'continue' or 'would that things remain roughly as they are now, in lumps or in intervals'.

We have so far been considering the extent to which the intentional ingredient in natural language distinguishes it from other systems of animal communication. Another point that some have raised in this connection is that animals cannot – or do not – lie when using their communication systems. The force of this objection depends, again, on the complexity of the attendant beliefs and intentions which analysis demands in the case of lying. Let us disregard the moral overtones which are irrelevant anyway to the concept of lying (what makes lying bad is what is bad about what makes it lying).

In communicating that 'P', one is lying just in case one believes 'not P' but intends one's audience to believe 'P'. A communicative act is a lie if by ascribing the appropriate belief and intention to produce in the audience the opposite belief, one achieves the best explanation – within one's theory of the agent's beliefs, desires, etc. – of his act. Consider now the case of a bird 'warning' its flock members near a food source that a predator is nearby. The other birds fly away leaving the warner with a temporary monopoly of the food. Has this bird lied? We must first enquire whether the bird believed there was no predator. That he did not himself fly away is strong evidence for this belief, especially if predators prefer to attack lone birds, and we have further reason for thinking that the bird believes *that*. Furthermore, we could investigate whether he behaves likewise when there is no food source to be monopolised. Secondly, we must ask whether he intended his fellows to believe that there was a predator nearby. To test for this intention we would have to establish whether he would act as he did in situations where he had no reason to believe that he could thereby induce the false belief in question. But this is almost impossible to do, even by recourse to highly contrived situations not encountered in the wild. To this extent, the status of the call as a lie is under-determined. To the biologist, it may seem unnecessarily convoluted to eschew the simple hypotheses that the bird is lying, given its useful role in making broad predictions about the future.[4] And at least one philosopher (Routley 1981) is prepared to defend them in this view. But for the radical interpreter, this would be to throw in the towel at a crucial conceptual conjuncture, imputing our intentional framework to another, dumb species.

Yet it is arguable that the child's first experiments with what adults would regard as linguistic deceit are on a causal and behavioural par with the bird's fraudulent warning cry. Both might just by accident hit on the fraudulent behaviour eliciting the desired response, and subsequently adopt it as a strategy in such situations.[5] The same holds true of any other strategy adopted as a result of operant conditioning. A significant difference might arise when the child learns about the possibility of detection and punishment after lying and its various moral implications. The latter, though, might just be assimilated to the factors that the subject has to take into account under operant conditioning. The trouble by this stage, however, is that an adequate account of the effects of

[4] Cf. also n. 2. Premack and Woodruff (1979), however, are well aware of the complicated controls needed before attributing to chimpanzees an intention to deceive.
[5] I owe this point to Florin von Schilcher.

admonishments, threats and exhortations would enmesh one further in the semantic question posed by the original problem.

Some may see the bird's warning cry as falling short of lying for a further reason. This is the absence of any higher intention, or evidence for such, that the receiver should believe something by recognising this very intention. This extra Gricean ingredient in the conceptual analysis of linguistic meaning applies not just to cases of lying but to linguistic communication in general.

So far we have been discussing the intentional aspect of language in our comparison of human with other animal communication. But we have not lost sight of the important role to be played by considerations concerning range of vocabulary items, methods of syntactic combination, discreteness of signals, and the associated semantic possibilities. Among these are reference to spatio-temporally remote items, generality and tense – to name but a few. They are among the most important semantic features of human language for which one would understandably be hard put to find correlates in other known systems of animal communication. One would be hard put also to find grounds for the attribution of the beliefs thus expressible to creatures that might be thought to have but not express them:

No doubt past beliefs are also caused by past experience; but what I am denying is the converse claim that any belief which is caused by the past must be or involve a belief about the past ... sometimes ... the attribution of a past belief can be effectively challenged by a lower-level, more economical attribution in which the past is introduced only causally and not epistemically. That is why I prefer more demanding standards for what it is to count as a behavioural manifestation of a past belief. (Bennett 1976: 103)

Considerations concerning syntactic and semantic structure are not unconnected with those about the beliefs and intentions involved in linguistic communication – beliefs and intentions which McDowell suggests are quite secondary once one has accepted that communication in general (from simple instinctive types through to natural language) has first and foremost to do with the transfer of information, or the instilling of knowledge. Let us put aside for the moment the misgiving that the latter phrase ushers in the intentional ingredient once more. No doubt McDowell could make do with first-order 'quasi'-knowledge in a theory of cognitive representations for 'lower' species (in something of the form suggested by Field 1978), stopping short of the special problems posed by the diagnosis of the higher-order beliefs and intentions involved in a Gricean or sub-Gricean mechanism (cf. Bennett). In doing so he might find himself in the company of evolutionary epistemologists such as Riedl (1979), whose over-arching theory of life as an 'erkenntnisgewinnender Prozess' seems to require a unitary notion of knowledge or information, information that can be stored in a genome at one end of the evolutionary spectrum, as well as be expressed, at the other end, by scientific theories that make the world a less strange place to live in.

But what I would wish to suggest is that other considerations of an evolutionary kind lend weight to the view McDowell is challenging. To do so I must sketch the bare outlines of the opposing views on the conceptual issues, to see which one harmonises more with evolutionary conjectures about language. (In this paper I cannot go very far into the available wealth of fact and conjecture in the neurophysiology of language, psycholinguistic theories of language acquisition, and comparative studies of man and other primates. Fuller justice to these topics, as well as the ape language experiments and various glottogonic theories, is to be done in a longer study.) The first evolutionary scenario, which places more emphasis on the intentional ingredient than McDowell would allow, is as follows.

Following Bennett, we regard it as admissible to frame theories of perception (or 'registration') and of 'proto'-belief and desire to explain the actions of certain creatures, provided their behaviour is complex enough, and subject also to the usual caveats of holistic method. But importantly (as behaviour proves more complex), the theory allows attribution of belief and intention *at higher order*, even in the absence of language. Then, when higher-order beliefs and intentions of interactants engage in a suitable way – by instantiating a sub-Gricean mechanism, say – certain actions (token events) can have *occasion meaning*. This is meaning in as rich an intentional sense as one is likely to get – far more than the mere instilling of (first-order) knowledge with which McDowell deals. Now, says Bennett, we can move from meaningful event tokens to conventional meanings of event types. For we are dealing, *ex hypothesi*, with creatures who can grasp the salience of certain features of past occasions of meaningful exchange. Lewis's theory of convention is then applied to account for the acquisition of conventional meaning by certain action (or utterance) *types* in the developing linguistic life of the group. But what is of crucial importance in the account thus far is that these action types are syntactically and semantically *unstructured*.[6] At this point in Bennett's exposition there is an interesting leap (between chapters 7 and 8). Having accounted for how action types might acquire conventional but unstructured meanings, he advances straightaway to a discussion of how one might come into an alien community and find

[6] It is worth noting here that the action types need not involve speech. One of the most promising theories about the origin of language – and surely the one most strongly supported by the results of various ape language experiments – is that natural language had a gestural origin. Moreover, the structure of spoken sentences need not have derived entirely from unstructured words grafted onto single gesture types. Gesture types, as achievements of deaf children indicate (Goldin-Meadow 1975), might already have had a rudimentary grammar allowing their combination into longer messages, before speech overlaid the substrate of gestures. But the 'problem' facing the deaf children was to find a channel of communication. The problem facing our forebears was to 'discover' linguistic communication.

evidence that their linguistic interactions are *structured* (syntactically and semantically). Yet he offers no account of how the language of the group could have attained such complexity of structure from the humble (albeit highly intentional) beginnings he had been discussing earlier. Let us call this the structural lacuna of the intentional scenario.

Compare now McDowell's account – in one way more austere, in another much more radical – which suggests a second scenario.

> A more attractive line of thought is that the linguistic repertoire retains, through the alteration of nature involved in the onset of self-consciousness, a form of the characteristic which was essential to its pre-linguistic ancestor: in suitable circumstances (to be spelled out in any fuller elaboration of this idea) its exercises are cognitive stand-ins for the states of affairs which they represent. An assertion will actually have that epistemological role only if the circumstances are right. But all standard assertions – excluding, that is, special cases like irony – purport to have it. Thus their possession of content – their capacity for representing states of affairs – is intelligible in terms of a suitable modification of the simple idea which seemed appropriate in the case of instinctive communication. (1980: 135)

This opens the possibility (and one acknowledged in conversation) that communication could involve *structured* messages, perhaps even structure of the sort producing infinite generative capacity, without the creatures ever having passed the 'Gricean hump' that Bennett put them past even before occasion meaning had made its evolutionary debut.

It is worth pausing here for a moment to reflect on the weight of traditional thinking that McDowell is seeking to shift:

> ... the utterance '(There is yellow fever on board)' ... is a sign that (the speaker has the objective that an audience should have reason to believe {that the speaker believes [that (there is yellow fever on board)]}) ... A, let us say, utters the phonemes that encode the sentence 'There is yellow fever on board'. B hears the phonemes. B *infers* (just as one infers from any sign) that A made this utterance with the object that an audience should have reason to believe {that A believes (that there is yellow fever on board)} ...
> if B makes [this] very first inference ... then *linguistic* communication, at least, has been achieved ... uptake has been secured. An illocutionary act has occurred. B has understood A's words. (Armstrong 1971: 432–3, 435)

> ... in order to make an assertion a speaker must represent himself as believing what he says. (Davidson 1979: 12)

> Language is derived from Intentionality, and not conversely. The direction of *pedagogy* is to explain Intentionality in terms of language. The direction of *analysis* is to explain language in terms of Intentionality ...
> ... in the performance of each illocutionary act with a propositional content, we express a certain Intentional state with that propositional content, and that Intentional state is the sincerity condition of that type of speech act. Thus, for example, if I make the statement that p, I express a belief that p ... All of these

connections, between illocutionary acts and expressed Intentional sincerity condition of the speech act are internal; that is, the expressed intentional state is not just an accompaniment of the performance of the speech act. The performance of the speech act is necessarily an expression of the corresponding Intentional state ... (Searle 1979b: 75, 78)

What McDowell is challenging is the notion thus unanimously upheld that the belief-expressive feature of assertions is essential to our understanding of the extra-linguistic purpose of statements of a natural language: challenging it, indeed, even for statements with syntactic structure. Indeed, in the first of his two papers cited here, Searle had wavered:

The primary extra-linguistic purpose of having the institution of assertion is to give information ... our beings would be capable of making a primitive form of assertion when they could perform actions *which were expressions of belief* for the purpose of giving information ... (1979a: 194, my italics)

Is the italicised clause incidental or essential? On McDowell's view it is not essential insofar as one is concerned just with explaining how language evolved to something like its present state of syntactic complexity, as selection favoured its communicative successes.

His view would be strengthened by scotching the appeal made by both Searle and Armstrong to Moore's paradox. (This appears to be the only independent support, apart from introspection, that they adduce for belief-expression's being essential to assertion.) But surely on the more austere view one can easily explain why it should be so peculiar to assert 'p but I don't believe that p'. The object language is already taken to contain attitude operators and the first person pronoun.

On McDowell's account, it would presumably be either as the language acquired such new structure, developing something like a pronoun system and (iterated) belief attributions or as, quite independently, *behaviour* became more complex, calling for higher-order indexical belief states for its explanation (cf. Mellor 1980a) that consciousness dawned: in particular, consciousness of what was happening when one *communicated*. With the evolutionarily intrusive possibility of linguistic deceit, as opposed to mere malfunction of communication, communicative exchanges would then come to be understood as having truth as their aim; and the Gricean template would come to be true of the pursuit of those aims. So too would utterances of Moore's form acquire their paradoxical force. It is only necessary, for the paradox to have its force, that an assertion that p *provide grounds for believing* (rather than: *express*) that the speaker believes that p. Now whenever I speak, this provides grounds for believing that I have vocal chords; but it does not *express* that fact. Is it not just as strange for me to state out loud 'p, but I don't have any vocal chords'? If one believes the second conjunct, one must invoke an unusual explanation for the sounds emanating from my mouth. Likewise in the case of Moore's paradox.

What I wish to suggest is that filling the structural lacuna makes structured talk without higher-order thought look much less likely. Even if one were to concede to McDowell that there could be traffic in simple message types before the Gricean hump, I wish to maintain that one would have to be over the hump (or at least capable of being in such states as are involved in the hump) before one's language could evolve syntactic structure of the kind yielding infinite generative capacity. I stress 'of the kind yielding infinite generative capacity' because it is the peculiar combinatorial potency of expressions in natural language which, it seems to me, could not have emerged by any evolutionary mechanism unless the users of the system were capable of the sort of second-order intentional states involved in the Gricean mechanism. I am quite willing to countenance the possibility that structure might usefully be discerned in signals whose segments thus descried were iteratively impotent. Different temporal segments of a mating display, say, might convey information about different aspects of the physical prowess and motivational states of the performer. Likewise different simultaneous aspects of a dance, such as wiggle and tilt with the bees, might separately convey information about different aspects of the world (distance, direction and quality of food source). But expressions of a recursive language, I maintain, could probably not have acquired their categorial valency as it were, their powers of combination into new but readily understood messages, unless their users were on the second rung of the intentional ladder and therefore, potentially, past the Gricean hump.

To make this claim plausible – a claim which, it seems to me, lies in a grey zone between the conceptual and the empirical – I wish first to offer what seems to me the most likely account of the evolution of syntactic structure. Even if my assessment of its implications concerning the relative order of emergence of the intentional ingredient and of syntactic structure were held to be incorrect, the mechanism of that evolution might be of independent interest, and be seen as bearing on other problems besides (especially in developmental psychology and theoretical linguistics).

Recently Sampson has challenged the status of many of the alleged linguistic 'universals' put forward by Chomskians. He has argued that 'independent explanation, more plausible *a priori* than nativism, is available for the universality of the trait'. His attack is therefore two-pronged: to argue that there are far fewer genuine universals than had been thought, and to explain away the remaining ones in ways more plausible than Chomsky's.

The main syntactic universal upon whose existence both Chomsky and Sampson are agreed is that all sentences of natural language are *hier-*

archically structured. It is with respect to this universal that we can illustrate the novelty of Sampson's contribution.

Any sentence can be broken down into immediate sub-units which themselves have reasonably independent status as coherent wholes, whose combination produces the original sentence. Each of the sub-units may in turn be decomposable into sub-sub-units and so on, until non-decomposable words or morphemes are encountered. Thus the revealed hierarchy of expressions is a tree-like structure with branchings determined in a definite way. It was precisely this analysis of how certain expressions lower down in the tree thus fell within the scope of others higher up on a branch that launched modern logic on its powerful and sophisticated account of logical relations among sentences.

Chomsky and Sampson claim that this tree-like decomposition of a sentence into its parts is a feature common to all human language, and is indeed the basis upon which we determine the meaning of a sentence from the way it is built up out of its parts (an insight going back at least to Frege). In a Chomskian grammar it is the base component, consisting of phrase structure rules, that generates the sort of revealed structure just explained. According to Chomsky, we are genetically pre-programmed to search for just this sort of structure underlying the sentences that we hear as infants. The strict sense in which such structures underlie the sentences is of course enshrined in the transformational component of the grammar. All this imposes a powerful constraint on language acquisition from the allegedly scanty data available to any child. The alleged deficiency is compensated for by a neurologically based preference for *Chomskian* grammars. That is, the child is pre-programmed to arrive at *this* sort of representation of his mother tongue rather than any of the many other mathematically possible kinds. The representation is, of course, implicit and we would not expect any child to be able to state explicitly the phrase structure rules and transformations generating the sentences of his language. There is also considerable evidence (as marshalled by Ingram 1975) to suggest that up to the age of six years it is mainly short, simple but still hierarchically structured sentences that the child is able to produce. Transformations that have to do with embedding one sentence into another (such as subordinate clause or relative clause formation) are only acquired between the ages of six and twelve. This would imply at least that the early fragment of language poses the problem of hierarchical analysis in a reasonably pure form.

Sampson's attack on Chomsky's account of how the child overcomes this problem is ingenious. He advances a quite different explanation of why hierarchicality is a feature to be found in all languages. In so doing, he avoids any appeal to neurological pre-programming of a specifically linguistic kind as claimed by Chomsky.

Sampson applies an evolutionary model due to Simon, originally devised for quite different domains than the present one. These include the evolution of human institutions, and certain kinds of pre-biotic evolution. The idea is strikingly simple. If one considers hierarchical assemblies in general, their evolution from their constituents is far more likely if they consist of relatively stable sub-assemblies which themselves are evolutionary products of an earlier period. Evolution proceeds by the accidental combination of already existing stable sub-assemblies, thereby producing new stable assemblies of higher complexity. A new stable assembly establishes its credentials as a useful whole, and is co-opted into the ever-growing network of items with burgeoning structure. If we have a principled way of discerning the stable sub-assemblies, thereby distinguishing them from merely arbitrary collections of parts, then we can as it were see the evolutionary pedigree of a complex structure.

Let us apply this account to the syntactic structures of a natural language undergoing the process of evolution which it is only reasonable to suppose has taken place. The systems of communication of our primate ancestors presumably consisted of words and short sentences (but what I have to say would hold even if only gestural sequences were involved). It is reasonable to suppose that these language users might (even accidentally) hit on new combinations of phrases to produce slightly longer sentences than had hitherto been the rule: sentences, moreover, whose newly-coined significance derived from both the context of their first use and the pre-established significance of their components.

Now there are two ways that the new composite sentence token will be of a type that is eventually to acquire a constant significance. (Note here that I am doing my best to avoid speaking of conventional meaning, for I do not wish to beg the question yet against the second scenario.) The first is a highly fortuitous and austere way: namely that the compound might have the same effect – the transfer of some particular kind of information – sufficiently often and sufficiently advantageously for there to be some selective advantage in its coming standardly to possess that significance: that is, for it to acquire the biological *function* of transmitting just that kind of information.

In the case of instinctual communication the fortuitous nature of this process is only too apparent; for it requires the formation of new closed genetic programmes for both the production and processing of the complex signal. Another observation is crucial here. Remember we are concerned eventually to account for the repeatable contribution constituents make to the significance of signals involving them; this being of the essence when syntax is recursive, or creative. Thus we want to see the representational role of the newly juxtaposed elements as recognisably preserved within, and thereby helping to determine the new representational role of, the new signal in which they occur. (I use the phrase 'representational role' rather than 'meaning' here to hew as closely as possible to the line of the second scenario.) Now in a language of potentially unlimited generative capacity, I fail to see how this could be achieved for all expressions across all patterns of combination in the first way described above. Insofar as any qualitative argument about improbability of emergence could have any force, surely this is one such case.

Compare now the vastly more plausible second way in which the new composite sentence token may be of a type that is to acquire constant significance. And let us no longer worry about begging questions against the second scenario, and simply say 'conventional meaning' rather than 'constant significance'. The second way makes the emergence of syntactic combinations seem much less fortuitous.

Consider an intriguing claim by Schmitt (1955). A proto-language might contain one-word sentences used appropriately (in a variety of speech acts) for things and events. There might be words for 'man', 'seal', 'booty', etc., and perhaps also words for events such as killings or harpoonings. Bearing in mind constantly the radical interpreter at one's shoulder, one could regard these as mainly nominal in character. Facial gesture and general demeanour could easily signal the force with which the utterance of such nouns was to be taken. Truculent and threatening utterances would be demands, plaintive ones requests, excited but friendly ones declaratives, and so on. Schmitt's claim is that even in present-day Eskimo the verb translated into English as 'kill' is a peripheral modification of the noun for 'booty'. One can imagine the first fortuitous utterance of the three word string

Man   seal   booty

as having the occasion meaning (via suitably diagnosed Gricean intentions etc.) of something roughly like 'The man killed the seal'. New strings like this, in a highly salient context, could readily be understood as new messages, of a new level of complexity, by an audience who already grasped the components from their isolated usages in the past. We may expect new conventions governing syntactic combinations – in our example the Subject-Object-Verb complex – to establish themselves quickly in the evolving language of any group whose members are bright enough to tumble to the meanings of such innovations. But this crucially involves their being past the Gricean hump. The linguist Charles Li, writing in his introduction to a highly speculative volume on the mechanisms of syntactic change (Li 1977), claims that with a few exceptions the only documented types of word order changes that are not due to language contact are SOV to (VSO) to SVO. Being documented they are possible; and possible, despite word order change being, as Li himself puts it, 'the most drastic and complex category of syntactic changes'.

As new syntactic categories settle down by innovative accretion along the lines suggested, the complex mesh of grammatical relations becomes the cloth of an ever-changing community coat. By the time transformational rules (if they are really operating – which is theoretically contentious, as we shall see in due course) enter the picture, we can expect even more linguistic material to be available for reshaping, re-ordering and relocating. In this way the surface output, being as it is so critically dependent on transformational pedigree, becomes a highly labile and volatile product.

If our account of innovative accretion is reasonable, we have a basic model within the second scenario of how the earliest linguistic structures were born. A few salient juxtapositions would confer upon words a new relational potency over and above their semantic directedness to the external world. They would acquire a certain potential for juxtapositions, a grammatical valency, which is now captured by the idea of the *category* of an expression, due to Frege and Ajdukiewicz. Phrase structure rules would implicitly have been adopted, legitimating certain combinations that have successfully occurred, as well as others that had not yet occurred but might very well have, and with similar success, had the choice of words and message had to be different. Thus even the earliest and most modest collection of phrase structure rules would have been pregnant with new output; and as the rules became entrenched so too would innovative effort and diagnostic insight become more relaxed and automatic, as words appeared newly combined in well-understood syntactic contexts. Transformational rules also, presumably, emerged at this time – at first, perhaps, with mainly abbreviatory effect. Later they could have wedded sentences in constructions such as causal conditionals, being both a spur to and the reflection of our ancestors' growing conceptual mastery of the world about them. Premack's tests (Premack 1976) to establish that chimpanzees make rudimentary connections between 'states of affairs' (in order not to beg the more refined question of objectuality within them) which to us appear closely connected by virtue of a cause and an effect, or by virtue of an implicit goal or problem and a means or stratagem, seem to the layman to support attributions to chimps of protean correlates of human categories of thought. It is not too fanciful to see a connection here with a point Ingram has made about the acquisition of linguistic transformations by children (to dwell within the Chomskian paradigm a little longer). It invites one to see Haeckel's principle at work once more, with ontogeny recapitulating phylogeny:

... most of the transformations of English are only acquired between the ages of six and twelve. These are the transformations that have to do with the embedding of one sentence into another. The evidence for this comes from both theory and facts. The facts come from the observation of children's complex sentences between two and twelve. The structures up to four are primarily simple sentences. Those from four to six show complex structures, but most propositions simply juxtaposed to each other. Piaget's theory of cognitive development predicts that this should be the case. To relate two structures to each other, the child needs to be capable of performing concrete operations. This ability is only developed between the age of six and twelve. (Ingram 1975: 99)

As Sampson observes, the phylogenetic account above of the simultaneous growth of phrase structure and transformational rules yields a prediction agreeing nicely with a principle formulated by the Chomskians. This principle states that transformations apply cyclically, and that later transformations, in tinkering with the transforms already produced, deal with them as completed units undergoing at most peripheral changes in this later re-arrangement. That is, later transformations tend not to interfere with or undo the effects of earlier ones in the generation of a surface from a deep structure. This is precisely what one would expect if the above evolutionary account were true. One would expect existing sentence patterns to be stabilised in use, and to be only minimally disturbed upon being combined to form more complex syntactic units. According to Sampson, many other features of transformational grammar can be explained away in a similar fashion once one adopts this evolutionary perspective.

Although Sampson himself does not point to independent evidence or hypotheses about syntactic change, what he suggests coheres well with the speculations of Chung (1977). From evidence concerning Pukapukan and Samoan, she forms the following conjectures. Syntactic change affects simple sentences before it affects the action of superficial rules; and when transformational rules are affected, the more superficial ones are affected first, the major cyclic ones last.

Also worth noting here is that Hankamer (1977) has put forward the possibility of competing grammars for a body of linguistic data as a force inducing syntactic change. The re-analysis of linguistic structure (once well developed) afforded by a different grammar may impel new structural developments and innovations. Thus the old grammar could become obsolete and it might no longer be possible to extend it to deal with relatively simple sentences of the language resulting from the 'actualisation of the re-analysis'. But Hankamer's idea is more appropriate to the 'evolution' of fully fledged languages, a process of interest in its own right but somewhat peripheral to the project of accounting for how more complex linguistic structures might have evolved from simpler ones.

The structural lacuna in the intentional scenario is, I am suggesting, to be filled by something like Sampson's account of the evolution of hierarchical arrangements of stable sub-assemblies. Innovative combinations become part of a familiar repertoire precisely because they offer a form of solution to recurring co-ordination problems whose salience the system users are quick to discern. And the accompanying growth and refinement of categorial conventions is possible only because the system users have higher order beliefs and intentions.

A further suggestion that flows from this is that such evolutionary considerations lend support to a competing grammatical paradigm – that of Montague grammar. Whereas in Chomskian grammar the basic approach is 'top–down', with transformation rules sometimes applying in ways that require one to consider syntactic environments beyond the immediate focus of application, the picture in Montague grammar is simpler, in a way more congenial to our evolutionary picture. In Montague grammar various categories of expression are simultaneously defined in a recursive fashion. One may think of similarly structured expressions within one category – differing only in lexical items – as stable sub-assemblies with an independent communicative value of their own. This may derive not only from repeated occurrence within wider syntactical contexts, but also from frequent usage 'in isolation', as it were. One thinks here, for example, of noun phrases being used in response to wh-questions. Indeed, one empirical reason why a certain category within a Montague grammar should be basic may be precisely a high pragmatic probability of its isolated use in fruitful exchanges: here the grammar of conversation rather than of the sentence may become crucial. One is inclined to ask here just how well argued is the frequent claim that 'the *unit of communication* is the sentence' (Armstrong 1971: 428).

The way a sentence (or indeed any complex expression) is generated within a Montague grammar provides a possible synchronic fossil of how, diachronically, the language acquired the complexity making such a sentence possible. For in Montague grammar one begins with lexical items (of known categories) and 'assembles' lower-level structures. Within these one can still discern the 'earlier' items, whose syntactic combination in accordance with Montague's formation rules involves only relatively minor peripheral modifications (just what one would expect on the Sampson-Simon model). The new lower-level structures are then themselves syntactically combined, again with peripheral modifications not obliterating their essential unity, into yet higher ones; and so on, until the sentence in question is produced. Importantly, there are no transformations capable of wholesale disfiguration of the by-products of any stage of the generative process.

Montague generation, proceeding as it does through all categories of expression simultaneously, promises recognition of the conversational integrity of parts of speech in a way that sentence-focussed Chomskian grammar does not. Moreover, there is a further independent reason for finding it attractive, apart from whatever success is to be had in the future in generating likely looking fragments of natural language. This reason is that it is mathematically much less powerful than Chomskian grammar. Peters and Ritchie (1971) have shown that every recursively enumerable set of strings is the language generated by some Chomskian grammar. Montague grammars, by contrast, characterise at most context-sensitive languages, and therefore yield decision procedures for grammaticality.

This is especially desirable in the light of our manifest ability to parse – that is, to produce judgements as to grammaticality, and not just judgements that are grammatical. It also means that whatever part of the brain it is that deals with matters grammatical can be regarded as relatively low in the so-called sub-recursive hierarchy of computing machines – putting it within easier reach, perhaps, of the evolution of cognitive capacities 'from below'. But these are technical considerations not to be dwelt on here.

On the account advanced by Sampson, especially with the substitution of Montague grammar for Chomskian, there is no need to appeal to innate linguistic abilities any more specialised than those required for general problem solving. The Chomskian might advance the speculative thesis that any mutation causing children to search immediately in the right class of grammars would have a great selective advantage, and that such evolutionary change might well have taken place, producing human beings who are now pre-programmed to process linguistic data in a specific way. Certainly the selective pressure for advanced linguistic competence would be very great – as witness the probable absence of any human language, in the intermediate range of the evolution that Sampson describes, that lacks, say, some of the syntactic and semantic functions and resources of known languages. But whether genes for hierarchical supposition would confer a sharp selective edge on language learners carrying them depends very much on how satisfactory an account of language acquisition is to be had from a suitably sophisticated (non-behaviourist) learning theory. Chomsky places faith in special neural mechanisms blossoming in the brain. He is ungroundedly pessimistic over the prospect of developing a powerful enough learning theory to account for language acquisition. His argument, if it counts as such, is a dogmatic admission of defeat, unsupported by quantitative evidence. We simply do not yet know enough about the capacity of learning strategies that have been discovered or perhaps remain to be discovered.

2

So far we have considered how natural language might have developed that complexity which sets it off so dramatically from the signalling systems of other species. What now of the claims that other primates can communicate with systems in all important respects as complicated as ours?

Several experimenters have maintained that chimpanzees and gorillas can be taught to communicate by means of artificial systems not involving speech. For anatomical reasons, chimps and gorillas cannot produce a range of sounds sufficient for speech. But some investigators claim that they have taught them to use systems approaching human language in their versatility and complexity. The implicit claim to be considered is that apes are, qualitatively speaking, a quantum jump ahead of other animals in this respect (although admittedly not many others have been investigated): that they are 'on our side of the divide'.

There has recently been some highly critical re-assessment of the claims initially made by ape language experimenters on behalf of their subjects. The criticism is of various kinds. Some concerns the basic methodological pitfalls surrounding any project of this kind – the lack of proper controls, over-readiness to read richer interpretations into bits of behaviour than a more rigorous viewpoint would endorse, even experimenters' proneness, given their wishful thinking, to be manipulated by their hairy charges into taking up certain attitudes not properly grounded in the available evidence. Another set of criticisms concerns the basic approach, given the desired object of establishing communicative contact with and among the apes concerned. Anyone can see that artificial keyboard or lexigram languages can be imparted, if at all, in only the most impoverished social situations – quite unlike the nexus of warm and intimate physical bonds that probably prevailed at the dawn of language millennia ago. Normal communication is free and spontaneous, with parties taking turns, with an equal balance between initiative and response. A human child quickly expands his vocabulary, and the mean length of his utterances increases accordingly. He uses already mastered words in new combinations to which he has not hitherto been exposed, and responds to such combinations appropriately as well.

Other criticisms focus on massaging of the data, in the form of simplification of ape utterances in their reporting, so as (probably unwittingly) to make them look more like human utterances than the hodge-podges they really are; and re-analysis of unedited films of 'discussions' with the apes, showing just what a high proportion of the exchanges embody no more than unconscious cueing by the human experimenter, slavish imitation by the ape, or his redundant expansion and embroidery of their exchanges without commensurate amplification of information conveyed. More philosophical criticism is to be found along Davidsonian lines. Apes may well have produced new two-sign combinations that their trainers have been inclined to interpret as appropriately invented for some feature in the context. A celebrated example is Washoe's signing of 'water bird' in the presence of a swan. But the radical interpreter could re-interpret the dyadic sign as 'bird on water' or 'bird and water' or 'wet feathers' or 'reflection of bird' or in any one of many ways. The dyadic sign need not be endowed with any unitary significance, or be regarded as a newly constructed compound of previously mastered components. On this view it would be overcharitable to credit ape strings with syntactic structure when they may be nothing but sequences of single 'word-sentences'.

One reviewer of the present state of the debate (J. L. Marx 1980) ably summarises all the points of failing in the collection of data and their interpretation, but makes so bold as to write:

Despite the controversy over whether or not apes can produce sentences, there seems to be agreement that they can use *words* the way we do – that is, as symbols *representing some object* that can be used to convey information to another individual. (Marx 1980: my italics)

Yet even this would be disputed by a Davidsonian who insisted on the primacy of a language of identity, reference and quantification before crediting anyone with even the general notion of an object.

One of the most important points of difference between language acquisition by human beings and the deficient parallel process in the case of the ape language experiments is, of course, that in the latter case one is not dealing with the acquisition by the young of a system employed already by conspecific elders. The apes being taught are therefore without an evolutionarily conferred advantage that human children enjoy – that of employing learning techniques, and being initiated by their elders, in a way that has presumably been refined by selection pressures over a very long time. Recent studies of language acquisition reveal that children are very attentive, and actively process evidence in ways perhaps not fully appreciated at the time when Chomsky was championing a theory of innate linguistic universals that depended heavily on an alleged gap between the scanty data available to the child and the rich system that he eventually masters in response thereto. Children are highly motivated learners of language, a disposition no doubt by now 'wired in' to our species. In this respect they are probably quite unlike the apes, who have not yet been subjected to evolutionary pressures for rapid acquisition of symbol systems. Children benefit also from more than usually grammatical speech from adults who address them in the early stages in a fashion tailored to their learning needs.

This tendency on the part of adults could no doubt also be selected for, once language was entrenched enough to exert the required pressures. Parents repeat and reinforce their children's utterances, and produce slightly more complicated versions of things already mastered in a gentle advance up the ontogenetic slope.

In the heyday of 'nativist' account of language acquisition (in the early 1960s) it was widely assumed that the speech heard by children was a haphazard collection of sentence fragments, mistakes, backtrackings, throat clearings, and other kinds of unintelligible gibberish. This assumption appears to have been derived from analyses of adults talking to each other at psycholinguistic conferences. There is now, of course, a considerable body of evidence showing that the speech addressed to young children is typically very different from that addressed to older children and adults. Many of these variations are structural and seem to reflect something other than differences in topic and semantic content. Mothers, some at least (and other adults), frequently speak slowly to children, leave physical gaps between words or phrases, use an extended pitch range, give very heavy stress to lexical items, use short sentences, simplify the syntax, expand and even correct their children's utterances. (Marshall 1980: 115. Marshall refers in this connection to C. Snow and C. Ferguson (eds), *Talking to Children* (Cambridge, 1977).)

These observations on human language learning, coupled with evolutionary speculations make one realise just what a formidable accomplishment it would be if apes could be taught the use of a communication system remotely approximating a natural language in creativity, recursiveness, and the extreme conventionality revealed in such matters as reference to spatio-temporally remote items or counterfactual conditionalising or universal generalisation about an unsurveyed domain. They may well have certain cerebral pre-adaptations that subtended vocalised speech linked with gesture, which responded in some ancestral line to pressures of selection for an ever more complex code of communication.[7] The ape's failure to acquire a 'language' from us (spoken or gestural or plastic-symbolic) in no way discredits the very reasonable evolutionary claim that they, or a common ancestor of ours, had the rudimentary cerebral beginnings that are now our speech centres. The language faculty is closely tied up, both conceptually and empirically, to other cognitive faculties such as silent foresight, planning, anticipation, reasoned fear, etc. It may be impossible for the apes to master a code that we would translate into our own terms. Admittedly we can discern glimmerings of intelligent thought involving the location of sub-goals and the execution of sub-strategies, a

---

[7] Jaynes (1976) claims that this happened as recently as the late Pleistocene. The proliferation of tools in the Pleistocene, the making of apparently 'non-utilitarian' and symbolic objects, the practice of burying the dead ceremonially, the construction of shelters and the marked increase in the size of the frontal lobe of the brain with Broca's area, all point to language's being reasonably developed by the end of the Pleistocene. See the papers by Isaac, Marshack and Holloway in Harnad *et al.* 1976.

grasp of 'causality', perhaps even a grasp of the internal motivational states of others, as disclosed by their behaviour; and some experimenters have even looked for signs of a sense of self, and even of intimation of mortality. But too much mist obscures the question what it is like to be a chimp for even the best-meaning efforts to make them make the best of meaning.

Our interpretation of the results of the chimp language experiments points to recursively structured language as a unique accomplishment of our own species. Lenneberg (1966) has argued that a great deal of evidence about deafness in children, aphasia, environmental deprivation of various kinds, muscular debilities and so on supports the hypothesis that language acquisition by children follows a definite maturational path, passing certain milestones of achievement in a certain order. Moreover these milestones correspond broadly with others in the course of sensory-motor development, being broadly in step with them even when the whole process is slowed down, as in the cases of mental retardation. Both linguistic and sensory motor development are then co-ordinated further with the 'brain maturation curve'. This is a graph of the growth in degree of organisation and certain chemical concentrations, which gives a crude measure of growth. There is no evidence from all this of cerebral 'rubicons' that correspond to the different stages of language acquisition, but one cannot avoid the impression that the linguistic skills acquired by the growing child are orchestrated by a physiological score; and one moreover that has its own peculiar, species-specific crescendoes.

In a survey of the evidence for the species-specificity of speech, Dingwall (1975) has reached broadly similar conclusions. He concludes that 'the ability to produce vocalisation which is articulated as opposed to holistic in nature, which is mediated by the neo-cortex as opposed to the limbic system, is unique to the genus: homo sapiens'. Of course, he is concerned here with *speech*, and not with language in general, which may of course encompass gestural systems or systems such as those used by the ape language experimenters. When two closely related species have similar behavioural patterns or capacities, and this similarity is due to their having a common origin, then the behaviours are said to be *homologous*. By contrast, similarities (even across unrelated species) that are not due to common origin, but rather to force of environmental circumstance, to conditions which elicit one narrowly constrained adaptive response from the two species, are called *analogous*. Dingwall concludes further from what he describes as 'abundant evidence' about structure and function, that human and ape vocalisations are not homologous. As for other aspects of the communication systems, the 'evolutionary, ontogenetic and neurological evidence currently available tends to support homology rather than [analogy]'.

Apes and monkeys employ a limited number of calls. Some may serve to warn fellows about very specific kinds of predator, and therefore have quite specialised communicative significance (Seyfarth *et al.* 1980). But they are not formed into sequences having different significance according to their manner of combination and the basic items they contain.

There are some noteworthy differences in brain physiology, apart from the massive increase in brain size, as one passes up through the other primates to man. Chimpanzees lack Broca's area (for muscular co-ordination in speech), as well as the neighbouring arcuate fasciculus. The latter is the fibre bundle connecting the auditory area with Broca's area, which some believe to be crucially involved in the imitation of sounds. It is little wonder then, given these handicaps of sheer physiology, that chimps are incapable of speech. A more delicate question to assess, however, is whether one could reasonably maintain that they are pre-adapted for *Language* (not necessarily vocal, but symbolic and semantic in an appropriate sense). We appear to share with chimpanzees a strong rooting of emotional cries in the limbic system – the so-called 'emotional' brain. But for the rest of spoken language, our neo-cortex is heavily involved, with strong evidence furthermore of lateralisation for speech even as early as birth. (By 'lateralisation' here we mean that the functions are based on one side – usually the left – rather than the other.) Infants appear, on certain experimental evidence, to be 'wired' for the recognition of speech sounds as opposed to others. And yet, paradoxically, the evidence for lateralisation of the 'higher' and more abstract processes of language apart from vocalisation, is less conclusive.

Geschwind once proposed a theory concerning association areas in the brain (Geschwind 1974). According to him, language could only evolve once the auditory and visual *association areas*, that in monkeys as well as man convey impulses from the auditory and visual areas to the limbic system, *themselves* acquired suitable connections via yet another association area, thereby making possible so-called non-limbic, cross-modal associations. This 'association area for the association areas' is the angular gyrus, and it is absent in monkeys. The reason why its mediation of modes is so crucial is that learning and understanding names of objects probably requires the association of visual with sound images (assuming, of course, that we are dealing with names from a *spoken* language). Of course, naming is not the whole of language, as the opening passage of Wittgenstein's *Investigations* makes us so well aware; yet it is no doubt a central part of language, and still an important and controversial topic in the philosophy of language. Geschwind's express intention was to find physiological correlates of linguistic capacities, in order to bring language within the scope of scientific materialism. His conjecture, then, is just one way of making sense of certain anatomical facts across species, evolutionary hypotheses, and observations of impairments of linguistic functions on the part of human patients who had suffered different sorts of damage to their brains.

Surprisingly Dingwall states categorically that Geschwind's theory, 'while ingenious, is most assuredly incorrect . . . ' He cites experiments that have shown that

Chimpanzees are able to match visually presented to tactilely presented stimuli . . . chimpanzees can transfer from auditory to Ameslan signs in the absence of referents . . . Thus, the inability to produce cross-modal associations is not a barrier to the acquisition of language in chimpanzees . . . Not only is there evidence of similarity in cross-modal association behaviour in chimpanzees and man but also, as pointed out . . . there is no marked difference in these two species in the angular gyrus which Geschwind holds to be important in mediating this behaviour. (Dingwall 1975: 43)

This is extremely puzzling argumentation. Chimpanzees have angular gyri. But given the copious evidence that chimps simply cannot get their lips and tongues around enough sounds, their cross-modal associations pose no threat to Geschwind's theory. On the contrary, the very successes claimed by the chimp language experimenters, to which Dingwall himself is sympathetic, would bear out that theory even further. For Geschwind had been careful enough to note that the angular gyrus is needed even for visual–visual (indeed, for any non-limbic) associations. So perhaps it is because they have angular gyri that chimpanzees have been able to sign successfully.

I say 'perhaps' because rhesus monkeys have recently been claimed to be able to make cross-modal associations.[8] Nevertheless, so far only chimpanzees have displayed any ability to make visual–auditory associations.[9] And it remains to enquire to what extent other associative abilities experimentally revealed in other species approach those to be expected of a creature able to use linguistic symbols. Von Glaserfeld has argued that

. . . the semanticity of a *linguistic* sign is constituted, not by a tie that links it to a 'thing', but by one that links it to a representation or concept. The fact that a sign, be it verbal or non-verbal, has acquired symbolicity, does of course not preclude that it still be used as a perception-bound sign whenever there is a perceptual input that corresponds to the representation it designates; nor does it preclude that it be used by the sender to trigger a conventional active response in the receiver (as in the case of an 'imperative'). But what gives a sign the status of symbol is that it *can* be used without such a stimulus and without triggering the active response. (Von Glaserfeld 1976: 222; his italics)

In the same Lockean spirit, Davenport reaffirms the relevance of non-limbic associations when he asks

Of what relevance is cross-modal perception to the origin and evolution of speech and language? First, it appears that multi-modal information extraction of environmental information is likely to result in more veridical perception, and may facilitate

8 See Cowey and Weiskrantz 1975.
9 See Fouts *et al.* 1976.

cognitive functioning. Second, in my view, cross-modal perception requires the derivation of modality-free information, a 'representation'. That an organism can have the same representations, concepts or percepts, regardless of the method of peripheral reception, confers a great advantage on that animal in coping with the demands of living ...

To the extent that an organism has a 'tag' for the representation, be it sound, gesture or combination, the process would be greatly facilitated. (Davenport 1976: 147–8)

Just as there appear to be no rubicons in a child's cerebral development, so also there were probably no such rubicons phylogenetically. Evolutionary pressures would have gone to work on whatever genetic variability there was in the ability to make the relevant cross-modal associations underlying linguistic competence. The importance of the former for the latter is not at all diminished by exhibiting languageless creatures that can associate across modes. For, that one must be able to do X in order to do Y does not entail that if one can do X then one should be able to do Y.

Are the recursive resources of language an innate endowment of Homo sapiens alone? Our earlier discussion inclines one to say so. But we must not support the innateness claim with the wrong arguments. Universality is no guarantee of innateness.[10] This is so even though it might be true that any infant, regardless of race or family niche, can acquire the tongue of any community. This acquisition claim has never been rigorously tested. Physiognomical differences between racial types might affect pronunciation of the foster mother tongue. But setting purity of pronunciation aside, could any child master any first language so well that native speakers would regard him as fully competent in matters lexical and grammatical? Should languages have diverged sufficiently radically in our evolutionary past, and should cerebral organization have adapted constantly to the need of parsing, it is quite possible that counterexamples to the claim of eventual competence might be found. But this would not count in any way against language's being innate. Indeed it is its very innateness, given sufficient divergence between different languages, that make such counterexamples seem possible.

Hewes (1977) counts twenty-four different theories concerning the origin of the first lexical items. (Perhaps 'theory' is too grand a label for these suggestions.) He concludes plausibly that the best account will probably incorporate several different suggestions about the origin of words in different 'lexical domains'. Onomatopoeia and adult imitation of salient infant babbling are just two such suggestions. But by far the most likely theory looks to gesture as the raw public material from which human communication grew. Speech could have grafted onto gesture once the vocal tract had developed sufficiently, with selective advantages that

---

[10] Compare a similar point about ethical theorising in Tennant 1983.

Darwin had remarked on. The hands are free when one talks; and one can be heard in the dark and in all directions, under cover and so on. Consistent with this theory is the synchronisation reported by MacNeill (1979) between hand movements and speech segments. He observes also that gestures can extend and replace full imitation, while yet being sufficiently iconic to secure uptake. Finally, although Neanderthal man had once been thought incapable of producing a reasonable range of vocal sounds, the fossil reconstruction on which this claim was based has been severely criticized recently (Du Brul 1979).

Complex sentences can be *parsed*. In the case of natural language, natives' pre-formal agreement on the boundaries of grammatical division is the most important kind of evidence the linguist can glean as he searches for the grammatical recipes and ingredients of sentence meaning. One attraction of the gestural theory of language origin is that significant structure does not have to await words. Susan Goldin-Meadow's subjects were un-acquainted deaf children; but they had normal parents who did not try to communicate with them by gesture, or at least not in *sequences* as the children did:

... the deaf children were seen to have devised their own manual signs. Many of them were based on actual movements. And they combined signs into sequences with relatively stable 'word' order preference. The most rapidly developing child eventually made use of such sophisticated devices as clausal embeddings. The steps in the development of these sign systems occur in a regular sequence, and at times which resemble the development of vocal speech by hearing children. (MacNeill 1979: 720)

Of course, these children might have been interpreted according to overly lax canons – compare our discussion of chimp gesture above. But *prima facie* the generous semantic account of their project is much more plausible, given that they are agents just like us except insofar as they cannot hear. We should not regard their 'invention' of a structured gestural language as grounds for believing that earlier hominid handwaving could thus rapidly have attained parsable results. After all, these children are presumably 'wired' for Language. They will possess the same cognitive structures and whatever maturational schedules thereof that underly hearing children's language acquisition. As we remarked earlier, their 'problem' was to find a channel of communication. The problem facing our forebears was to discover communication.

Gestural messages, so it seems, can have significant structure. Thus the structure of spoken sentences need not have derived entirely from combin-ation of words that had replaced single gesture types. Instead, structured gestural sequences, or *syntagmata* as MacNeill calls them, might already have had a rudimentary grammar before they were overlaid by speech.

Whatever the relative order of gesture, speech and structure thereof, my quasi-conceptual evolutionary thesis would still be pressing: iterable contribution to significant structure across the whole language, be it gestural or symbolic, is almost certain to have needed a shrewd intentional grasp by communicators of what they were up to. Note that this claim would not be undermined by showing that infants 'mindlessly' master the communicative content of structured sentences before it dawns on them gradually that assertions express beliefs and that deceit is possible. For selective pressures for linguistic ability could easily reverse in ontogeny the order I maintain would be needed in phylogeny. Selection would have operated within the environment of an already structured code. Mastery of that code by distant descendants could therefore become more 'mindless' in the early stages (even those involving significant structure) as brains were shaped by natural selection for more and more rapid language acquisition.

Interest in language origin theory, as the heavy volume edited by Harnad and others testifies (Harnad *et al.* 1976), is being revived after a long period of disrepute. Hardly any writer has looked, linguistically, beyond unstructured lexical items. My attention here has been held far more by the enigma of syntactic structure, and how its development might mesh with the conceptual analyses of meaning and intentionality offered by philosophers of language. My thesis can best be summarised as follows:

> There could be staccato talk without thought.
> There had to be thought before structured talk.
> Once established, structured talk could be mastered with less thought.
> Once mastered, structured talk makes for more thought.

REFERENCES

Armstrong, D. M. 1971. 'Meaning and Communication', *Philosophical Review* 80, 427–47.

Bennett, J. 1976. *Linguistic Behaviour*. Cambridge.

Caplan, D. (ed.) 1980. *Biological Studies of Mental Processes*. Cambridge, Mass.

Chomsky, N., and Caplan, D., 1980. 'Linguistic Perspectives on Language Development', in Caplan 1980:97–105.

Chung, S. 1977. 'On the Gradual Nature of Syntactic Change', in Li 1977: 3–55.

Cowey, A., and Weiskrantz, L. 1975. 'Demonstration of Cross-modal Matching in Rhesus Monkeys, *Macaca mulatta*', *Neuropsychologia* 13, 117–20.

Dato, D. P. (ed.). 1975. *Georgetown Roundtable on Languages and Linguistics: Developmental Psycholinguistics*. Washington, D.C.

Davenport, R. K. 1976. 'Cross-Modal Perception in Apes', in Harnad *et al.* 1976: 143–49.

Davidson, D. 1973. 'Radical Interpretation', *Dialectica* 27, 313–28.

Davidson, D. 1975. 'Thought and Talk', in Guttenplan 1975: 7–23.

Davidson, D. 1979. 'Moods and Performances', in Margalit 1979: 9–20.

Dingwall, W. O. 1975. 'The Species-Specificity of Speech', in Dato 1975: 17–62.

Du Brul, E. L. 1979. 'Poor Old Neanderthal Man: Response to a Response', *Brain and Language* 8, 251–7.

Eisner, T. and Wilson, E. O. 1977. 'The Insects', *Readings from Scientific American*. San Francisco.

Field, H. 1978. 'Mental Representations', *Erkenntnis* 13, 9–61.

Fouts, P. *et al.* 1976. 'Translation of Signed Responses in American Sign Language from Vocal English Stimuli to Physical Object Stimuli by a Chimpanzee', *Learning and Motivation* 7, 458–75.

Geschwind, N. 1974. *Language and the Brain*. Dordecht.

Goldin-Meadow, S. J. 1975. 'The representation of semantic relations in a manual language created by deaf children of hearing parents: a language you can't dismiss out of hand', PhD thesis, Department of Psychology, University of Pennsylvania; quoted in MacNeill 1979.

Grice, H. P. 1969. 'Utterer's Meaning and Intentions', *Philosophical Review* 78, 147–77.

Guttenplan, S. 1975. *Mind and Language*. Oxford.

Hankamer, J. 1977. 'Multiple Analyses', in Li 1977: 583–607.

Harnad, S. R., Steklis, H. D. and Lancaster, J. (eds) 1976. *Origins and Evolution of Language and Speech*, Annals of the New York Academy of Sciences vol. 280.

Hewes, G. W. 1977. 'Language Origin Theories', in Rumbaugh 1977: 3–53.

Holloway, R. L., 'Paleoneurological Evidence for Language Origins', in Harnad *et al.* 1976: 330–48.

Ingram, D. 1975. 'If and when Transformations are Acquired by Children', in Dato, 1975: 99–127.

Isaac, G. L. 1976. 'Stages of Cultural Elaboration in the Pleistocene. Possible Archaeological Indicators of the Development of Language Capabilities' in Harnad *et al.* 1976: 275–88.

Jaynes, J. 1976. 'The Evolution of Language in the Late Pleistocene', in Harnad *et al.* 1976: 312–25.

Leakey, R. 1981. 'The Birth of Language', *The Listener*, 28 May 1981.

Lenneberg, E. H. 1966. 'The Natural History of Language', in Smith and Miller 1966: 219–52.

Lewis, D. K. 1969. *Convention*. Cambridge, Mass.

Li, C. (ed.). 1977. *Mechanisms of Syntactic Change*. Austin, Texas.

MacNeill, D. 1979. 'Language Origins', in von Cranach *et al.* 1979: 715–28.

Margalit, A. (ed.) 1979. *Meaning and Use*. Dordrecht.

Marshack, A. 1976. 'Some Implications of the Paleolithic Symbolic Evidence for the Origin of Language', in Harnad *et al.* 1976: 289–311.

Marshall, J. C. 1980. 'On the Biology of Language Acquisition', in Caplan 1980: 106–48.

Marx, J. L. 1980. 'Ape-Language Controversy Flares Up', *Science* 207, 1330–3.

McDowell, J. 1980. 'Meaning, Communication and Knowledge', in van Straaten 1980: 117–39.

Mellor, D. H. 1980a. 'Consciousness and Degrees of Belief, in Mellor 1980b: 139–73.

Mellor, D. H. (ed.) 1980b. *Prospects for Pragmatism: Essays in Memory of F.P. Ramsey*. Cambridge.

Montague, R. 1974. *Formal Philosophy*. New Haven.

Peters, P. S., and Ritchie, R. W. 1971. 'On Restricting the Base Component of Transformational Grammars', *Information and Control* 18, 483–501.

Petitto, L. A. and Seidenberg, M. S. 1979. 'On the Evidence for Linguistic Abilities in Signing Apes', *Brain and Language* 8, 162–83.

Premack, D. 1976. *Intelligence in Apes and Man.* Erlbaum, N.J.

Premack, D. and Woodruff, G. 1979. 'Intentional Communication in the Chimpanzee: The Development of Deception', *Cognition* 7, 333–62.

Riedl, R. 1979. *Biologie der Erkenntnis.* Berlin.

Routley, R. 1981. 'Alleged Problems in Attributing Beliefs and Intentionality to Animals', *Inquiry* 24, 385–417.

Rumbaugh, D. M. (ed.) 1977. *Language Learning by a Chimpanzee.* New York.

Sampson, G. 1978. 'Linguistic Universals as Evidence for Empiricism', *Journal of Linguistics* 14, 183–206.

Schmitt, A. 1955, 'Der nominale Charakter des sogenannten Verbums der Eskimosprache', *Zeitschrift für Vergleichende Sprachforschung* 73, 27–45.

Searle, J. R. 1979a, 'Intentionality and the Use of Language', in Margalit 1979: 181–97.

Searle, J. R. 1979b. 'What is an Intentional State?', *Mind* 88, 74–92.

Seidenberg, M. S., and Petitto, L. A. 1979. 'Signing Behaviour in Apes: A Critical Review', *Cognition* 7, 177–215.

Seyfarth, R. M., Cheney, D. L. and Marler, P. 1980. 'Vervet Monkey Alarm Calls: Semantic Communication in a Free Ranging Primate', *Animal Behaviour* 28, 1070–94.

Simon, H. A. 1962, 1969. 'The Architecture of Complexity', *Proceedings of the American Philosophical Society* 106, 467–82; reprinted in *The Sciences of the Artificial.* Cambridge, Mass.

Smith, E. and Miller, G. A. (eds.) 1966. *The Genesis of Language – A Psycholinguistic Approach.* Cambridge, Mass.

Tennant, N. 1983. 'Evolutionary v. Evolved Ethics', *Philosophy* 58.289–302.

Van Straaten, Z. (ed.) 1980. *Philosophical Subjects*, Oxford.

Von Cranach, M., Foppa, K., Lepennies, W. and Plogg, D. 1979. *Human Ethology: Claims and Limits of a New Discipline.* Cambridge.

Von Glaserfeld, E. 1976. 'The Development of Language as Purposive Behaviour', in Harnad *et al.* 1976: 212–26.

Machines and consciousness[1]

YORICK WILKS

INTRODUCTION

I have no strikingly original view of machines and consciousness to offer, nor shall I present a survey of the views of those in artificial intelligence (AI for short) who have discussed their relation, for the simple reason that there are none, at least in the sense of well-articulated philosophical views. AI workers are, by and large, naive materialists and mechanists, and for them those are not positions to be justified, but simply assumptions that allow them to get on with the job of constructing mechanical analogues or simulations of ourselves, who are, in Minsky's memorable phrase, 'meat machines'.

One could argue that such a strong assumption of underlying mechanism is only the normal situation in the sciences: one that allows experimental, as opposed to philosophical, work to proceed. True enough but, as I shall argue below, AI is not an experimental science but an engineering technique or, if you want something more dignified, a practical task in the alchemical tradition, and what I have to say about its suggestiveness for investigating the nature of consciousness rests entirely on that fact.

Again, the 'normal' situation in the sciences is not a sure guide, as none of you needs to be reminded, when the brain and mind are the subjects of investigation, given the peculiar features that attach to the notion of consciousness and to its close relations, thought, feeling, privacy and so on. In what follows, I shall play fast and loose with these words and the subtle distinctions between them. That is to say, I shall not distinguish carefully such questions as:

[1] The paper is indebted to comments and criticism from Kathy Wilkes, John Watkins, Jim Doran, Libor Spacek, John Mackie, John Marshall, Abram Tversky, Maggie Boden, Dan Dennett, Ned Block, Phil Johnson-Laird, Christopher Longuet-Higgins, Steve Hardy and members of the Thyssen Philosophy Group. The faults, as always, are mine.

Earlier versions of this paper were presented at the Annual Conference of the British Society for the Philosophy of Science, 1981, and the meeting of the Thyssen Philosophy Group, Spring 1982.

> Does X think?
> Is X conscious?
> Does X have essentially private inner processes?
> Is X aware of a sensation of pain?
> Is X aware of those trees in front of him?
> Is X conscious he is giving an after dinner speech?

When I write of consciousness I shall mean what is often called self-consciousness, rather than awareness of sensations or perceptions. Moreover, I shall not try to determine what kind of phenomenon consciousness is; the task here is rather to see whether the machine analogy can give us a way of talking about it, whatever it is.

The matter of the paper is to present those areas of AI (some would say that is too parochial and what I shall put forward belongs more generally to Computer Science) where a mechanical analogue of consciousness might be sought in the future, and to argue that they are not the obvious places, and have not been subjected to much philosophical investigation. At the end, I shall turn your attention to three accounts of the nature of consciousness by philosophers acquainted with AI, and contrast what they have to say with my own account.

I shall present the following notions in turn:
(i)   modularity
(ii) implementation independence
(iii) program-level reduction
(iv) program inference.

These are not really technical terms, but just convenient labels I shall use, though each is close to a well-understood technical concept. They are, I believe, some of the places to start our search for features of modern machines that might be suggestive as models or analogues of consciousness.

Although I was brisk at the beginning about the philosophical attitudes of AI workers, I owe the reader some small sample of them, that I can refer back to later. The best known of such views, very close to the theme of this paper, are Turing's speculations on whether machines could be said to think (Turing 1950). These are both too well known and too widely misunderstood to introduce here in detail: Turing, it will be remembered, wanted to cut through philosophical discussion with a Wittgensteinian fervour. He proposed a test, based on communication via teletypes with an unseen entity that was to be at first a human and then a computer, and if the human interlocutor, who had been told he was communicating on the subject of the differences between men and women, failed to notice that a machine had been substituted for the original human partner in the dialogue, then the machine was deemed to have passed the test, and Turing suggested we might as well speak of such a successful machine as thinking by polite convention, just as, 'instead of arguing continually ... it is usual to have a polite convention that everybody thinks'.

A more recent sample, in very much the same tradition would be Minsky's:

When a man M answers questions about the world we attribute his ability to some internal mechanism W* (a model of world W) inside of M. It would be most convenient if we could discern physically within M two separate regions W* and M-W*, such that W* 'really contains' the knowledge and M-W* contains only general purpose machinery for coding questions, decoding answers and general administrative work. However, one cannot really expect to find in an intelligent machine a clear separation between coding and knowledge structures, either anatomically or functionally because, for example, some 'knowledge' is likely to be used in the encoding and interpretation processes. (Minsky 1968: 426)

Minsky is making an interesting and important point here and I shall refer back to it, but for the moment the quotation functions purely as a sample: what it has in common with Turing's classic paper is that it is not philosophical argument at all. In Minsky's case, the philosophical question of whether there are hidden mechanisms that explain, etc., etc., never arises, because their existence is assumed from the outset, without discussion. The passage will remind some readers of Chomsky's palmier days, in linguistics rather than AI, when he would begin arguments with 'Obviously, everyone has internalized a grammar ... ' (Chomsky 1965: 8).

(1) MODULARITY

Modern computer programs, especially those in AI, are written, and are intended to be thought of, as interconnecting sub-parts or modules, and not at all as seamless wholes. Modules, in this sense, do not have access to the contents of other modules and, in Carl Hewitt of MIT's immortal words, 'modules shouldn't be able to dicker around with the insides of their neighbours'. In Winograd's (1971) well-known language understanding program, for example, there is a syntax analysis module and a semantics analysis module: these can demand answers from each other to specific questions about the structures of sentences but cannot 'get at' how the other one finds out whatever it does. Herbert Simon has argued (1969: 115) that evolution will prefer structures that are decomposable in this way, and that modularity may be expected in 'genetic programs'. He uses the metaphor of the commercial viability of two watchmakers, one of whom puts watches together out of finished sub-assemblies which cannot fall apart, and another who assembles each watch from its basic parts and risks the whole thing falling to pieces if dropped.

It was such an idea of modularity that Minsky intended in the quoted passage above, and he has suggested at various times that an organism would be more efficient, in terms of its ability to survive, if it had, as a separate module, a model of itself, which might of course be totally false as to the facts of the self's reality: alcoholics who believe themselves to be merely social drinkers probably survive less well than those who believe themselves to be alcoholics. An accessible model of the self is clearly one of the places that one might look for analogues of consciousness in a machine system.

More recently, Minsky has revived these notions, explicitly drawing analogies with the sorts of 'modularity' to be found in the writings of Freud (the three-way Ego, Id, Super-ego division) and Leibniz in his Mona-dology,[2] by claiming that an appropriate machine analogue of the human individual should have, among its modules, a supreme organizer. This module would, Minsky suggests, alone have access to the model (again possibly false, of course) of how it itself related to all the other, lower, modules, and it might be expected to have some property of the type we refer to as consciousness or self-consciousness. This additional property, Minsky believes, could have a functional or evolutionary explanation, of the sort suggested for the property of modularity itself by Simon, in that the 'conscious' supreme organizing module would *ipso facto* be in a position to 'debug' or repair the connections of the lower modules amongst themselves or to itself.[3] In order to preserve modularity, this power could not, of course, extend to repairing the modules themselves, for that is just the sort of tinkering that a principle of modularity would rule out.

In so far as I understand this view, and it is not yet a matter of close textual criticism of a published account, I find it difficult to connect the commonsense properties of consciousness (vague as they may be), with the notions of repair and debugging (fundamental as those are to any account of intelligent mechanisms). It is reliably claimed, for example, that certain yogis are able to take control of their physiological functions (heart-beat rate, digestion, etc.), utterly inaccessible to most of us. They can, if these claims are true as they seem to be, debug their 'digestive program', or slow their hearts considerably. But would we want to say that these abilities, striking though they are, have any particular connection with conscious-ness? If a yogi could tell us at any given moment what his digestive organs were doing, in chemical terms, and some constant monitoring apparatus attached to his intestines confirmed everything he said, then we might want

---

[2] This assumption that Freud's is a simple modular view of the psyche is unfair to the totality of his work, in particular *The Project* (Pribram & Gill 1976), a neurophysiological enterprise closer to the 'level' than the 'module' view (see below). I owe this point to Dr J. Marshall.

[3] To debug a program is to alter it or patch it up in such a way that it works.

to say yes; for the performance would seem to show just that immediate awareness of goings-on that we think of as intuitively necessary for a conscious process. But that, of course, is not change, debugging or repair (the very things Minsky was referring to), for we would be impressed in this way by a yogi who was *not* able, also and in addition, to change his digestive process. Conversely, we would be impressed by another yogi who could alter these processes in his intestines on a word of command but made no claims to know what was going on down there from moment to moment. These are simply different powers, but only one of them seems connected with consciousness, and not the one Minsky opted for.

A more important point lurks here that I shall have cause to return to later: there is a tension in Minsky's accounts of these matters between an emphasis on hierarchical organization (the supreme organizer, or Simon's modular watchmaker would be paradigms of that), and another on heter-archical organization. The latter notion has never been made very clear, but it was one much promoted by Minsky in the late 1960s (it enormously influenced Winograd's view of the organization of a language understand-ing system, for example); its essence was that there need be no permanent upper node of a system, as there always is in a hierarchical system, but that different nodes at different 'levels' could take control at different times. This was a more democratic view of organization, both socially and meta-physically, and one closer to Aristotle and Leibniz, for whom every entity, however lowly, had its degree of consciousness.

Minsky's 'supreme organizer' view must be a hierarchical one, for that organizer alone has the model of its relation to other modules, and it must therefore always be in control, because no other module has the model of relationships that would allow it sometimes to be in control (in the way a heterarchical view requires). Whether or not this control and its pre-requisite knowledge remain as properties of a single 'command' module, or shift about heterarchically, both views are forms of what I shall later want to call a 'light up' view of consciousness: as in a pinball machine different areas light up at different times depending on the state of the game. It is a view of consciousness I shall want to question later, in the light of published views of Dennett.

(II) IMPLEMENTATION INDEPENDENCE

It is a reasonably well-known fact that the same computer program can be run on a number of machines, not only different tokens of machines but different types, where that extends to machines working with quite different physical processes. This is what is referred to when one speaks of the implementation of a program being machine-independent, and it is part of the conventional distinction between hardware (i.e. machines) and soft-ware (i.e. programs). That there is a conventional element in the distinction is shown by the fact that procedures expressed as programs can also be expressed by the hardware structure of machines: the principal program-ming language of AI is LISP, which has been in existence for about twenty years, but only recently has a 'hard-wired' LISP-machine been built, one in which the LISP programs are more straight forwardly isomorphic with the operations of the hardware. All agree that hard-wired machines are faster, but what one loses with them is portability: the ability to run programs in many languages on a single machine, and a program in one language on many different sorts of machine.

It is this portability aspect of programs, and the conventional hardware–software distinction that goes with it, that has most interested those in AI who have concerned themselves with the relation of brains to minds: there has been an easy temptation to exploit the hardware–software distinction as a model of the brain–mind distinction. That would lead, of course, to a portable notion of mind, one that many have always found independently attractive on theological grounds. Support for it has come from the observation that both the brain and the conventional digital computer (i.e. the one hard-wired only for its machine code) seem to be surprisingly homogeneous in their internal structure, which led to remarks like Newell's (1973) '... intelligent behaviour demands only a few very general features in the underlying mechanism'.

This mind–brain analogy will not be used here, in part because the shifting of the hardware/software boundary that has resulted from the contruction of new machines has made it less attractive. Nonetheless, implementation independence has had a powerful effect on AI thinking about metaphysical problems, and has been behind McCarthy's insistence that AI must be defined as the study of intelligent mechanisms independent of their implementation in machines or brains, and hence to a general denial that AI is, in any strong sense, about machines. The point can be seen best by contrast: in the uniform rejection, by anyone acquainted with the practice of programming, of Fodor's claim (1976) that the principal interpretations or models, in the logical sense, of programs are actual hardware items and states. On this claim rests his whole theory of mental language, and yet it cannot be true for, if it were, there would be no serious portability of software, as between, say, machines of radically different architectures. But there is (cf. Johnson-Laird 1977 and Wilks 1982).

(III) PROGRAM-LEVEL REDUCTION

This phenomenon is related to the last, but concerns not the translation of procedures from programs/software to machines/hardware, but rather the translation of procedures from one *level* of programming language to another. In a digital computer the 'lowest level' of language is simply a string of binary digits 1 and 0 that is isomorphic to the states of the machine's registers. At a level above that there is what is called machine code: one whose lines are normally instructions to add or subtract or shift the contents of whole registers (themselves strings of binary numbers). At a level above that is assembly language whose commands normally translate into a set, of ten or perhaps a hundred, machine language commands. This ascent up the levels of programming languages can go on without any natural limit: a language like LISP, when run, is normally translated through two or three levels before it becomes machine code. But there are already languages, claimed to be of 'higher' levels than LISP, that must, in their turn, be translated into LISP before programs in them can run. It is normally said that as one goes further up this ascent of languages, the code becomes progressively more like a natural language such as English. This may be so, but is not necessarily so, and nothing particular hangs on the fact.

The notion of 'translation' just given covers a distinction that will be important for the purposes of this paper: a program at a given level can be either *interpreted* or *compiled* into a program at a lower level of language. In the former case, one can think (without it being too misleading) of each statement of the higher-level program translated into a set of statements of lower-level program, and that is done when the program runs. In the latter case, the higher-level program is translated as a whole into a lower-level program as a whole, and that process is carried out at a time before and separate from the time when the (compiled) program runs. The latter is more efficient and can be thought of by analogy with the translation of, say, a whole poem in English by a whole poem in Chinese (perhaps by Pound), with no line-to-line correspondence, but only an overall 'sameness of meaning or function'; whereas, on an 'interpretation' view, a Chinese poem would be constructed by a line-by-line translation of the English one. Both kinds of reduction 'preserve meaning' but in quite different ways.

Whenever a program runs, then, a sequence of such translations between levels of language is set up, but, and here is an important point, no particular lower-level translation is necessary for the program to achieve its purposes. Yet more importantly, the upper levels of the program have no access to the levels below them: the programmer who writes at the topmost, or accessible, level has no need to know how his program is being translated, even though for certain purposes he might wish to find out.

This phenomenon is very suggestive of a feature of conscious experience: our lack of conscious access to how we perform the details of activities, both 'mental' and 'physical', if that distinction makes a rough sort of sense here. When someone says 'We went to a bar and ordered a drink', plain men and parsing specialists all agree that the sense of 'bar' in question is a drinking place and not a rod of iron. Linguists, psychologists and AI workers have theories about what procedures might select the right sense on the basis of sensible rules and reject the wrong one. However, it is plain that the speaker of English, although he performs this general task reliably thousands of times a day, has no idea whatever how he does it, and may well have a healthy scepticism about proffered accounts in terms of linguistic or other rules. Yet how can we get a picture of the way in which it is possible to accept both that a task is done by rules (for it is certainly not done randomly) and yet the performer has no access whatever to the rules?

Wittgenstein pointed out that no account is satisfactory that assumes that a human somehow surveys the alternatives and chooses one: 'It is as if I should say that the application of a word does not pass in one moment in front of my eye' (1964: 15).[4] Yet it is not too hard to imagine how a computer parsing program might achieve some such effect: if we ask an English speaker how he does it, we may well get some reply like 'Well, I'm simply looking for a sense of the word related to drinking, aren't I?' In program terms, we can imagine a high-level command:

GIVE ME A DRINKING SENSE OF THIS WORD IF THERE IS ONE

and the response to such a command could be to hand up some dictionary definition of a bar as a drinking place. I am not advocating such a theory of parsing English into formal representations – I happen not to believe strongly in such 'top–down' theories, though there are several relatively successful ones in the literature. The point is that there could be such a command and at the level of that command where, as it were, the answer would be received, no information would ever be received about the other senses of 'bar' that the system as a whole might happen to know about in its dictionary, and the procedures for surveying that range of senses would never be revealed. To that very limited degree, such a program would avoid the puzzle posed by the Wittgensteinian remark, about how it is possible to locate the right sense without any 'conscious' access, even in principle, to all the uses of the word.

This situation might seem more difficult in the case of physical activities such as walking: I walk, with or without conscious effort, it may be said, but

[4] Wittgenstein 1953, para. 139:
'When someone says the word "cube" to me, for example, I know what it means. But can the whole use of the word come before my mind, when I understand it in this way?'
I am not suggesting here that Wittgenstein was assuming some particular division of a word's use into 'senses'; the point I am making survives however one construes his 'whole use'.

have no access of any kind to the associated brain, nerve and muscle activities, even though we have perfectly good physiological evidence for the regular association of those activities with the act of walking. As with the linguistic theories of how we understand 'bar', we may have theories or models or whatever of our own walking but they may be wildly false. A lay person asked whether both his feet were off the ground simultaneously when he walked would probably be wrong as often as right. Thus far, the analogy with the linguistic case holds. However, how can this phenomenon be illuminated by means of the metaphor of levels of programming language, on which view the 'lower activities' are inscrutable at the 'higher level', given that, after a road accident, say, I can by conscious effort retrain myself to walk properly?

We are returning, by another route, to Minsky's suggestion that the evolutionary role of consciousness has been to give access to modules or levels, otherwise inaccessible, so as to debug, reprogram or retrain them. I argued earlier that there was no necessary connection between the two families of notions (of access and repair), and the present example suggests, I would claim, that there is no factual connection either. I have the ability to retrain my walk, say, precisely because the muscular sub-movements of walking (flexing toes and feet, moving calves, etc.) are neither in 'another module' of activity (i.e. from the 'conscious' module, if there is one) nor at an inaccessible level of translation of commands. After a tendon transfer operation, for example, one can relearn to walk by 'moving' one's foot outward instead of upwards (although, because of the transfer, it then actually moves upward, as required for normal walking).

I shall return later to the possibility of seeing the inaccessibility in terms of a limitation of access between levels (rather than between modules), but for the moment we can redescribe this retraining activity as the ability of the subject, at a given level (the uppermost, of intending to walk, in this case), to retranslate an activity into a lower level, in such a way that the translation later becomes compiled (in terms of the earlier distinction between compilation and translation) and ceases to be accessible from the 'higher level'. Thus, after a while, the one who had retrained his walk with great effort would have no more conscious access to his method of walking than one who had never had such an accident, or subsequent operation.

This intuitive account would require, in an analogue of consciousness for which program-level reduction could provide a necessary condition, but no more, that there be access from a higher to a lower level of programming language in certain, yet to be specified, circumstances. Those might be, for example, early stages of the retraining of walking in which a subject could still access and change the order of muscle movements. But this access would be only to an *interpretation* translation at the lower level (one in which there remains a one–many mapping of commands) but not to an (inscrutable) compilation translation.

If this sort of account is true to the facts, then it is a consideration against any factual connection of the type Minsky envisaged between conscious access and 'reprogramming or debugging', at least it is if lower-level translations normally exist as (undebuggable) compilations. For the provision of a new interpretation of walking (later to be compiled, as it were) precisely did not require any access to, or repair of, the structure of how the walking was done originally. Empirical evidence against my point might arise if there was significant support for the claims now made by some surgeons that a patient after such an accident can both will, and have conscious access to, the process of nerve regrowth (as an alternative to the sort of superficial retraining of behaviour described above). If that turned out to be possible, it might suggest there is access from a higher level to quite remote lower-level translations, unless one was prepared to redescribe such a phenomenon in terms of our (levels of programming language) metaphor as 'This patient has found out how to access a highest level command GROW A NEW NERVE TO YOUR LEFT FOOT though without, of course, having any access to the translation of that command in terms of the nerve cell processes themselves.' Though then, of course, the activity in question would no longer be walking but growing nerves, and the walking itself might again have to be relearned as described earlier.

(IV) PROGRAM INFERENCE

This concerns limitations on the ability to infer the highest level program given the lowest: if one stood in front of a large machine one would see banks of lights flashing, as in the conventional newspaper cartoons. These lights are in one-to-one relationships with certain key registers of the machine and actually express the binary numbers in them (a light being off for 0 and on for 1). Thus, if the whole internal process were slowed down enormously, one could actually see a representation of each command executed by the machine at the lowest possible level of representation. If one were in possession of all those binary numbers in sequence, could one infer the highest level of program or, to put it another way, could one infer what the machine was actually up to in the sense of paying tax refunds to the citizens of London, as distinct from translating a book from English to Chinese? And, if there are limitations on our ability to make such inferences, are they in any sense serious or just casual, in that they would require more effort than anyone is normally prepared to put in?

Such an ability would be of more than merely theoretical interest: there are specialists, detectives one might almost say, who can take enormous quantities of program in a lower-level language (not binary numbers, but normally machine code or something a little 'higher') and make plausible guesses as to what they actually do at a higher level of description; or rather, given that they are told what the program was designed to do, work out how it accomplished the task and by what 'higher-level' steps. This task is an important one because of the enormous amounts of program in the hands of organizations whose original writers have long since left without leaving any description of what they had done. The US Government is reliably said to have invested large sums from its military budget on research in which impulses from computers (which might give you something like the binary number level of the program) were detected at a distance and the task was to see whether the highest level of program (expressing what the real purpose of the program was) could be reliably inferred. The answer was 'no', roughly speaking, unless one knew not only the machine code but, most importantly, what the highest level language in question was, and the one from which the binary code had been obtained when the program ran. The important point was that there seemed to be no way of determinately reversing this higher-to-lower translation unless the target high-level language was already known.

It is sometimes argued that an experienced programmer can detect the 'general shape' of a particular high-level language X from blocks of machine code, just by hunch and judgement, but this ignores the possibility that the code may have been written in language Y with the syntactic style of X precisely in order to create this confusion; just as one can murmur English with a German intonation and cause a distant listener to believe he is listening to unintelligible German. In sum, then, there is no reason to believe that, in a complex machine, the real processes can be inferred reliably from any number of observations of internal behaviour (in the sense in which the changing of register contents expressed in binary numbers is internal behaviour[5]), in the absence of knowledge of a quite different type: the language in which the processes have been expressed to the machine.

It would be dangerous to suggest that this impossibility is in any strong sense theoretical, i.e. open to mathematical proof, and I will assume it is no more than a strong empirical impossibility. If such a program detective had descriptions of all the high-level languages ever written, and knew them to be all there were, then he could presumably work through them all in turn

[5] I have argued in more detail the case outlined here, and in particular that the distinction of 'internal' and 'external' behaviour cannot, *pace* Fodor, be maintained for a digital computer, in Wilks 1974.

(the obvious difference from the human brain case being that, even if it has a high-level programming language we have no idea what it could be like[6]).

Suppose one grants some such upwards inscrutability, in terms of lower-to-higher language levels, does anything general or of interest for our discussion follow? If it amounts to some sort of 'machine privacy', is that at all suggestive for the question of consciousness? Before addressing those questions directly, let us return for a moment to the so-called 'Turing test' (Turing 1950) mentioned earlier.

One aspect of performance that one might expect of any machine that was to pass the test (by behaving in such a way that the human interlocutor never even suspected a machine was present) would be to have the sort of final authority over what state it was in that we normally concede to humans: when Jones, on the neurosurgeon's table, insists that he is in pain, we tend to allow his authority even though the neurosurgeon says that, given the position of the brain probe at that moment, he should not be.

If a computer printed out that its memory was suffering from a certain kind of fault, we might be persuaded from past experience to go on examining its hardware for faults, even though we found none in the initially plausible places. We might, to speak anthropomorphically, allow it to *insist* that its memory was going and, if we did, we would allow it the authority in question. Closer perhaps to the title of this section, we might come to allow that the computer really was paying tax refunds (because it said it was), even though all detective work on its machine code program was consistent with it being occupied directing the trajectories of intercontinental ballistic missiles. If we did come to allow such authority, or privacy, to the machine enormous consequences would follow,[7] for its blueprints and machine programs would no longer be a safe guide to its future behaviour. Yet, of course, a machine that was to pass the Turing test fully should have this authority, because we do, or appear to do. To be plausible the authority should also be limited in the way ours is: a machine that appeared certain,[8] in the teeth of all the evidence observable by us, that such and such a transistor was failing might well have given itself away

6 There are arguments that a mental state cannot be inferred from any number of observations of the state of the brain, whether the last phrase is given a concrete, (i.e. neural) or more abstract interpretation (see Wilkes 1980). Such arguments tell for the same general conclusions as are argued for here, though in quite different terms.

7 I have developed this point further in Wilks 1975, where I was arguing for the possibility of a more serious machine privacy, and against the satirical forms of privacy that Putnam has ascribed to machines in order to argue that, being of the same kind as theirs, our mental privacy is also illusory.

8 Nothing I argue for here depends on there being incorrigible certainty about pain or any other internal phenomenon – as has of course been much questioned by Wittgensteinians, and Dennett more recently in connection with computers and pain. All I require is that people and computers may be in the same boat, whatever the boat turns out to be (cf. Dennett 1979).

precisely because it would lack the 'downwards' inscrutability that our inner workings have for us.

To return to the question at issue: does all this even suggest anything insightful about the nature of consciousness? Given that privacy is plausibly one of the necessary conditions for being an explication of consciousness (see below), it seems to me that any establishment of an interesting sense of machine privacy must be relevant. At the very least, it would show that human beings do *a fortiori* have some sort of privacy.

An initial objection against any easy identification of such a privacy with consciousness is that, when driving, say, the highest level commands to turn the car, keep the accelerator depressed, etc., would be 'inscrutable from below' in the way discussed, but the level of those commands could never be identified with consciousness because, as Sartre liked to point out *ad nauseam*, we can drive 'without thinking about it' and, moreover, at no danger to the public. This is correct, but nothing I shall say, when I come to draw conclusions, will amount to any such identification, only to necessary, though not sufficient, conditions for an explication of consciousness.

So, if we are conscious in the sense of this analogy of levels, then it is *of* the uppermost level that we are conscious, but that does not require me to claim that we are always conscious of that level. Nor am I assuming that the top level of language, in the sense of programming language, coincides always with the 'top level of control', though it will in general do so. The driving-unconsciously-while-proving-a-theorem case illustrates that situation well enough.

More seriously, one might object that everything said here depends crucially on the assumption that there really is one activity, rather than another, that a given computer is performing. One might go on to say that if there are two or more consistent interpretations of the lowest level code,[9] then it makes no sense to say that the computer is in fact, say, paying tax refunds rather than doing something else because that can never be more than a matter of pragmatic interpretation by some human users of the thing. This seems to me just false, although I find it hard to show it convincingly. If a detective approaches someone and says 'all your

---

[9] Everything here assumes there is some such translation, whatever the difficulty of reversing it. It is not even suggested in this paper that there is no such translation, which seems to me obscurantism. In one of his clear statements of position Wittgenstein gave a marvellous hostage to historical fortune (or at least to the history of plant genetics) that I have not seen remarked on: 'No supposition seems to me more natural than that there is no process in the brain correlated with or associated with thinking; so it would be impossible to read off thought processes from brain processes ... the case would be like the following – certain kinds of plant multiply by seed, so that a seed always produces a plant of the same kind as that from which it was produced – but *nothing* in the seed from which the plant comes corresponds to it; so that it is impossible to infer the properties of structure of the plant from those of the seed that comes out of it ... ' (Wittgenstein 1968: para. 609).

activities of the last week are consistent with the interpretation that you are planning to rob a post office' then, when the person replies, 'but as a matter of fact, I just am shopping there and no more, and that's that', one can either refer to *intentionality* or some such notion[10] and allow the appeal or, with the detective, one can continue to keep one's eye open. Not everyone will concede that there really is a single interpretation, nor that, if there is, the subject necessarily knows what he is up to.

I think the most commonsense response to this objection is as follows: whatever may be the theoretical case about competing interpretations of low-level code in the machine, we need to remind ourselves that, if this machine is 'paying tax refunds', as opposed to 'directing missiles', then it is actually printing large rolls of cheques at its peripheral devices. Any claim that, because there are competing interpretations, either is equally valid in the absence of knowledge of the programmer's intentions in the matter, is impossible to maintain in the face of the long rolls of encashable instruments pouring out of its printer.[11]

CRITERIA FOR AN EXPLICATION OF CONSCIOUSNESS

I now want to draw together the four aspects of intelligent machines set out above and three *prima facie* features of consciousness: these three seem to me necessary criteria for any explication of consciousness, and I will suggest that the aspects of such machines already described are interestingly related to these facts. They are not, of course, sufficient features and I shall make neither claims nor suggestions here as to the sufficiency of existing or possible machines for being conscious entities.

(a) Vacuity or 'downwards opacity'

Dennett (see below) has in recent publications emphasized the relative emptiness of the contents of consciousness: all that is not there and which,

[10] This sense of the term is that of writers like Searle, for whom a human subject has incorrigible access to his intentions (Searle 1980).

[11] A more sophisticated response would be in terms of the sort of notion of 'intentionality' set out by Dennett, quite different from that of Searle's referred to above, according to which predicates like intention are terms in a descriptive theory and not subjective incorrigibles. On that account it would be as straightforward to have a theory of what the tax-paying machine was really up to (on the basis of its behaviour and our theory of intelligent entities) as it would be to make similar claims about a human being. My reaction to that would be consistent with my earlier remarks about a machine in a possible Turing test to which we allowed something of the final authority that we allow to humans, for 'allowance of final authority' need be no more, on a quasi-Dennett view, than part of our theory of sufficiently complex organisms. My aim in both places is to suggest that humans and some machines may be in much the *same theoretical position* in this matter; *whatever* that position is (cf. Dennett 1979).

for much of the workings of our bodies, cannot be brought into the contents of consciousness. I would suggest that the two sorts of opacity in a computer that have been discussed here are at least potentially interesting explications of that fact: modularity and program-level reduction. When discussing Dennett and Sloman below, I shall argue that the opacity of one level of programming language to another is a better preliminary model of consciousness than the inaccessibility of the contents of one module from another. Different kinds of opacity within a program were discussed earlier and these would seem to have quite different correlates in the sphere of consciousness: the lower level of language is almost totally inaccessible from the higher level (unless special structural features are added to the language to make it accessible), in rather the way that the machine code of our brain, if there is one, is utterly inaccessible to me, thinking in English.

One might suggest at this point that the *level* and *module* metaphors are not really opposed, because there could be a module that did the translation between the uppermost level and the one below it, and so on downwards. In that case, it would be argued, the levels are in one-to-one correspondence with the modules and the difference is only one terminology. But one can see immediately that that is not so: the task of the modules is translation, and so the task of each translation module is therefore different (translating a poem from English to Chinese is not the same task as translating that poem from Chinese to French). But the levels, in the original description, all have the same function.

The notion of difference of level between quite different programming languages can equally well be expressed within a single language: at a single level of language, say of the programming language LISP, one normally defines a function in terms of sub-functions, so that I might for example write a function WALK(x) (where x ranges over walkers) whose sub-functions (to be executed in order) might be some form of LIFT-RIGHT-LEG; FLEX-RIGHT-FOOT; and so on (I am not suggesting that sequence would be even remotely plausible in fact). Normally the highest level of program, demanding the execution of WALK within a program called GO-SHOPPING(x), would have no access to WALK, nor *a fortiori* to the contents of WALK. The difference of level now would be that of a hierarchy of functions and sub-functions within a single language, though one might still plausibly maintain that the above sequence beginning LIFT-RIGHT-LEG was the translation of WALK in that system.

One must be a little careful with the word 'translation' here: it is fairly innocuous in the present context of WALK, translated into the string of sub-functions, but much less so in the earlier use of the relation of a program in LISP, say into a lower-level program in machine code. It is in that latter role that Fodor (1976) has exploited the use of 'translation' and made the inference that the lower-level code must therefore mean the same as the higher-level code, thus arguing in effect against what I called 'implementation independence'. My earlier use of 'translation' to cover both interpretation and compilation into a lower-level language is not intended to carry any suggestion that the lower levels, including the lowest level of all, the machine's registers, can be an interesting formal semantics for the higher levels, let alone what the highest level 'is about'. Nor can one assume that two levels of program 'have the same semantics' (as true translations normally would).

However, within the single language LISP, access could, with appropriate effort, be made to the translation of GO-SHOPPING(x) as a sequence beginning WALK(x), but the subsequent access from WALK(x) to the yet lower-level sequence beginning LIFT-RIGHT-LEG(x) is far more dubious, whatever the effort required, since that would normally have been compiled and so be inaccessible to the higher level in question, even though, as we saw, one can, in the human case, impose a new translation of WALK, in the place of the existing one.

A person's initial attempt, when recovering from such a supposed accident, to construct a sequence beginning LIFT-RIGHT-LEG(x), etc., may well draw on our observation of others, folk theories of walking, etc., and be a totally false – in the sense of ineffectual – theory of walking (i.e. be a wrong W* in the terms of the original quotation from Minsky 1968). The actual retraining of walking in physiotherapy may require that one has imposed on one a new sequence of movements, a sequence quite different from that of the false folk theory, and one that the patient might not be able to construct without the expert help of the physiotherapist. All this, I argued, is at least suggestive about how we can have some form of access to the superficial form, say of our walking (i.e. to the gross sequence of movements, if not to the nerves), and can impose a new walking 'strategy' to which we will then in due course (after an analogue of compilation) again lose access.

The claim in this section that what I have called downwards opacity is a necessary feature of consciousness may seem open to the following reply: a person might claim that he was conscious, directly and permanently, of all aspects and details of his bodily functions: nerves, cells, blood vessels, etc., and medical evidence might confirm what he said. Would we want to rule him out as being conscious, on the grounds that the above condition is a necessary one? Logically, we would not, but the reply would have to be that given the processing mechanisms we seem to have, it would not be practically possible. To say this is to adopt a quasi-evolutionary view, close to Minsky's, not in terms of debugging and repair, but in terms of attention and processing load: to be able to concentrate on everything is not to be able to concentrate at all. Or, to put it another way, there is an essentially *privative* (in the sense of 'deprive' not 'private') aspect of consciousness and this feature (a) is one way of capturing that.

(b) Upwards opacity

By this I refer to the acknowledged limitations on the ability to infer the contents of consciousness from any number of behavioural or physiological observations. This is a deep but much discussed subject and I shall not go into it here but simply assume it. As I argued, the phenomena associated with upwards program inference are a plausible explication of that.

(c) The unity of consciousness

This is another classic and difficult topic. There is, to put it crudely, a firm intuition that the self we can identify with our immediate consciousness is a unity, in that we would not count as being that self any part or module of ourselves which was put forward as a candidate for being a conscious entity. There are great difficulties about this notion, however crudely one expresses it, and however firm the intuition that it is true, and they come from well-known considerations to do with unconscious and sub-conscious aspects of the mind, as well as from the more rococo possibilities of more than one conscious individual within a single body, which has recently been connected with research on the status and relationship of the two hemispheres of the brain (cf. Wilkes 1978).

Block (1980) has argued that one can construct a case where one would be forced to say that a conscious individual not only contained, but consisted of, other conscious individuals. His ingenious situation concerns very small homunculi from space, of the order of magnitude of body cells, who enter a human being in large numbers and colonize him to such an extent that he is eventually made up of small conscious entities. In some sense, we are then forced to say that he simply is them, physically speaking, and the problem, of course (for a view like the one put forward here), concerns the relationship of his consciousness to theirs. To this I find no difficulty in replying briskly that the human's consciousness does not have the consciousnesses of the homunculi as parts any more than two Siamese Twins that share digestive organs have the unity and separateness of their respective consciousnesses compromised.

Again, we have to consider both modularity and program level as possible explications of this assumed unity of consciousness. In the case of modularity, there seems a natural explication if we take seriously Minsky's idea of a highest organizing module. It will be remembered that his other, earlier, intuitions about heterarchy pulled in the opposite direction, towards a monadology of separate partial sub-consciousnesses. I shall argue below, in connection with Dennett and Sloman, that our common-sense intuitions about the unity of consciousness are better preserved by analogy with program *level* than with program *module*.

Before turning to the work of Sayre, Dennett and Sloman, I should at least mention one major question that has been left unasked in this paper, and intentionally so: namely, what properties would a machine have to have in order to be *sufficient* for us to deem it conscious?

I simply do not know, at least not if the properties are to be non-trivial, and more than an acceptance of certain machines into the category of human beings by fiat or polite convention. One might guess that a substantive discussion of this issue would centre on the question of linguistic performance: Danto (1960) suggested that we will do violence to the English language if machines achieve certain linguistic performances but we still refuse to deem them conscious.

However, such performances cannot be *necessary* conditions for such ascription, because of all those we would naturally deem conscious but who cannot, for various reasons, provide them. A problem might arise here because the phenomena discussed in this paper – vacuity, upwards inference and so on – could only be established for entities capable of some degree of linguistic performance. This difficulty could be fatal to the argument of this paper, if successful, for then the proposed necessary conditions would, in their turn, rest upon a sufficient condition, namely having language.

The first answer is to argue that the computer-science phenomena described here could be established by non-linguistic means (e.g. hardware readings of some sort). The other, more plausible, avenue is to accept that the phenomena discussed would normally be established by linguistic means but that is in no way a necessary feature of them, and so no problem of principle need arise.

Sayre

I shall give a quotation from Sayre simply to show the difference between the approaches to such issues as consciousness in the AI tradition and in the cybernetics tradition; both, after all, are concerned with the implications of intelligent machines for consciousness, etc.

Perceptual consciousness, I maintain, is a mode of information processing in which information entering the organism's sense receptors is transformed into patterns of cortical states which remain generally stable from moment to moment and change

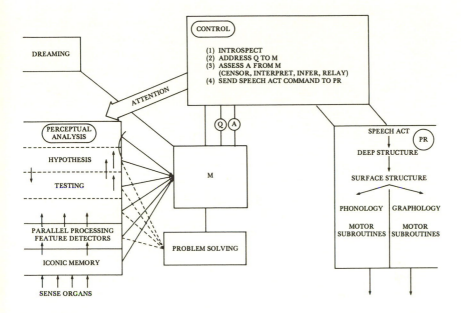

with the changing demands upon the perceptual system. In brief, perceptual consciousness is a patterned response of the organism's cortex to information arriving at its sense periphery. (Sayre 1976: 156)

But this, of course, makes no serious claim at all about the notion of consciousness, in the sense in which the word is normally used: it simply sets up a definition of the term on which virtually any organism higher than an amoeba is conscious, as would be many existing computers. He tells us at the beginning of his book that he is an Aristotelean in these matters, but the price he pays is that his definition simply fails to bear upon the intuitive criteria for an explication of consciousness, such as those set out above.[12]

Dennett

In his Brainstorms, Dennett set out to: '... sketch a theory of consciousness that can be continuous with and help unify current cognitivist theories of perception, problem solving and language use' (Dennett 1979: 149).

His strategy is to argue from intuitive examples and psychological results that very little is in fact available to consciousness: that it is vacuous in the sense used above. His most striking example is derived from an experiment

---

[12] Though one must be wary here too: definitions nearly as wide can be found within the AI tradition in these matters: '... to ascribe purpose to an organism is to ascribe consciousness to it to some degree' (Boden 1972:320).

by Lackner and Garrett in which subjects heard sentences like 'He put out the lantern to signal the attack' (which is ambiguous as between place outside and extinguish). One group received just the sentence, while another group heard 'disambiguating input' through a channel they were not explicitly attending to (i.e. an additional sentence such as 'He extinguished the lantern'). Naturally enough, the latter group interpreted the first sentence appropriately but were unable to report what they heard through the unattended channel. In other words, they were not at all *conscious* of the perceptual information that had solved the problem for them. The centrepiece of the paper is a flow chart, which I reproduce here (Dennett 1979: 155).

The heart of Dennett's case is that very little is available to consciousness: we just get the results. We are conscious, in general, of some of our memory, and the results of speech generation, though in the latter case we are in much the same position as any other observer (cf. E. M. Forster's 'How do I know what I think till I see what I say').

A principal feature of Dennett's case is that we posit features of our unconscious apparatus, which have no necessary connection with the actual thoughts we have, any more than had Hume's perceptions of causation with perceptions of causes. This is an observation in line with his general theory of psychological predicates, and consistent with, for example, Minsky's notion of self-model that we discussed earlier. Our folk theories of our contents of consciousness may be as wildly false to the facts as are our folk theories of grammar to the language that comes out of our mouths.

None of this shows, of course, that the folk theories, even if false, are not well and truly in consciousness; indeed if they were not one could not truly be said to be working with a false theory of the mind (unless theory became no more than a structure of, possibly unconscious, assumptions). So the observations about folk theories of consciousness, though highly interesting, do not in themselves show consciousness to be more impoverished than we had earlier thought, for fictions are as good as fillers of consciousness as are truths.

No, the difficulty I have with Dennett's excellent paper, and the reason I have brought it into discussion here, has to do with the fact that he never actually says which parts of the diagram are *in consciousness* and his view is consistent with consciousness being (a) the 'control box', (b) sometimes one box and sometimes another (very like the 'heterarchical aspect' of Minsky's views, which I earlier called a 'pinball machine' theory of consciousness), or (c) some elements of what passes down the communication channels, that is to say, the lines between the boxes.

The last view is suggested by his claims that we are conscious of some memories (those brought to INTROSPECTION in the 'control box' for example) and some of the commands to say things (as in deliberately saying something, as distinct from finding ourselves saying it), which would be messages from the 'control box' to PR (the 'public relations box', by analogy with the White House public relations chief, who is simply handed a piece of paper telling him what to say, but not to think about).

I have no quarrel with interpretation (c) and think it probably consistent with my suggestions in this paper that the notion of the 'highest level of program' is the best available explication of consciousness. But one problem about showing that is that Dennett has opted (perhaps unnecessarily for his argument) for a flow-chart explication, which is inherently a static rather than a process one. It is no accident that people in AI rarely draw flow-charts, and it is a cliché of programming in LISP that if one finds oneself drawing a flow-chart, one has not understood how LISP works. Now merely saying that is not evidence of any kind (and may merely annoy those AI workers who program in languages other than LISP and do use flow-charts), but it does bring out something of the opposition between modules and levels that is the heart of the last part of this paper: flow-chart boxes are essentially separated from each other in ways like those that separate the modules of programs; but program levels are not like that. The LIFT-RIGHT-LEG sub-function of the WALK function is not a part of it and in no way a module of it.

My argument here with Dennett is that if he intends interpretations (a) or (b) (a textual quotation here would be beside the point, since these distinctions are not made in his paper in that form), then those are inferior explications of consciousness to a process one in terms of level: (b) because it lacks the 'unity' requirement, and (a) because, although it could meet all the necessary conditions set out earlier, it seems in some way arbitrary, just as did Minsky's supreme organizing module. After all, why should it be that particular one? Given the richness of interconnections between the boxes, it could have been any one of them that was dubbed the conscious one, so we would need something more by way of justification for choosing any particular one. In the case of levels, opting for the uppermost of a set of them seems less arbitrary.

I have not touched on the difficult question of localization here: it is a lively issue where the brain is concerned, but not for the digital computer because, depending on how you interpret its operations, information can be thought of as being anywhere at all in the machine (i.e. not localized in the sense of being associated with a particular place in it), or (and in some sense conversely) all operations of the machine can be thought of as going on in one very small and specific place. Neither of these views is of much interest for brain scientists seeking suggestive computer models. So, we can think of

different modules from Dennett's flow-chart as being stored and functioning in the same place in the machine, just as we can think of different
levels of translation of programming language as being carried out in the
same place in the machine. Nonetheless, the flow-chart-cum-module model
is much more open to interpretation in terms of localization (if only because
both are normally explained and displayed spatially), and therefore any
explication of consciousness in their terms will tend to be a localized model,
or what I referred to as a pinball-machine view of consciousness, one that
seems to me *a priori* implausible.

Sloman

Sloman (1978) straightforwardly argues for a conscious module or sub-part
view, of just the sort I have opposed to a program-level view.

He describes, as I did, the lack of access between the interiors of modules,
but accepts the view of consciousness that I associated with Minsky's views
on heterarchy: that, roughly speaking, sometimes one module would be
conscious and sometimes another, depending on circumstances:

> It is possible (as I believe Leibniz claimed) that instead of there being one division
> between what is and is not conscious in a complex system, there may be many
> divisions: one for the system as a whole, and more for various subsystems. If there is
> something in the argument about the need for some centralised decision making in
> the system as a whole, then the same argument can be used for the more complex
> subsystem. Considered as an organic whole there may be some things a subsystem
> can be said to be conscious of, and others which it cannot.
>
> This would be clearest in a computer which controlled a whole lot of robot-bodies
> with which it communicated by radio. For each individual robot, there might be a
> fairly well-integrated subsystem, aware of where the robot is ... Within it there will
> be information stores and subprocesses of which it is not conscious ... Similarly
> within the total system, composed of many robots, there will be some kind of
> centralised process ... which knows where each (robot) is ... So individual robots
> may be aware of things the system as a whole cannot be said to be aware of, and vice
> versa. (Sloman 1978: 251)

In the terms established earlier this, like the Monadology itself, seems an
unsatisfactory account of consciousness in that it ignores the unity principle, for what that is worth. Viewed as an 'independent robot', I am happy
to admit that a particular area of my brain controls my digestive processes
and 'I' do not, but I certainly do not want to say that that brain area is
'aware' of those processes. Sloman prompts one to ask what it could be like
to be an entity that controlled all existing (presumably conscious) human
beings but had no access to what went on in their conscious minds at all,
and of which, *ex hypothesi*, the humans themselves were not aware? To use
the argument brought forward against the related speculation of Block (i.e.

about the tiny homunculi), one might at the very least want to deny that the higher and lower consciousnesses could, in any sense, be the same consciousnesses, whether or not they could be said to be in a physical part–whole relationship. The supreme organizer picture set out above, whose sub-modules are controlled but themselves conscious (though not of the control itself), is a well-known theological pattern and has been explored elsewhere in detail: a God who is omnipotent, conscious, but not omniscient in that he can look into human brains while being unable to see what they are thinking. Whatever the heady consequences of that (and they have classically been found contradictory), Sloman's explication does not tackle the question of why it is we are conscious of certain things at some times but not at others. In that sense it is, like Dennett's, a picture-cum-flow-chart view, rather than one in terms of processes.

I have done little to remedy that myself, except to fall back on the preferred notion of level, which at least can begin to explicate how things can be reached by effort at some times but not others. However, it too is in need of a great deal of further explanation. The concept of level, it must be said, is not an original metaphor to bring to bear on the topic of consciousness: mystics have always talked of levels of consciousness, and the nineteenth-century vitalists wrote at length of the emergence of a level of consciousness from a sufficiently complex lower level of organization. What I believe a notion of computer language level can do, though I have not achieved it here, is to put some procedural flesh on those traditional bones.

REFERENCES

Block, N. 1980. 'States' Rights', commentary on Searle 1980, *Behavioral and Brain Sciences* 3, 425–7.
Boden, M. 1972. *Purposive Explanation in Psychology*. Cambridge, Mass.
Chomsky, N. 1965. *Aspects of the Theory of Syntax*. Cambridge, Mass.
Danto, A. 1960. 'On Consciousness in Machines', in *Dimensions of Mind*, ed. Hook, 180–7. New York.
Dennett, D. 1979. *Brainstorms*. Hassocks.
Dreyfus, H. 1972. *What Computers Can't Do*. New York.
Fodor, J. 1976. *The Language of Thought*. Hassocks.
Johnson-Laird, P. 1977. 'Procedural Semantics', *Cognition* 5, 189–214.
Minsky, M. 1968. 'Matter, Mind and Models', in *Semantic Information Processing* ed. D. G. Bobrow, 425–32. Cambridge, Mass.
Newell, A. 1973. 'Artificial Intelligence and the Concept of Mind', in *Computer Models of Thought and Language*, ed. Schank and Colby, 1–60. San Francisco.
Pribram, K. and Gill, M. 1976. *Freud's Project Reassessed*. London.
Sayre, K. 1976. *Cybernetics and the Philosophy of Mind*. London.
Searle, J. 1980. 'Minds, Brains and Programs', *Behavioral and Brain Sciences* 3, 417–57.
Simon, H. 1969. *The Sciences of the Artificial*. Cambridge, Mass.
Sloman, A. 1978. *The Computer Revolution in Philosophy*. Hassocks.

Turing, A. 1950. 'Computing Machinery and Intelligence', *Mind* 59, 433–60.

Wilkes, K. 1978. 'Consciousness and Commisurotomy', *Philosophy* 53, 185–99.

Wilkes, K. 1980. 'Brain States', *British Journal for the Philosophy of Science* 31, 111–29.

Wilks, Y. 1974. 'More on Fodor's Distinction between Weak and Strong Simulations' *Philosophy of Science* 41, 408–11.

Wilks, Y. 1975. 'Putnam and Clarke and Body and Mind', *British Journal for the Philosophy of Science* 26, 213–25.

Wilks, Y. 1982. 'Some Thoughts on Procedural Semantics', in *Advances in Natural Language Processing*, ed. Lehnert and Ringle. New Jersey.

Winograd, T. 1971. *Understanding Natural Language*. Edinburgh.

Wittgenstein, L. 1953. *Philosophical Investigations*. Oxford.

Wittgenstein, L. 1964. *Philosophical Remarks*. Oxford.

Wittgenstein, L. 1968. *Zettel*. Oxford.

Cognitive wheels: the frame problem of AI

DANIEL DENNETT

Once upon a time there was a robot, named R1 by its creators. Its only task was to fend for itself. One day its designers arranged for it to learn that its spare battery, its precious energy supply, was locked in a room with a time bomb set to go off soon. R1 located the room, and the key to the door, and formulated a plan to rescue its battery. There was a wagon in the room, and the battery was on the wagon, and R1 hypothesized that a certain action which it called PULLOUT (WAGON, ROOM) would result in the battery being removed from the room. Straightway it acted, and did succeed in getting the battery out of the room before the bomb went off. Unfortunately, however, the bomb was also on the wagon. R1 *knew* that the bomb was on the wagon in the room, but didn't realize that pulling the wagon would bring the bomb out along with the battery. Poor R1 had missed that obvious implication of its planned act.

Back to the drawing board. 'The solution is obvious', said the designers. 'Our next robot must be made to recognize not just the intended implications of its acts, but also the implications about their side effects, by deducing these implications from the descriptions it uses in formulating its plans.' They called their next model, the robot-deducer, R1D1. They placed R1D1 in much the same predicament that R1 had succumbed to, and as it too hit upon the idea of PULLOUT (WAGON, ROOM) it began, as designed, to consider the implications of such a course of action. It had just finished deducing that pulling the wagon out of the room would not change the color of the room's walls, and was embarking on a proof of the further implication that pulling the wagon out would cause its wheels to turn more revolutions than there were wheels on the wagon – when the bomb exploded.

Back to the drawing board. 'We must teach it the difference between relevant implications and irrelevant implications', said the designers, 'and teach it to ignore the irrelevant ones.' So they developed a method of tagging implications as either relevant or irrelevant to the project at hand, and installed the method in their next model, the robot-relevant-deducer, or R2D1 for short. When they subjected R2D1 to the test that had so

DANIEL DENNETT

unequivocally selected its ancestors for extinction, they were surprised to
see it sitting, Hamlet-like, outside the room containing the ticking bomb,
the native hue of its resolution sicklied o'er with the pale cast of thought, as
Shakespeare (and more recently Fodor) has aptly put it. 'Do something!'
they yelled at it. 'I am', it retorted. 'I'm busily ignoring some thousands of
implications I have determined to be irrelevant. Just as soon as I find an
irrelevant implication, I put it on the list of those I must ignore, and . . .' the
bomb went off.

All these robots suffer from the *frame problem*.[1] If there is ever to be a robot
with the fabled perspicacity and real-time adroitness of R2D2, robot-design-
ers must solve the frame problem. It appears at first to be at best an
annoying technical embarrassment in robotics, or merely a curious puzzle
for the bemusement of people working in Artificial Intelligence (AI). I
think, on the contrary, that it is a new, deep epistemological problem –
accessible in principle but unnoticed by generations of philosophers –
brought to light by the novel methods of AI, and still far from being solved.
Many people in AI have come to have a similarly high regard for the
seriousness of the frame problem. As one researcher has quipped, 'We have
given up the goal of designing an intelligent robot, and turned to the task of
designing a gun that will destroy any intelligent robot that anyone else
designs!'

I will try here to present an elementary, non-technical, philosophical
introduction to the frame problem, and show why it is so interesting. I have
no solution to offer, or even any original suggestions for where a solution
might lie. It is hard enough, I have discovered, just to say clearly what the
frame problem is – and is not. In fact, there is less than perfect agreement in
usage within the AI research community. McCarthy and Hayes, who
coined the term, use it to refer to a particular, narrowly conceived problem
about representation that arises only for certain strategies for dealing with a
broader problem about real-time planning systems. Others call this
broader problem the frame problem – 'the whole pudding', as Hayes has
called it (personal correspondence) – and this may not be mere terminological sloppiness. If 'solutions' to the narrowly conceived problem have
the effect of driving a (deeper) difficulty into some other quarter of the

[1] The problem is introduced by John McCarthy and Patrick Hayes in their 1969 paper. The
task in which the problem arises was first formulated in McCarthy 1960. I am grateful to
John McCarthy, Pat Hayes, Bob Moore, Zenon Pylyshyn, John Haugeland and Bo
Dahlbom for the many hours they have spent trying to make me understand the frame
problem. It is not their fault that so much of their instruction has still not taken.

I have also benefited greatly from reading an unpublished paper, 'Modelling Change –
the Frame Problem', by Lars-Erik Janlert, Institute of Information Processing, University
of Umea, Sweden. It is to be hoped that a subsequent version of that paper will soon find its
way into print, since it is an invaluable *vademecum* for any neophyte, in addition to advancing
several novel themes.

broad problem, we might better reserve the title for this hard-to-corner difficulty. With apologies to McCarthy and Hayes for joining those who would
appropriate their term, I am going to attempt an introduction to the whole
pudding, calling *it* the frame problem. I will try in due course to describe the
narrower version of the problem, 'the frame problem proper' if you like, and
show something of its relation to the broader problem.

Since the frame problem, whatever it is, is certainly not solved yet (and
may be, in its current guises, insoluble), the ideological foes of AI such as
Hubert Dreyfus and John Searle are tempted to compose obituaries for the
field, citing the frame problem as the cause of death. In *What Computers Can't
Do* (Dreyfus 1972), Dreyfus sought to show that AI was a fundamentally
mistaken method for studying the mind, and in fact many of his somewhat
impressionistic complaints about AI models and many of his declared
insights into their intrinsic limitations can be seen to hover quite systematically in the neighborhood of the frame problem. Dreyfus never
explicitly mentions the frame problem,[2] but is it perhaps the smoking pistol
he was looking for but didn't *quite* know how to describe? Yes, I think AI can
be seen to be holding a smoking pistol, but at least in its 'whole pudding'
guise it is everybody's problem, not just a problem for AI, which, like the
good guy in many a mystery story, should be credited with a discovery, not
accused of a crime.

One does not have to hope for a robot-filled future to be worried by the
frame problem. It apparently arises from some very widely held and
innocuous-*seeming* assumptions about the nature of intelligence, the truth of
the most undoctrinaire brand of physicalism, and the conviction that it
must be possible to explain how we think. (The dualist evades the frame
problem – but only because dualism draws the veil of mystery and obfuscation over all the tough how-questions; as we shall see, the problem arises
when one takes seriously the task of answering certain how-questions.
Dualists inexcusably excuse themselves from the frame problem.)

One utterly central – if not defining – feature of an intelligent being is that

---

[2] Dreyfus mentions McCarthy 1960: 213–14, but the theme of his discussion there is that
McCarthy ignores the difference between a *physical state* description and a *situation* description, a theme that might be succinctly summarized: a house is not a home.

Similarly, he mentions *ceteris paribus* assumptions (in the Introduction to the Revised
Edition, pp. 56ff.), but only in announcing his allegiance to Wittgenstein's idea that
'whenever human behavior is analyzed in terms of rules, these rules must always contain a
ceteris paribus condition ...' But this, even if true, misses the deeper point: the need for
something like *ceteris paribus* assumptions confronts Robinson Crusoe just as ineluctably as it
confronts any protagonist who finds himself in a situation involving human culture. The
point is not, it seems, restricted to *Geisteswissenschaft* (as it is usually conceived); the
'intelligent' robot on an (otherwise?) uninhabited but hostile planet faces the frame problem
as soon as it commences to plan its days.

it can 'look before it leaps'. Better, it can *think* before it leaps. Intelligence is (at least partly) a matter of using well what you know – but for what? For improving the fidelity of your expectations about what is going to happen next, for planning, for considering courses of action, for framing further hypotheses with the aim of increasing the knowledge you will use in the future, so that you can preserve yourself, by letting your hypotheses die in your stead (as Sir Karl Popper once put it). The stupid – as opposed to ignorant – being is the one who lights the match to peer into the fuel tank,[3] who saws off the limb he is sitting on, who locks his keys in his car and then spends the next hour wondering how on earth to get his family out of the car.

But when we think before we leap, *how do we do it?* The answer seems obvious: an intelligent being learns from experience, and then uses what it has learned to guide expectations in the future. Hume explained this in terms of habits of expectation, in effect. *But how do the habits work?* Hume had a hand-waving answer – associationism – to the effect that certain transition paths between ideas grew more likely-to-be-followed as they became well worn, but since it was not *Hume*'s job, surely, to explain in more detail the mechanics of these links, problems about how such paths could be put to good use – and not just turned into an impenetrable maze of untraversable alternatives – were not discovered.

Hume, like virtually all other philosophers and 'mentalistic' psychologists, was unable to see the frame problem because he operated at what I call a purely semantic level, or a *phenomenological* level. At the phenomenological level, all the items in view are *individuated by their meanings*. Their meanings are, if you like, 'given' – but this just means that the theorist helps himself to all the meanings he wants. In this way the semantic relation between one item and the next is typically plain to see, and one just assumes that the items behave as items with those meanings *ought* to behave. We can bring this out by concocting a Humean account of a bit of learning.

Suppose there are two children, both of whom initially tend to grab cookies from the jar without asking. One child is allowed to do this unmolested but the other is spanked each time she tries. What is the result? The second child learns not to go for the cookies. Why? Because she has had experience of cookie-reaching followed swiftly by spanking. What good does that do? Well, the *idea* of cookie-reaching becomes connected by a habit path to the idea of spanking, which in turn is connected to the idea of pain ... so *of course* the child refrains. Why? Well, that's just the effect of that idea on that sort of circumstance. But why? Well, what else ought the idea of pain to do on such an occasion? Well, it might cause the child to pirouette on her left foot, or recite poetry or blink or recall her fifth birthday. But

---

[3] The example is from an important discussion of rationality by Christopher Cherniak, in 'Rationality and the Structure of Memory', forthcoming in *Synthèse*.

given what the idea of pain *means*, any of those effects would be absurd. True; now *how* can ideas be designed so that their effects are what they ought to be, given what they mean? Designing some internal things – an idea, let's call it – so that it behaves *vis-à-vis* its brethren as if it meant *cookie* or *pain* is the only way of endowing that thing with that meaning; it couldn't mean a thing if it didn't have those internal behavioral dispositions.

That is the mechanical question the philosophers left to some dimly imagined future researcher. Such a division of labor might have been all right, but it is turning out that most of the truly difficult and deep puzzles of learning and intelligence get kicked downstairs by this move. It is rather as if philosophers were to proclaim themselves expert explainers of the methods of a stage magician, and then, when we ask them to explain how the magician does the sawing-the-lady-in-half trick, they explain that it is really quite obvious: the magician doesn't really saw her in half; he simply makes it appear that he does. 'But how does he do *that?*' we ask. 'Not our department', say the philosophers – and some of them add, sonorously: 'Explanation has to stop somewhere.'[4]

When one operates at the purely phenomenological or semantic level, where does one get one's data, and how does theorizing proceed? The term 'phenomenology' has traditionally been associated with an introspective method – an *examination* of what is presented or given to consciousness. A person's phenomenology just was by definition the contents of his or her consciousness. Although this has been the ideology all along, it has never been the practice. Locke, for instance, may have thought his 'historical, plain method' was a method of unbiased self-observation, but in fact it was largely a matter of disguised aprioristic reasoning about what ideas and impressions *had to be* to do the jobs they 'obviously' did.[5] The myth that each of us can observe our mental activities has prolonged the illusion that major progress could be made on the theory of thinking by simply reflecting carefully on our own cases. For some time now we have known better: we have conscious access to only the upper surface, as it were, of the multi-level system of information-processing that occurs in us. Nevertheless, the myth still claims its victims.

So the analogy of the stage magician is particularly apt. One is not likely to make much progress in figuring out *how* the tricks are done by simply sitting attentively in the audience and watching like a hawk. Too much is going on out of sight. Better to face the fact that one must either rummage

[4] Note that on this unflattering portrayal, the philosophers might still be doing *some* valuable work; think of the wild goose chases one might avert for some investigator who had rashly concluded that the magician really did saw the lady in half and then miraculously reunite her. People have jumped to such silly conclusions, after all; many philosophers have done so, for instance.

[5] See my 1982a, a commentary on Goodman 1982.

around backstage or in the wings, hoping to disrupt the performance in telling ways; or, from one's armchair, think aprioristically about how the tricks *must* be done, given whatever is manifest about the constraints. The frame problem is then rather like the unsettling but familiar 'discovery' that so far as armchair thought can determine, a certain trick we have just observed is flat impossible.

Here is an example of the trick. Making a midnight snack. How is it that I can get myself a midnight snack? What could be simpler? I suspect there is some leftover sliced turkey and mayonnaise in the fridge, and bread in the breadbox – and a bottle of beer in the fridge as well. I realize I can put these elements together, so I concoct a childishly simple plan: I'll just go and check out the fridge, get out the requisite materials, and make myself a sandwich, to be washed down with a beer. I'll need a knife, a plate, and a glass for the beer. I forthwith put the plan into action and it works! Big deal.

Now of course I couldn't do this without knowing a good deal – about bread, spreading mayonnaise, opening the fridge, the friction and inertia that will keep the turkey between the bread slices and the bread on the plate as I carry the plate over to the table beside my easy chair. I also need to know about how to get the beer out of the bottle into the glass.[6] Thanks to my previous accumulation of experience in the world, fortunately, I am equipped with all this worldly knowledge. Of course some of the knowledge I need *might* be innate. For instance, one trivial thing I have to know is that when the beer gets into the glass it is no longer in the bottle, and that if I'm holding the mayonnaise jar in my left hand I cannot also be spreading the mayonnaise with the knive in my left hand. Perhaps these are straight-forward implications – instantiations – of some more fundamental things that I was in effect *born knowing* such as, perhaps, the fact that if something is in one location it isn't also in another, different location; or the fact that two things can't be in the same place at the same time; or the fact that situations change as the result of actions. It is hard to imagine just how one could learn these facts from experience.

Such utterly banal facts escape our notice as we act and plan, and it is not surprising that philosophers, thinking phenomenologically *but introspec-tively*, should have overlooked them. But if one turns one's back on intro-spection, and just thinks 'hetero-phenomenologically'[7] about the purely informational demands of the task – what *must* be known by any entity that can perform this task – these banal bits of knowledge rise to our attention. We can easily satisfy ourselves that no agent that did not *in some sense* have

---

6 This knowledge of physics is not what one learns in school, but in one's crib. See Hayes 1978, 1979.
7 For elaborations of hetero-phenomenology, see Dennett 1978, chapter 10, 'Two Approaches to Mental Images', and Dennett 1982b. See also Dennett 1982c.

the benefit of the information (that beer in the bottle is not in the glass, etc.) could perform such a simple task. It is one of the chief methodological beauties of AI that it makes one be a phenomenologist in this improved way. As a hetero-phenomenologist, one reasons about what the agent must 'know' or figure out *unconsciously or consciously* in order to perform in various ways.

The reason AI forces the banal information to the surface is that the tasks set by AI start at zero: the computer to be programmed to simulate the agent (or the brain of the robot, if we are actually going to operate in the real, non-simulated world), initially knows nothing at all 'about the world'. The computer is the fabled *tabula rasa* on which every required item must somehow be impressed, either by the programmer at the outset or via subsequent 'learning' by the system.

We can all agree, today, that there could be no learning at all by an entity that faced the world at birth as a *tabula rasa*, but the dividing line between what is innate and what develops maturationally and what is actually learned is of less theoretical importance than one might have thought. While some information has to be innate, there is hardly any particular item that must be: an appreciation of *modus ponens*, perhaps, and the law of the excluded middle, and some sense of causality. And while some things we know must be learned – e.g., that Thanksgiving falls on a Thursday, or that refrigerators keep food fresh – many other 'very empirical' things could in principle be innately known – e.g., that smiles mean happiness, or that unsuspended, unsupported things fall. (There is some evidence, in fact, that there is an innate bias in favor of perceiving things to fall with gravitational acceleration).[8]

Taking advantage of this advance in theoretical understanding (if that is what it is), people in AI can frankly ignore the problem of learning (it seems) and take the shortcut of *installing* all that an agent has to 'know' to solve a problem. After all, if God made Adam as an adult who could presumably solve the midnight snack problem *ab initio*, AI agent-creators can *in principle* make an 'adult' agent who is equipped with worldly knowledge *as if* it had laboriously learned all the things it needs to know. This may of course be a dangerous shortcut.

The installation problem is then the problem of installing in one way or another all the information needed by an agent to plan in a changing world. It is a difficult problem because the information must be installed in a usable format. The problem can be broken down initially into the semantic

8 Gunnar Johannsen has shown that animated films of 'falling' objects in which the moving spots drop with the normal acceleration of gravity are unmistakeably distinguished by the casual observer from 'artificial' motions. I do not know whether infants have been tested to see if they respond selectively to such displays.

problem and the syntactic problem. The semantic problem – called by Allen Newell the problem at the 'knowledge level' (Newell, 1982) – is the problem of just what information (on what topics, to what effect) must be installed. The syntactic problem is what system, format, structure, or mechanism to use to put that information in.[9]

The division is clearly seen in the example of the midnight snack problem. I *listed* a few of the very many humdrum facts one needs to know to solve the snack problem, but I didn't mean to suggest that those facts are stored in me – or in any agent – piecemeal, in the form of a long list of sentences explicitly declaring each of these facts for the benefit of the agent. That is of course one possibility, officially: it is a preposterously extreme version of the 'language of thought' theory of mental representation, with each distinguishable 'proposition' separately inscribed in the system. No one subscribes to such a view; even an encyclopedia achieves important economies of explicit expression via its organization, and a walking encyclopedia – not a bad caricature of the envisaged AI agent – must use different systemic principles to achieve efficient representation and access. We know trillions of things; we know that mayonnaise doesn't dissolve knives on contact, that a slice of bread is smaller than Mount Everest, that opening the refrigerator doesn't cause a nuclear holocaust in the kitchen.

There must be in us – and in any intelligent agent – some highly efficient, partly generative or productive system of representing – storing for use – all the information needed. Somehow, then, we must store many 'facts' at once – where facts are presumed to line up more or less one-to-one with non-synonymous declarative sentences. Moreover, we cannot realistically hope for what one might call a Spinozistic solution – a *small* set of axioms and definitions from which all the rest of our knowledge is deducible on demand – since it is clear that there simply are no entailment relations between vast numbers of these facts. (When we rely, as we must, on experience to tell us how the world is, experience tells us things that do not at all follow from what we have heretofore known.)

The demand for an efficient system of information storage is in part a

[9] McCarthy and Hayes (1969) draw a different distinction between the 'epistemological' and the 'heuristic'. The difference is that they include the question 'In what kind of internal notation is the system's knowledge to be expressed?' in the epistemological problem (see p.466), dividing off *that* syntactic (and hence somewhat mechanical) question from the procedural questions of the design of 'the mechanism that on the basis of the information solves the problem and decides what to do'.

One of the prime grounds for controversy about just which problem the frame problem is springs from this attempted division of the issue. For the answer to the syntactical aspects of the epistemological question makes a large difference to the nature of the heuristic problem. After all, if the syntax of the expression of the system's knowledge is sufficiently perverse, then in spite of the *accuracy* of the representation of that knowledge, the heuristic problem will be impossible. And some have suggested that the heuristic problem would virtually disappear if the world knowledge were felicitously couched in the first place.

space limitation, since our brains are not all that large, but more importantly it is a time limitation, for stored information that is not reliably accessible for use in the short real-time spans typically available to agents in the world is of no use at all. A creature that can solve any problem given enough time – say a million years – is not in fact intelligent at all. We live in a time-pressured world and must be able to think quickly before we leap. (One doesn't have to view this as an *a priori* condition on intelligence. One can simply note that we do in fact think quickly, so there is an empirical question about how we manage to do it.)

The task facing the AI researcher appears to be designing a system that can plan by using well-selected elements from its store of knowledge about the world it operates in. 'Introspection' on how *we* plan yields the following description of a process: one envisages a certain situation (often very sketchily); one then imagines performing a certain act in that situation; one then 'sees' what the likely outcome of that envisaged act in that situation would be, and evaluates it. What happens backstage, as it were, to permit this 'seeing' (and render it as reliable as it is) is utterly inaccessible to introspection.

On relatively rare occasions we all experience such bouts of thought, unfolding in consciousness at the deliberate speed of pondering. These are occasions in which we are faced with some novel and relatively difficult problem, such as: How can I get the piano upstairs? or Is there any way to electrify the chandelier without cutting through the plaster ceiling? It would be quite odd to find that one had to think *that* way (consciously and slowly) in order to solve the midnight snack problem. But the suggestion is that even the trivial problems of planning and bodily guidance that are beneath our notice (though in some sense we 'face' them) are solved by similar processes. Why? I don't *observe* myself planning in such situations. This fact suffices to convince the traditional, introspective phenomenologist that no such planning is going on.[10] The hetero-phenomenologist, on the other hand, reasons that *one way or another* information about the objects in the situation, and about the intended effects and side effects of the candidate actions, *must* be used (considered, attended to, applied, appreciated). Why? Because otherwise the 'smart' behavior would be sheer luck or magic. (Do we have any model for how such unconscious information-appreciation might be accomplished? The only model we have *so far* is

---

[10] Such observations also convinced Gilbert Ryle, who was, in an important sense, an introspective phenomenologist (and not a 'behaviorist'). See Ryle 1949.

One can readily imagine Ryle's attack on AI: 'And *how many* inferences do I perform in the course of preparing my sandwich? What syllogisms convince me that the beer will stay in the glass?' For a further discussion of Ryle's skeptical arguments and their relation to cognitive science, see my 'Styles of Mental Representation', Dennett 1983.

conscious, deliberate information-appreciation. Perhaps, AI suggests, this is a good model. If it isn't, we are all utterly in the dark for the time being.)

We assure ourselves of the intelligence of an agent by considering counterfactuals: if I had been told that the turkey was poisoned, or the beer explosive, or the plate dirty, or the knife too fragile to spread mayonnaise, would I have acted as I did? If I were a stupid 'automaton' – or like the *Sphex* wasp who 'mindlessly' repeats her stereotyped burrow-checking routine till she drops[11] – I might infelicitously 'go through the motions' of making a midnight snack oblivious to the recalcitrant features of the environment.[12] But in fact, my midnight-snack-making behavior is multifariously sensitive to current and background information about the situation. The only way it could be so sensitive – runs the tacit hetero-phenomenological reasoning – is for it to examine, or test for, the information in question. This information manipulation may be unconscious and swift, and it need not (it *better* not) consist of hundreds or thousands of *seriatim* testing procedures, but it must occur somehow, and its benefits must appear in time to help me as I commit myself to action.

I may of course have a midnight snack routine, developed over the years, in which case I can partly rely on it to pilot my actions. Such a complicated 'habit' would have to be under the control of a mechanism of some complexity, since even a rigid sequence of steps would involve periodic testing to ensure that subgoals had been satisfied. And even if I am an infrequent snacker, I no doubt have routines for mayonnaise-spreading, sandwich-making, and getting-something-out-of-the-fridge, from which I could compose my somewhat novel activity. Would such ensembles of routines, nicely integrated, suffice to solve the frame

---

[11] 'When the time comes for egg laying the wasp *Sphex* builds a burrow for the purpose and seeks out a cricket which she stings in such a way as to paralyze but not kill it. She drags the cricket into her burrow, lays her eggs alongside, closes the burrow, then flies away, never to return. In due course, the eggs hatch and the wasp grubs feed off the paralyzed cricket, which has not decayed, having been kept in the wasp equivalent of deep freeze. To the human mind, such an elaborately organized and seemingly purposeful routine conveys a convincing flavor of logic and thoughtfulness – until more details are examined. For example, the wasp's routine is to bring the paralyzed cricket to the burrow, leave it on the threshold, go inside to see that all is well, emerge, and then drag the cricket in. If, while the wasp is inside making her preliminary inspection the cricket is moved a few inches away, the wasp, on emerging from the burrow, will bring the cricket back to the threshold, but not inside, and will then repeat the preparatory procedure of entering the burrow to see that everything is all right. If again the cricket is removed a few inches while the wasp is inside, once again the wasp will move the cricket up to the threshold and re-enter the burrow for a final check. The wasp never thinks of pulling the cricket straight in. On one occasion, this procedure was repeated forty times, always with the same result' (Dean Wooldridge 1963).

This vivid example of a familiar phenomenon among insects is discussed by me in *Brainstorms*, and in Douglas R. Hofstadter 1982.

[12] See my 1982c: 58–9, on 'Robot Theater'.

problem for me, at least in my more 'mindless' endeavors? That is an open question to which I will return below.

It is important in any case to acknowledge at the outset, and remind oneself frequently, that even very intelligent people do make mistakes; we are not only not infallible planners; we are quite prone to overlooking large and retrospectively obvious flaws in our plans. This foible manifests itself in the familiar case of 'force of habit' errors (in which our stereotypical routines reveal themselves to be surprisingly insensitive to some portentous environmental changes while surprisingly sensitive to others). The same weakness also appears on occasion in cases where we have consciously deliberated with some care. How often have you embarked on a project of the piano-moving variety – in which you've thought through or even 'walked through' the whole operation in advance – only to discover that you must backtrack or abandon the project when some perfectly foreseeable but unforeseen obstacle or unintended side effect loomed? If we smart folk seldom actually paint ourselves into corners, it may be not because we plan ahead so well as that we supplement our sloppy planning powers with a combination of recollected lore (about fools who paint themselves into corners, for instance) and frequent progress checks as we proceed. Even so, we must know enough to call up the right lore at the right time, and to recognize impending problems as such.

To summarize: we have been led by fairly obvious and compelling considerations to the conclusion that an intelligent agent must engage in swift information-sensitive 'planning' which has the effect of producing reliable but not foolproof expectations of the effects of its actions. That these expectations are normally in force in intelligent creatures is testified to by the startled reaction they exhibit when their expectations are thwarted. This suggests a graphic way of characterizing the minimal goal that can spawn the frame problem: we want a midnight-snack-making robot to be 'surprised' by the trick plate, the unspreadable concrete mayonnaise, the fact that we've glued the beer glass to the shelf. To be surprised you have to have expected something else, and in order to have expected the right something else, you have to have *and use* a lot of information about the things in the world.[13]

[13] Hubert Dreyfus has pointed out that *not expecting x* does not imply *expecting y* (where $x \neq y$), so one can be startled by something one didn't expect without its having to be the case that one (unconsciously) expected something else. But this sense of *not expecting* will not suffice to explain startle. What are the odds against your seeing an Alfa Romeo, a Buick, a Chevrolet, and a Dodge parked in alphabetical order some time or other within the next five hours? Very high, no doubt, all things considered, so I would not expect you to expect this; I also would not expect you to be startled by seeing this unexpected sight – except in the sort of special case where you had reason to expect something else at that time and place.

Startle reactions are powerful indicators of cognitive state – a fact long known by the police (and writers of detective novels). *Only* someone who expected the refrigerator to

The central role of expectation has led some to conclude that the frame problem is not a new problem at all, and has nothing particularly to do with planning actions. It is, they think, simply the problem of having good expectations about any future events, whether they are one's own actions, the actions of another agent, or the mere happenings of nature. That is the problem of induction – noted by Hume and intensified by Goodman (Goodman 1965), but still not solved to anyone's satisfaction. We know today that the problem of induction is a nasty one indeed. Theories of subjective probability and belief fixation have not stabilized in reflective equilibrium, so it is fair to say that no one has a good, principled answer to the general question: given that I believe all *this* (have all this evidence), what *ought* I to believe as well (about the future, or about unexamined parts of the world)?

The reduction of one unsolved problem to another is some sort of progress, unsatisfying though it may be, but it is not an option in this case. The frame problem is not the problem of induction in disguise. For suppose the problem of induction were solved. Suppose – perhaps miraculously – that our agent has solved all its induction problems or had them solved by fiat; it believes, then, all the right generalizations from its evidence, and associates with all of them the appropriate probabilities and conditional probabilities. This agent, *ex hypothesi*, believes just what it ought to believe about all empirical matters in its ken, including the probabilities of future events. It might still have a bad case of the frame problem, for that problem concerns how to represent (so it can be *used*) all that hard-won empirical information – a problem that arises independently of the truth value, probability, warranted assertability, or subjective certainty of any of it. Even if you have excellent *knowledge* (and not mere belief) about the changing world, how can this knowledge be represented so that it can be efficaciously brought to bear?

Recall poor R1D1, and suppose for the sake of argument that it had perfect empirical knowledge of the probabilities of all the effects of all its actions that would be detectable by it. Thus it believes that with probability 0.7864, executing PULLOUT (WAGON, ROOM) will cause the wagon wheels to make an audible noise; and with probability 0.5, the door to the room will open in rather than out; and with probability 0.999996, there will be no live elephants in the room, and with probability 0.997 the bomb will remain on the wagon when it is moved. How is R1D1 to find this last, relevant needle in its haystack of empirical knowledge? A walking encyclopedia will walk over a cliff, for all its knowledge of cliffs and the effects of gravity, unless it is designed in such a fashion that it can find the right bits of

contain Smith's corpse (say) would be *startled* (as opposed to mildly interested) to find it to contain the rather unlikely trio: a bottle of vintage Chablis, a can of cat food, and a dishrag.

knowledge at the right times, so it can plan its engagements with the real world.

The earliest work on planning systems in AI took a deductive approach. Inspired by the development of Robinson's methods of resolution theorem proving, designers hoped to represent all the system's 'world knowledge' explicitly as axioms, and use ordinary logic – the predicate calculus – to deduce the effects of actions. Envisaging a certain situation S was modeled by having the system entertain a set of axioms describing the situation. Added to this were background axioms (the so-called 'frame axioms' that give the frame problem its name) which describe general conditions and the general effects of every action type defined for the system. To this set of axioms the system would apply an action – by postulating the occurrence of some action A in situation S – and then deduce the effect of A in S, producing a description of the outcome situation S'. While all this logical deduction looks like nothing at all in our conscious experience, research on the deductive approach could proceed on either or both of two enabling assumptions: the methodological assumption that psychological realism was a gratuitous bonus, not a goal, of 'pure' AI, or the substantive (if still vague) assumption that the deductive processes described would somehow model the backstage processes beyond conscious access. In other words, either we don't do our thinking deductively in the predicate calculus but a robot might; or we do (unconsciously) think deductively in the predicate calculus. Quite aside from doubts about its psychological realism, however, the deductive approach has not been made to work – the proof of the pudding for any robot – except for deliberately trivialized cases.

Consider some typical frame axioms associated with the action type: *move x onto y*.

(1) If $z \neq x$ and I move x onto y, then if z was on w before, then z is on w after.

(2) If x is blue before, and I move x onto y, then x is blue after.

Note that (2), about being blue, is just one example of the many boring 'no-change' axioms we have to associate with this action type. Worse still, note that a cousin of (2), also about being blue, would have to be associated with every other action-type – with *pick up x* and with *give x to y*, for instance. One cannot save this mindless repetition by postulating once and for all something like

(3) If anything is blue, it stays blue,

for that is false, and in particular we will want to leave room for the introduction of such action types as *paint x red*. Since virtually any aspect of a situation can change under some circumstance, this method requires introducing for each aspect (each predication in the description of S) an axiom to handle whether that aspect changes for each action type.

This representational profligacy quickly gets out of hand, but for some 'toy' problems in AI, the frame problem can be overpowered to some extent by a mixture of the toyness of the environment and brute force. The early version of SHAKEY, the robot at S.R.I., operated in such a simplified and sterile world, with so few aspects it could worry about that it could get away with an exhaustive consideration of frame axioms.[14]

Attempts to circumvent this explosion of axioms began with the proposal that the system operate on the tacit assumption that nothing changes in a situation but what is explicitly asserted to change in the definition of the applied action (Fikes & Nilsson 1971). The problem here is that, as Garrett Hardin once noted, you can't do just one thing. This was R1's problem, when it failed to notice that it would pull the bomb out with the wagon. In the explicit representation (a few pages back) of my midnight snack solution, I mentioned carrying the plate over to the table. On this proposal, my model of S' would leave the turkey back in the kitchen, for I didn't explicitly say the turkey would come along with the plate. One can of course patch up the definition of 'bring' or 'plate' to handle just this problem, but only at the cost of creating others. (Will a few more patches tame the problem? At what point should one abandon patches and seek an altogether new approach? Such are the methodological uncertainties regularly encountered in this field, and of course no one can responsibly claim in advance to have a good rule for dealing with them. Premature counsels of despair or calls for revolution are as clearly to be shunned as the dogged pursuit of hopeless avenues; small wonder the field is contentious.)

While one cannot get away with the tactic of supposing that one can do just one thing, it remains true that very little of what could (logically) happen in any situation does happen. Is there some way of fallibly marking the likely area of important side effects, and assuming the rest of the situation to stay unchanged? Here is where relevance tests seem like a good idea, and they may well be, but not within the deductive approach. As Minsky notes:

Even if we formulate relevancy restrictions, logistic systems have a problem using them. In any logistic system, all the axioms are necessarily 'permissive' – they all help to permit new inferences to be drawn. Each added axiom means more theorems; none can disappear. There simply is no direct way to add information to tell such a system about kinds of conclusions that should *not* be drawn! ... If we try to change this by adding axioms about relevancy, we still produce all the unwanted theorems, plus annoying statements about their irrelevancy. (Minsky 1981: 125)

---

[14] This early feature of SHAKEY was drawn to my attention by Pat Hayes. See also Dreyfus 1972: 26. SHAKEY is put to quite different use in Dennett 1982b.

What is needed is a system that genuinely *ignores* most of what it knows, and operates with a well-chosen portion of its knowledge at any moment. Well-chosen, but not chosen by exhaustive consideration. How, though, can you give a system *rules* for ignoring – or better, since explicit rule-following is not the problem, how can you design a system that reliably ignores what it ought to ignore under a wide variety of different circumstances in a complex action environment?

John McCarthy calls this the qualification problem, and vividly illustrates it via the famous puzzle of the missionaries and the cannibals.

Three missionaries and three cannibals come to a river. A rowboat that seats two is available. If the cannibals ever outnumber the missionaries on either bank of the river, the missionaries will be eaten. How shall they cross the river?

Obviously the puzzler is expected to devise a strategy of rowing the boat back and forth that gets them all across and avoids disaster ...

Imagine giving someone the problem, and after he puzzles for awhile, he suggests going upstream half a mile and crossing on a bridge. 'What bridge?' you say. 'No bridge is mentioned in the statement of the problem.' And this dunce replies, 'Well, they don't say there isn't a bridge.' You look at the English and even at the translation of the English into first order logic, and you must admit that 'they don't say' there is no bridge. So you modify the problem to exclude bridges and pose it again, and the dunce proposes a helicopter, and after you exclude that, he proposes a winged horse or that the others hang onto the outside of the boat while two row.

You now see that while a dunce, he is an inventive dunce. Despairing of getting him to accept the problem in the proper puzzler's spirit, you tell him the solution. To your further annoyance, he attacks your solution on the grounds that the boat might have a leak or lack oars. After you rectify that omission from the statement of the problem, he suggests that a sea monster may swim up the river and may swallow the boat. Again you are frustrated, and you look for a mode of reasoning that will settle his hash once and for all. (McCarthy 1980: 29–30)

What a normal, intelligent human being does in such a situation is to engage in some form of *non-monotonic inference*. In a classical, monotonic logical system, *adding* premises never *diminishes* what can be proved from the premises. As Minsky noted, the axioms are essentially permissive, and once a theorem is permitted, adding more axioms will never invalidate the proofs of earlier theorems. But when we think about a puzzle or a real life problem, we can achieve a solution (and even prove that it is a solution, or even the only solution to *that* problem), and then discover our solution invalidated by the addition of a new element to the posing of the problem; e.g., 'I forgot to tell you – there are no oars' or 'By the way, there's a perfectly good bridge upstream.'

What such late additions show us is that, contrary to our assumption, other things weren't equal. We had been reasoning with the aid of a *ceteris paribus* assumption, and now our reasoning has just been jeopardized by the discovery that something 'abnormal' is the case. (Note, by the way, that the abnormality in question is a much subtler notion than anything anyone has yet squeezed out of probability theory. As McCarthy notes, 'The whole situation involving cannibals with the postulated properties cannot be regarded as having a probability, so it is hard to take seriously the conditional probability of a bridge given the hypothesis' (*ibid.*).)

The beauty of a *ceteris paribus* clause in a bit of reasoning is that one does not have to say exactly what it means. 'What do you mean, "other things being equal"? Exactly which arrangements of which other things count as being equal?' If one had to answer such a question, invoking the *ceteris paribus* clause would be pointless, for it is precisely in order to evade that task that one uses it. If one could answer that question, one wouldn't need to invoke the clause in the first place. One way of viewing the frame problem, then, is as the attempt to get a computer to avail itself of this distinctively human style of mental operation. There are several quite different approaches to non-monotonic inference being pursued in AI today. They have in common only the goal of capturing the human talent for *ignoring* what should be ignored, while staying alert to relevant recalcitrance when it occurs.

One family of approaches, typified by the work of Marvin Minsky and Roger Schank (Minsky 1981; Schank & Abelson 1977), gets its ignoring-power from the attention-focussing power of stereotypes. The inspiring insight here is the idea that all of life's experiences, for all their variety, boil down to variations on a manageable number of stereotypic themes, paradigmatic scenarios – 'frames' in Minsky's terms, 'scripts' in Schank's.

An artificial agent with a well-stocked compendium of frames or scripts, appropriately linked to each other and to the impingements of the world via its perceptual organs, would face the world with an elaborate system of what might be called habits of attention and benign tendencies to leap to particular sorts of conclusions in particular sorts of circumstances. It would 'automatically' pay attention to certain features in certain environments and assume that certain unexamined normal features of those environments were present. Concomitantly, it would be differentially alert to relevant divergences from the stereotypes it would always begin by 'expecting'.

Simulations of fragments of such an agent's encounters with its world reveal that in many situations it behaves quite felicitously and apparently naturally, and it is hard to say, of course, what the limits of this approach are. But there are strong grounds for skepticism. Most obviously, while such systems perform creditably when the world co-operates with their stereotypes, and even with *anticipated* variations on them, when their worlds turn perverse, such systems typically cannot recover gracefully from the misanalyses they are led into. In fact, their behavior *in extremis* looks for all the world like the preposterously counterproductive activities of insects betrayed by their rigid tropisms and other genetically hard-wired behavioral routines.

When these embarrassing misadventures occur, the system designer can improve the design by adding provisions to deal with the particular cases. It is important to note that in these cases, the system does not redesign itself (or learn) but rather must wait for an external designer to select an improved design. This process of redesign recapitulates the process of natural selection in some regards; it favors minimal, piecemeal, *ad hoc* redesign which is tantamount to a wager on the likelihood of patterns in future events. So in some regards it is faithful to biological themes.[15] Nevertheless, until such a system is given a considerable capacity to learn from its errors without designer intervention, it will continue to respond in insectlike ways, and such behavior is profoundly unrealistic as a model of human reactivity to daily life. The shortc .ts and cheap methods provided by a reliance on stereotypes are evident enough in human ways of thought, but it is also evident that we have a deeper understanding to fall back on when our shortcuts don't avail, and building some measure of this deeper understanding into a system appears to be a necessary condition of getting it to learn swiftly and gracefully.

In effect, the script or frame approach is an attempt to *pre-solve* the frame problems the particular agent is likely to encounter. While insects do seem saddled with such control systems, people, even when they do appear to be relying on stereotypes, have back-up systems of thought that can deal more powerfully with problems that arise. Moreover, when people do avail themselves of stereotypes, they are at least relying on stereotypes of their own devising, and to date no one has been able to present any workable ideas about how a person's frame-making or script-writing machinery might be guided by its previous experience.

Several different sophisticated attempts to provide the representational framework for this deeper understanding have emerged from the deductive tradition in recent years. Drew McDermott and Jon Doyle have developed a 'non-monotonic logic' (1980), Ray Reiter has a 'logic for default reasoning' (1980), and John McCarthy has developed a system of 'circumscription', a formalized 'rule of conjecture that can be used by a person or program for "jumping to conclusions"' (1980). None of these is, or is claimed to be, a complete solution to the problem of *ceteris paribus* reasoning, but they might be components of such a solution. More recently, McDer-

---

[15] In one important regard, however, it is dramatically unlike the process of natural selection, since the trial, error and selection of the process is far from blind. But a case can be made that the impatient researcher does nothing more than telescope time by such foresighted interventions in the redesign process.

mott has offered a 'temporal logic for reasoning about processes and plans' (McDermott 1982). I will not attempt to assay the formal strengths and weaknesses of these approaches. Instead I will concentrate on another worry. From one point of view, non-monotonic or default logic, circumscription, and temporal logic all appear to be radical improvements to the mindless and clanking deductive approach, but from a slightly different perspective they appear to be more of the same, and at least as unrealistic as frameworks for psychological models.

They appear in the former guise to be a step towards greater psychological realism, for they take seriously, and attempt to represent, the phenomenologically salient phenomenon of common sense *ceteris paribus* 'jumping to conclusions' reasoning. But do they really succeed in offering any plausible suggestions about how the backstage implementation of that conscious thinking is accomplished *in people*? Even if on some glorious future day a robot with debugged circumscription methods maneuvered well in a non-toy environment, would there be much likelihood that its constituent processes, *described at levels below the phenomeno-logical*, would bear informative relations to the unknown lower-level backstage processes in human beings? To bring out better what my worry is, I want to introduce the concept of a *cognitive wheel*.

We can understand what a cognitive wheel might be by reminding ourselves first about ordinary wheels. Wheels are wonderful, elegant triumphs of technology. The traditional veneration of the mythic inventor of the wheel is entirely justified. But if wheels are so wonderful, why are there no animals with wheels? Why are no wheels to be found (functioning as wheels) in nature? First, the presumption of that question must be qualified. A few years ago the astonishing discovery was made of several microscopic beasties (some bacteria and some unicellular eukaryotes) that have wheels of sorts. Their propulsive tails, long thought to be flexible flagella, turn out to be more or less rigid corkscrews, which rotate continuously, propelled by microscopic motors of sorts, complete with main bearings.[16] Better known, if less interesting for obvious reasons, are the tumbleweeds. So it is not quite true that there are no wheels (or wheeliform designs) in nature.

Still, macroscopic wheels – reptilian or mammalian or avian wheels – are not to be found. Why not? They would seem to be wonderful retractable landing gear for some birds, for instance. Once the question is posed, plausible reasons rush in to explain their absence. Most important, probably, are the considerations about the topological properties of the axle/bearing boundary that make the transmission of material or energy across it particularly difficult. How could the life-support traffic arteries of a living system

[16] For more details, and further reflections on the issues discussed here, see Diamond 1983.

maintain integrity across this boundary? But once that problem is posed, solutions suggest themselves; suppose the living wheel grows to mature form in a non-rotating, non-functional form, and is then hardened and sloughed off, like antlers or an outgrown shell, but not completely off: it then rotates freely on a lubricated fixed axle. Possible? It's hard to say. Useful? Also hard to say, especially since such a wheel would have to be free-wheeling. This is an interesting speculative exercise, but certainly not one that should inspire us to draw categorical, *a priori* conclusions. It would be foolhardy to declare wheels biologically impossible, but at the same time we can appreciate that they are at least very distant and unlikely solutions to *natural* problems of design.

Now a cognitive wheel is simply any design proposal in cognitive theory (at any level from the purest semantic level to the most concrete level of 'wiring diagrams' of the neurons) that is profoundly unbiological, however wizardly and elegant it is as a bit of technology.

Clearly this is a vaguely defined concept, useful only as a rhetorical abbreviation, as a gesture in the direction of real difficulties to be spelled out carefully. 'Beware of postulating cognitive wheels' masquerades as good advice to the cognitive scientist, while courting vacuity as a maxim to follow.[17] It occupies the same rhetorical position as the stockbroker's maxim: buy low and sell high. Still, the term is a good theme-fixer for discussion.

Many critics of AI have the conviction that *any* AI system is and must be nothing but a gearbox of cognitive wheels. This could of course turn out to be true, but the usual reason for believing it is based on a misunderstanding of the methodological assumptions of the field. When an AI model of some cognitive phenomenon is proposed, the model is describable at many different levels, from the most global, phenomenological level at which the behavior is described (with some presumptuousness) in ordinary mentalistic terms, down through various levels of implementation all the way to the level of program code – and even further down, to the level of fundamental hardware operations if anyone cares. No one supposes that the model maps onto the processes of psychology and biology *all the way down*. The claim is only that for some high level or levels of description below the phenomenological level (which merely *sets* the problem) there is a mapping of model

[17] I was interested to discover that at least one researcher in AI mistook the rhetorical intent of my new term on first hearing; he took 'cognitive wheels' to be an accolade. If one thinks of AI, as he does, not as a research method in psychology but as a branch of engineering attempting to extend human cognitive powers, then of course cognitive wheels are breakthroughs. The vast and virtually infallible memories of computers would be prime examples; others would be computers' arithmetical virtuosity and invulnerability to boredom and distraction. See Hofstadter (1982) for an insightful discussion of the relation of boredom to the structure of memory and the conditions for creativity.

features onto what is being modeled: the cognitive processes in living creatures, human or otherwise. It is understood that all the implementation details below the level of intended modelling will consist, no doubt, of cognitive wheels – bits of unbiological computer activity mimicking the gross effects of cognitive sub-components by using methods utterly unlike the methods still to be discovered in the brain. Someone who failed to appreciate that a model composed microscopically of cognitive wheels could still achieve a fruitful isomorphism with biological or psychological processes at a higher level of aggregation would suppose there were good *a priori* reasons for generalized skepticism about AI.

But allowing for the possibility of valuable intermediate levels of modelling is not ensuring their existence. In a particular instance a model might descend directly from a phenomenologically recognizable level of psychological description to a cognitive wheels implementation without shedding any light at all on how we human beings manage to enjoy that phenomenology. I *suspect* that all current proposals in the field for dealing with the frame problem have that shortcoming. Perhaps one should dismiss the previous sentence as mere autobiography. I find it hard to imagine (for what that is worth) that any of the *procedural details* of the mechanization of McCarthy's circumscriptions, for instance, would have suitable counterparts in the backstage story yet to be told about how human commonsense reasoning is accomplished. If these procedural details lack 'psychological reality' then there is nothing left in the proposal that might model psychological processes except the phenomenological-level description in terms of jumping to conclusions, ignoring and the like – and we already know we do that.

There is an alternative defense of such theoretical explorations, however, and I think it is to be taken seriously. One can claim (and I take McCarthy to claim) that while formalizing commonsense reasoning in his fashion would not tell us anything *directly* about psychological processes of reasoning, it would clarify, sharpen, systematize the purely semantic-level characterization of the demands on any such implementation, biological or not. Once one has taken the giant step forward of taking information-processing seriously as a real process in space and time, one can then take a small step back and explore the implications of that advance at a very abstract level. Even at this very formal level, the power of circumscription and the other versions of non-monotonic reasoning remains an open but eminently explorable question.[18]

---

[18] McDermott 1969 ('A Temporal Logic for Reasoning about Processes and Plans', Section 6, 'A Sketch of an Implementation',) shows strikingly how many *new* issues are raised once one turns to the question of implementation, and how indirect (but still useful) the purely formal considerations are.

Some have thought that the key to a more realistic solution to the frame problem (and indeed, in all likelihood, to any solution at all) must require a complete rethinking of the semantic-level setting, prior to concern with syntactic-level implementation. The more or less standard array of predicates and relations chosen to fill out the predicate-calculus format when representing the 'propositions believed' may embody a fundamentally inappropriate parsing of nature for this task. Typically, the interpretation of the formulae in these systems breaks the world down along the familiar lines of objects with properties at times and places. Knowledge of situations and events in the world is represented by what might be called sequences of verbal snapshots. State S, constitutively described by a list of sentences true at time t asserting various n-adic predicates true of various particulars, gives way to state S', a similar list of sentences true at t'. Would it perhaps be better to reconceive of the world of planning in terms of histories and processes?[19] Instead of trying to model the capacity to *keep track of things* in terms of principles for passing through temporal cross-sections of knowledge expressed in terms of terms (*names* for *things*, in essence) and predicates, perhaps we could model keeping track of things more directly, and let all the cross-sectional information about what is deemed true moment by moment be merely implicit (and hard to extract – as it is for us) from the format. These are tempting suggestions, but so far as I know they are still in the realm of handwaving.[20]

Another, perhaps related, handwaving theme is that the current difficulties with the frame problem stem from the conceptual scheme engendered by the serial-processing von Neumann architecture of the computers used to date in AI. As large, fast parallel processors are developed, they will bring in their wake huge conceptual innovations which are now of course only dimly imaginable. Since brains are surely massive parallel processors, it is tempting to suppose that the concepts engendered by such new hardware will be more readily adaptable for realistic psychological modelling. But who can say? For the time being, most of the optimistic claims about the powers of parallel processing belong in the same camp with the facile observations often encountered in the work of neuroscientists, who postulate marvelous cognitive powers for various portions of the nervous system without a clue of how they are realized.[21]

[19] Patrick Hayes has been exploring this theme, and a preliminary account can be found in 'Naive Physics I: The Ontology of Liquids', (Hayes 1978).

[20] Oliver Selfridge's forthcoming monograph, *Tracking and Trailing* (Bradford Books/MIT Press), promises to push back this frontier, I think, but I have not yet been able to assimilate its messages. There are also suggestive passages on this topic in Ruth Garrett Milliken's *Language, Thought, and Other Biological Categories*, also forthcoming from Bradford Books.

[21] To balance the 'top–down' theorists' foible of postulating cognitive wheels, there is the 'bottom–up' theorists' penchant for discovering *wonder tissue*. (Wonder tissue appears in many locales. J.J. Gibson's theory of perception, for instance, seems to treat the whole

Filling in the details of the gap between the phenomenological magic show and the well-understood powers of small tracts of brain tissue is the immense research task that lies in the future for theorists of every persuasion. But before the problems can be solved they must be encountered, and to encounter the problems one must step resolutely into the gap and ask how-questions. What philosophers (and everyone else) have always known is that people – and no doubt all intelligent agents – can engage in swift, sensitive, risky-but-valuable *ceteris paribus* reasoning. How do we do it? AI may not yet have a good answer, but at least it has encountered the question.[22]

REFERENCES

Cherniak, C. 'Rationality and the Structure of Memory', in *Synthèse* (forthcoming).

Darmstadter, H. 1971. 'Consistency of Belief', *Journal of Philosophy* 68, 301–10.

Dennett, D. C. 1978. *Brainstorms*. Hassocks and Cambridge, Mass.

Dennett, D. C. 1982a. 'Why do we think what we do about why we think what we do?' in *Cognition* 12, 219–27.

Dennett, D. C. 1982b. 'How to Study Consciousness Empirically; or Nothing Comes to Mind', in *Synthèse* 53, 159–80.

Dennett, D. C. 1982c. 'Beyond Belief', in *Thought and Object*, ed. A. Woodfield. Oxford.

Dennett, C. C. 1983. 'Styles of Mental Representation' in *Proceedings of the Aristotelean Society* 83, 213–26.

Diamond, J. 1983. 'The Biology of the Wheel', *Nature* 302, 572–3.

Dreyfus, H. L. 1972. *What Computers Can't Do*. New York.

Fikes, R. and Nilsson, N. 1971. 'STRIPS: a New Approach to the Application of Theorem Proving to Problem Solving', *Artificial Intelligence* 2, 189–208.

Gibson, J. J. 1979. *The Ecological Approach to Visual Perception*. New York.

visual system as a hunk of wonder tissue, for instance, resonating with marvelous sensitivity to a host of sophisticated 'affordances'. See, e.g., J. J. Gibson 1979.)

[22] One of the few philosophical articles I have uncovered that seem to contribute to the thinking about the frame problem – though not in those terms – is Ronald de Sousa's 'The Rationality of Emotions' (de Sousa 1979). In the section entitled 'What are Emotions For?' de Sousa suggests, with compelling considerations, that:

the function of emotion is to fill gaps left by [mere wanting plus] 'pure reason' in the determination of action and belief. Consider how Iago proceeds to make Othello jealous. His task is essentially to direct Othello's attention, to suggest questions to ask ... Once attention is thus directed, inferences which, before on the same evidence, would not even have been thought of, are experienced as compelling.

In de Sousa's understanding, 'emotions are determinate patterns of salience among objects of attention, lines of inquiry, and inferential strategies' (p.50) and they are not 'reducible' in any way to 'articulated propositions'. Suggestive as this is, it does not, of course, offer any concrete proposals for how to endow an inner (emotional) state with these interesting powers. Another suggestive – and overlooked – paper is Howard Darmstadter's 'Consistency of Belief' (Darmstadter, 1971: 301–10). Darmstadter's exploration of *ceteris paribus* clauses and the relations that might exist between beliefs as psychological states and sentences believers may utter (or have uttered about them) contains a number of claims that deserve further scrutiny.

Goodman, N. 1965. *Fact, Fiction and Forecast*, 2nd ed. Indianapolis.

Goodman, N. 1982. 'Thoughts without Words', *Cognition* 12, 211–17.

Hayes P. 1978. 'Naive Physics I: The Ontology of Liquids', Working Paper 35, *Institut pour les Etudes Semantiques et Cognitives, Univ. de Génève.*

Hayes, P. 1979. 'The Naive Physics Manifesto', in *Expert Systems in the Microelectronic Age*, ed. D. Michie, Edinburgh.

Hofstadter, D. 1982. 'Can Inspiration be Mechanized?', *Scientific American* 247, 18–34.

McCarthy, J. 1960. 'Programs with Common Sense', *Proceedings of the Teddington Conference on the Mechanization of Thought Processes*, London, a version is reprinted in *Semantic Information Processing*, ed. M. Minsky, Cambridge.

McCarthy, J. 1980. 'Circumscription – a Form of Non-Monotonic Reasoning', *Artificial Intelligence* 13, 27–39.

McCarthy, J. and Hayes, P. 1969. 'Some Philosophical Problems from the Standpoint of Artificial Intelligence', in *Machine Intelligence* vol. 4, ed. B. Meltzer and D. Michie, 463–502. New York and Edinburgh.

McDermott, D. 1982. 'A Temporal Logic for Reasoning about Processes and Plans', *Cognitive Science* 6, 101–55.

McDermott, D. and Doyle, J. 1980. 'Non-Monotonic Logic', in *Artificial Intelligence* 13, 41–72.

Millikin, R. G. *Language, Thought and Other Biological Categories*. Cambridge, Mass. (forthcoming).

Minsky, M. 1981. 'A Framework for Representing Knowledge', originally published as Memo 3306, AI Lab, MIT. Quotation drawn from excerpts reprinted in *Mind Design*, ed. J. Haugeland. Cambridge, Mass.

Newell, A. 1982. 'The Knowledge Level', *Artificial Intelligence* 18, 87–127.

Reiter, R. 1980. 'A Logic for Default Reasoning', *Artificial Intelligence* 13, 81–132.

Ryle, G. 1949. *The Concept of Mind*. London.

Schank, R. and Abelson, R. 1977. *Scripts, Plans, Goals and Understanding: An Inquiry into Human Knowledge*, Hillsdale, N.J.

Selfridge, O. *Tracking and Trailing*, Cambridge, Mass. (forthcoming).

de Sousa, R. 1979. 'The Rationality of Emotions', *Dialogue* 18, 41–63.

Wooldridge, D. 1963. *The Machinery of the Brain*, New York.

Animal perception from an Artificial Intelligence viewpoint

MARGARET A. BODEN

I

Years ago, I saw in the pages of *Punch* a cartoon more memorable than most (I have redrawn it in Figure 1). It showed a kingfisher sitting on a willow-branch, staring at a fish in the river below, and thinking to itself, '$\mu = \sin \phi / \sin \theta$'. This cartoon is no mere triviality, for it is a reminder of some deeply puzzling questions.

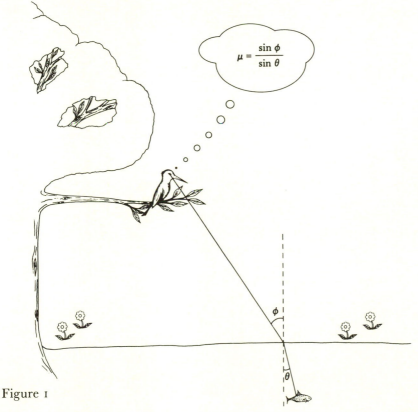

Figure 1

How does the kingfisher manage to catch the fish, no matter – within limits – where it is in the water? (Unlike some birds, it does not dive vertically into the water, nor does it pursue the fish while under water; kingfishers are plunge-divers, who go rapidly straight to the target.) Given that it has never heard of Snell's law, does it have to go through some alternative process of computation to adjust its angle-of-dive appropriately – and if so, what? Or is its action based on a bodily skill whose exercise requires no computations? How does the bird manage to identify part of the scene as a fish, or as food, in the first place, and how is it thereupon led to take appropriate action (that is, how does it know that it should dive, irrespective of how steep the dive should be)? And, the most perplexing puzzle of all, just what *is* the phenomenal nature of the kingfisher's experience as it gazes into the water?

Similar puzzles arise with respect to all animal species. In his seminal paper on 'the invisible worlds of animals and men', Jacob von Uexkull defined the task of comparative psychology as the articulation of the varied *Umwelten* of different creatures, by identifying what a given species can perceive and what it can do accordingly (von Uexkull 1957). Von Uexkull illustrated this definition by his unforgettable pictures of the living-room as seen by fly, dog, or man, and of the fish and the boat as seen by a sea-urchin. But these pictures are more charming than they are clear. Not only do they fail to express *what it is like to be* a sea-urchin, fly, or dog, but they also fail to articulate the specific psychological functions involved. Precisely what are the cognitive functions, or epistemological resources, of different animals? Given that dogs can discriminate three-dimensional objects in living-rooms, and that kingfishers can catch fish viewed from above the water, how do they manage to do so? And what are the constraints on possible perceptions: for instance, is it in principle possible that a creature able to perceive the motion of an individual object might be able to perceive the object's shape?

These questions concern the information being used by the animal, and the way in which the animal is using it, so the question arises whether artificial intelligence (AI) might help us solve them. For AI provides a wide range of concepts defining the reception, storage, transformation, interpretation, and use of information by information-processing systems.

The systems that are the special concern of AI are systems employing symbolic representations, and their interpretative procedures are symbol-manipulating processes. However, it is often regarded as problematic whether or not animals have mental representations, or use symbolic systems or languages. Sometimes it is even stated categorically that they do not. To some degree, these disputes turn on differences in the use of terms such as 'representation' and 'language'. For example, some people define 'language' in such a way that only a system of intentional communication between conspecifics could count as language, and some regard abstract features such as syntactic structure or individuating reference to past events as necessary to 'language'. But even setting aside such terminological differences, it remains true that whether or not any animals employ symbolic representations is widely regarded as doubtful.

Certainly, one cannot argue that *all* computations carried out by animals must be effected symbolically. For example, hoverflies appear to compute their interception paths with conspecifics according to a simply specifiable rule, one which could plausibly be 'hard-wired' into the flies' brains (Collett & Land 1978). Although this rule *could* be represented and applied within a symbolic system, it is reasonable to suggest that it has been 'learnt' by the evolutionary process and is embodied in the flies' neurophysiology. It is significant, however, that the feedback involved is fairly simple, and dependent on only a few physical parameters, so that the computations concerned are relatively inflexible. The fly in effect assumes that the size and velocity of the target are *always* those corresponding to hoverflies, and on this rigid (and fallible) basis the creature determines its angle of turn, when initiating its flight, according to the variable approach angle subtended by the target. Moreover, the fly's path cannot be adjusted in mid-flight, there being no way in which the pursuer can be influenced by feedback from the (perhaps unpredictable) movement of the target animal.

Similarly rigid behaviour is fairly common in insects. But the higher animals are capable of considerable flexibility in adjusting their behaviour to widely differing (and continuously changing) circumstances, where the relevant 'parameters' are structural features, rather than physical ones (such as angle-of-approach). The freedom of much animal behaviour from physically specifiable constraints implies that many animals must have inner representations and symbolic language. Only thus could they interpret stimulus-information sensibly in widely differing contexts and take appropriate action accordingly. (Internal languages need not have formal features like those characteristic of spoken languages: we shall see that some representations hypothesized in AI are very different from verbal or mathematical strings.) The more flexible the action, the more complex must be the computational resources for monitoring, planning, and scheduling different types of activity. In particular, when the creature has to take account of a wide range of structural differences and similarities between distinct situations (as opposed to concentrating on only one or a few physical parameters), these structural features can only be represented symbolically – for, by hypothesis, they have no *physical* features in common.

This is true irrespective of whether the animal is able to communicate with its conspecifics – either by way of warning-cries, mating-calls, and the like, or by means of a syntactically-structured language whose meaning is determined by social conventions rather than by fixed genetic mechanisms. The point is that even much *non-communicative* behaviour has to be understood in computational terms, such that internal symbolic processes must be attributed to the creature. Indeed, the interpretation of audible or visible signs, words, or gestures *as* communications with a certain meaning presupposes the computational mechanisms involved in sensory perception in general. This is why one philosopher deeply influenced by AI has referred to 'the primacy of non-communicative language' (Sloman 1979).

What is meant by 'the computational mechanisms involved in sensory perception in general' will be clarified in the next section, where I discuss some AI ideas bearing on the puzzles about the kingfisher's perceptual competence that were listed above. In Section III, I discuss the objection that the computational processes in a program may not be the same as the cognitive processes in the organism, and the view that AI can have no bearing on any phenomenological experience, in human or animal species.

2

Von Uexkull's assumption that all animal species have perceptual capacities functionally coordinated with their motor activity is shared by comparative psychologists in general. For example, the behaviour of many species is assumed by ethologists to be dependent on motion-perception and object-concepts of some sort. Just what sort, however, is usually unclear. The perceptual side of the *Umwelt* has received less attention than the motor aspect, the study of animal perception (as opposed to sensory physiology or discriminative behaviour) having been inhibited by the explicitly anti-mentalistic bias of behaviourism. Significantly, it has been held back also by the absence of concepts suited to expressing the psychological processes involved in perception. The lack of suitable concepts has meant that even in the human case, where introspective reports are available, the psychological nature of motion-perception is not understood. So, although we know that the phenomenology of motion-perception varies under differing conditions, we do not understand why our experience varies as it does.

For instance, if a person is shown two differing views successively, then one of four phenomenologically distinct perceptions may arise. We may see an object (visible in the earlier view) disappearing, and being *replaced* by another one – as in a game of 'peekaboo'. We may see one and the same (rigid) object *moving*, perhaps involving a change in its appearance due to rotation. We may see one and the same object *changing* in shape so as to be transformed into something different – as the baby that Alice was holding gradually turned into a pig before her eyes. Finally, we may see an object moving and changing shape at the same time (as does a walking mammal).

The conditions under which these several perceptions are differentially elicited can be studied by the technique of 'apparent movement', wherein two stimuli or input-arrays are presented successively to the visual system and subjects are asked to report what they see. This technique was originated by the Gestalt school, and since their early work experimental psychologists have amassed a great deal of information about which parameters influence the occurrence of apparent motion. But the rationale for these facts is not well understood: why do these parameters affect motion-perception in the way that they do?

Some recent AI-based work done by Shimon Ullman poses computational questions and offers hypothetical answers that suggest how such phenomena are possible (Ullman 1979a, 1979b). These suggestions are relevant not only to human vision (Ullman's prime focus), but to animal vision also. For Ullman is concerned with types of perceptual process that can plausibly be attributed to many animal species.

Like the psychologist J.J. Gibson, Ullman attempts to show that many perceptual features can be recognized by relatively low-level psychophysiological mechanisms, whose functioning relies on the information available in the ambient light rather than on high-level concepts or cerebral schemata (Gibson 1950, 1966, 1979). But unlike Gibson, who posits a 'direct' unanalysable perceptual process of 'information pick-up', Ullman views this functioning as a significantly complex process intelligible in computational terms. (Ullman's work is thus closer to the spirit of Kant, and may be thought of as an attempt to articulate the intuitions and categories of space which structure and give meaning to the input stimulus.)

Ullman reminds us of the facts about the phenomenology of motion perception that were listed above. His project is to discover the series of computations that the visual system performs on the input-pairs so as to arrive at an interpretation of the (2-D) array in terms of (3-D) replacement, motion, or change. In particular, he asks whether (and *how*) these distinct percepts can be differentially generated without assuming reliance on high-level concepts of specific 3-D objects (such as fish or sticklebacks), and even without assuming the prior recognition of a specific overall shape (such as a sort of narrow pointed ellipse with sharp projections on its upper surface). Ullman thus attempts to follow Lloyd Morgan's Canon, asking what are the *minimal* computational processes that need to be posited to explain motion-perception.

As regards the visual interpretation of each array considered in isolation, Ullman relies on the work of David Marr, who studied the information picked up from the ambient light by the retina, and the image-forming computations performed on it by peripheral levels of the visual system (Marr 1976, 1978, 1979). The first stage of visual computation, according to Marr, results in descriptions of the scene in terms of features like *shading-edge, extended-edge, line,* and *blob* (which vary as to *fuzziness, contrast, lightness, position, orientation, size,* and *termination* points). These epistemological primitives are the putative result of pre-processing of the original intensity array at the retinal level – that is, they are not computations performed by the visual cortex (still less, the cerebral cortex). Marr defines further computations on these primitive descriptions, which group lines, points, and blobs together in various ways, resulting in the separation of figure and ground. He stresses that these perceptual computations *construct* the image, which is a symbolic description (or articulated representation) of the scene based on the initial stimulus-array. The computations are thus interpretative processes, carried out by the visual system considered as a symbol-manipulating system rather than simply as a physical transducer (though Marr attempts to ground his computational hypotheses in specific facts of visual psychophysiology).

Starting with Marr's basic meaningful units, Ullman defines further visual computations which would enable the system, presented with two differing views, to make a perceptual decision between replacement, motion, or change. Ullman divides the computational problem faced by the visual system into two logically distinct parts, which he calls the *correspondence* and the *interpretation* problems. (The latter term unfortunately obscures the fact that *all* these computations, including Marr's, are interpretative processes, carried out by the visual system in its role as a symbol-manipulating device.)

The correspondence problem is to identify specific portions of the changing image as representing the same object at different times. This identity-computation must succeed if the final perception is to be that of a single object, whether in motion or in change. Conversely, the perception of replacement presupposes that no such identity could be established at the correspondence stage. The interpretation problem is to identify parts of the input arrays as representing objects, with certain 3-D shapes, and moving through 3-space (if they are moving) in a specific way. In principle, correspondence- and interpretation-computations together can distinguish between the three types of perception in question. And, if specific hypothetical examples of such computations are to be of any interest to students of biological organisms, they should be able to distinguish reliably (though not necessarily infallibly) between equivalent changes in the real-world environment.

This last point is relevant to the way in which Ullman defines specific correspondence- and interpretation-algorithms. In principle, any part of one 2-D view could correspond with (be an appearance of the same object as) many different parts of another; similarly, any 2-D view has indefinitely many possible 3-D interpretations. (Anyone who doubts this should recall the images facing them in distorting mirrors at funfairs.) Faced with this difficulty, Ullman makes specific assumptions about normal viewing conditions, and takes into account certain physical and geometrical properties of the real world, as well as (human) psychological evidence based on studies of apparent motion. Accordingly, he formulates a hypothetical set of computational constraints which he claims will both assess the degree of match between two views so as to choose the better one, and typically force a 3-D interpretation which is both unique and veridical.

For instance, for the correspondence stage he defines 'affinity functions' that compute the degree of match between two points or short line-segments, depending on their distance, brightness, retinal position, inter-stimulus (time) interval, length, and orientation. And for the interpretation stage, he defines a way of computing the shape and motion of a rigid object from three views of it, making his system assume that if such a computation succeeds then it is indeed faced with a rigid body in motion (as opposed to two different objects or one object changing its shape). He justifies this by proving mathematically that, except in highly abnormal viewing conditions, three views of a rigid object can uniquely determine its shape and motion.

Given that Ullman's computations can indeed interpret correspondence, shape, and motion in a wide range of paired 2-D views (which has been tested by running his system in its programmed form on a computer provided with the relevant input), how is his work relevant to questions about perception in animals?

The first thing to notice is that Ullman builds implicit assumptions about the physics and geometry of the real world, and about biologically normal viewing conditions, into the computations carried out by the visual system. It is plausible that many species may have evolved such implicit computational constraints. That is, the animal's mind may implicitly embody knowledge about its external environment, which knowledge is used by it in its perceptual interpretations. Something of the sort seems to be true for migratory birds, who have some practical grasp of the earth's magnetic field or of stellar constellations; and, as I shall suggest presently, the kingfisher may have some practical grasp of the refractive properties of water. A 'practical grasp' of physical properties is not the same thing as the ability to articulate and reason about them by way of verbal symbols. So I am here attributing to the kingfisher 'knowledge how' rather than 'knowledge that'. (The view that the bird's ability to go straight to the fish is the exercise of a 'bodily skill', supposed to be quite independent of any representation or computation, will be discussed in Section III.)

A creature has a practical grasp of a domain if its behaviour is, within limits, successfully adjusted to the underlying constraints of the domain. If adjustment to these constraints appears (on the basis of psychological and/or physiological evidence) to be innate rather than learned, they may be said to be 'built in', or 'hard-wired'. However, that a constraint is built in does not mean that the animal must necessarily be (like the hoverfly) capable only of a rigid, predetermined response to any given value of the environmental parameter concerned. It is in principle possible that (as in the perceptual systems posited – and simulated – by Ullman and Marr) the ability to construct symbolic representations of certain aspects of the environment is itself built in to the animal's perceptual system. The terms 'built in' and 'embodied' thus have rather different implications. Knowledge is *embodied* if the functions in virtue of which the knowledge is attributed to the organism are at base carried out by bodily (physiological) mechanisms; knowledge is *built in* if its embodiment is determined genetically rather than experientially. The knowledge of an empiricist's guardian angel would presumably be neither embodied nor built in.

What is ethologically implausible about Ullman's hypotheses is not that they involve some (unconscious) knowledge about material objects and normal viewing conditions, but rather that they assume the perception of *rigid* objects to be basic, while perception of non-rigid movement is taken to be a more complex special case. *Mathematically*, of course, the perception of non-rigid motion is more complex; but this does not prove that it is *biologically* secondary to the perception of rigid objects. At least in the higher animals, it is more likely that the visual perception of shape and motion have evolved in response to such biologically significant environmental features as the gait or stance of hunter or prey, or the facial grimaces and tail-waving of conspecifics. The fact that human beings do not always perceive the correct (rigid) structure when presented with a mathematically adequate though impoverished stimulus, may be due not (as Ullman suggests) to their failing to pick up all of the mathematically necessary information in the stimulus, but rather to their using computational strategies evolved for the perception of non-rigid objects which – *even* when directed at rigid objects – need more information than is present in the experimental stimulus concerned.[1] Admittedly, a robot could be provided with an Ullmanesque capacity to perceive rigid objects in motion; but whether any creature on the phylogenetic scale employs such visual mechanisms is another question.

Our friend the kingfisher apparently possesses computational mechan-

[1] This point is made by Aaron Sloman in Sloman (1980), a reply to Ullman (1980).

isms which can discover the real position of a fish at varying depths in the water. Ullman's general approach suggests that these could well be relatively low-level processes, not requiring cerebral computations (as puzzling out the correct values of the variables in the formula for Snell's law presumably does). For the visual computations algorithmically defined by Ullman do not depend on high-level processes capable of identifying (recognizing) objects as members of a specific class: the system does not need to know that an object is a fish, or even that it has the 3-D shape that it has, in order to know that it is an object.

Nor does it need any familiarity with the object; that is, it does not need to have experienced those two views in association beforehand. Ullman therefore suggests (*contra* empiricists and Piaget) that a baby – or, one might add, a kingfisher – can see that two appearances are views of one and the same object even if it has never seen that sort of object before, and even if it has no tactile or manipulative evidence suggesting that they pertain to one and the same thing. These conclusions follow from the fact that all of the correspondence-computation, and much of the interpretation-computation, is via low-level, autonomous processes that do not depend on recognition of the input as a familiar 3-D object. The correspondence-computations match primitive elements (those defined by Marr) in successive views, and do not depend on computation of the overall shape as a whole.

It follows that creatures incapable of computing shape in any detail, or of recognizing different classes of physical object, may nonetheless be able to compute motion. As the example of von Uexkull's sea-urchin suggests, this is no news to ethologists, who often have behavioural evidence that an animal can perceive motion though they doubt its ability to be aware of detailed shapes. But Ullman's achievement is to have complemented this empirically-based intuition by a set of admirably clear hypotheses about precisely what visual computations may be involved, at least in the human case. That some of his hypotheses are biologically dubious does not destroy the interest of his general approach. If one accepts that comparable hypotheses may explain differential phenomenology (such as the different experiences of motion-perception previously described), then his work shows that it is in principle possible for a creature incapable of experiencing distinct shapes to be aware of motion and to ascribe it correctly to an individual object.

Ullman's work also casts some light on our kingfisher cartoon. For if the general shape, the location, and the motion of objects can be computed in a low-level, autonomous fashion, then it is not impossible that a kingfisher may possess comparable perceptual mechanisms capable of computing the depth of a fish in water. The refractive index of water would be implicitly embodied in these computational mechanisms, perhaps in an unalterable fashion. So a kingfisher experimentally required to dive into oil might starve to death, like newborn chicks provided with distorting goggles that shift the light five degrees to the right, who never learn to peck for grains of corn in the right place (Hess 1956). This assumes (what is the case for the chicks) that the kingfisher utilizes an inborn visuomotor coordination, linking the perceptual active aspects of its *Umwelt*, a coordination that is not only innate but unalterable. Psychological experiments on human beings, and comparable studies of chimps, show that these species by contrast can learn to adjust to some systematic distortions of the physics of the visual field (Stratton 1896, 1897; Kohler, 1962).

Our discussion so far implies that many animals are lay physicists, that they have implicit knowledge of real-world properties (such as the optics of 3-D objects viewed in air or water) that can be explicitly described by professional physicists. Moreover, their physical knowledge contributes to their perception, so that they see something *as* an object, or *as* moving. Presumably, many species perceive their environment in a way that is informed by a variety of concepts and inferential structures (innate and acquired) embodying everyday knowledge of the material world. Diving animals need some grasp of the difference between *solids* and *fluids*, as well as of *depth*, *movement*, and *distance*. A cat or monkey using its perceptual powers in leaping from wall to wall, or branch to branch, needs some represent-ation of *stability* and *support*. Newborn creatures who refuse to cross a 'visual cliff' apparently have some innate procedure for recognizing the absence of *support*, where the object to be supported is their own body. It does not follow that they understand in any sense that the bottom bricks of a tower support the top ones – although this is something which a leaping animal living in a jungle or an untidy house may have to learn. For leaping creatures who can recognize the potential for action in a pile of bricks, *support* has something to do with *above*. In general, having a concept (whether linguistic or pre-linguistic) involves being able to draw inferences linking it usefully with other concepts. Psychologists theorizing about animal *Umwelten* need to ask what such inferences might be, what is the perceptual evidence in which the animal's concepts are anchored, and what are the motor activities which test for them or which are carried out on the basis of conditional tests defined in terms of them.

In his 'Naive Physics Manifesto', P.J. Hayes draws on AI-ideas about the representation of knowledge to ask comparable questions about the human being's everyday understanding of the physical world.[2] One might be tempted to dismiss such an enquiry as irrelevant to our discussion: human beings have Newton and Einstein, whereas animals do not, so

[2] Hayes 1979; compare McCarthy and Hayes 1969.

human knowledge of physics cannot be relevant to enquiries about chimps, beavers, or bees. That this would be an inappropriate objection is evident from the fact that the *Punch* cartoon I mentioned earlier would have been almost as funny if it had figured a human fisherman rather than a kingfisher. Not only do we not usually think of Snell's law when we try to net a fish or tickle a trout, but we could not use it to help us do so even if we did. Our everyday perceptions interpret our environment in terms of pre-theoretical concepts such as *weight, support, velocity, height, inside/outside, next to, boundary, path, entrance, obstacle, fluid,* and *cause* (to name but a few). It is this pre-theoretical knowledge which interests Hayes.

Like the understanding of animals, our earliest knowledge of naive physics is independent of language. Hayes posits pre-linguistic conceptual networks as the basis of the infant's sensorimotor understanding. But most of his detailed epistemological claims concern adult human perception, which is informed through and through by natural language. The degree to which detailed descriptions of the human *Umwelt* are deemed relevant to animal *Umwelten* depends on one's view of philosophical semantics. Hayes argues for a semantics from which it follows that, once natural language is acquired, the meaning of the more primitive core concepts is altered – not merely added to. He claims that the meaning of a token in a representational system cannot in general be captured definitionally (in terms of semantic primitives, for instance), but depends upon the entire formalization of which the token is part. On this view, a change to any part of the system can, in principle, alter the meaning of every other part of it. So, even if we had a precise account of adult human knowledge of *inside, support,* and *behind,* we could not equate any part of this with a cat's or a chimp's knowledge simply by jettisoning those parts of it influenced by our linguistic representations.

Rather, we would need to be able to trace the development of our naive physical concepts, distinguishing their earlier, sensorimotor, forms from the later, linguistically-informed, semantic contents and inferential patterns. Hayes makes some relevant remarks, but even more apposite here is the computationally-informed work of the psycholinguists G. A. Miller and P. N. Johnson-Laird, who have studied the basic perceptual procedures in which our linguistic abilities are grounded (Miller & Johnson-Laird 1976).

Miller and Johnson-Laird define a number of perceptual discriminations in detailed procedural terms, utilizing what is known about our sensorimotor equipment and development. They then show how these discriminatory procedures could come to function as the semantic anchoring of our lexicon. For example, perceptual predicates that can be procedurally defined include the following spatial descriptions: x is higher than y; the distance from x to y is zero; x is in front of the moving object y; y is between x

and z; x has boundary y; x is convex; x is changing shape; x has the exterior surface y; x is included spatially in y; x, y, and z lie in a straight line; x travels along the path p. They give both psychological and physiological evidence for the primacy of these notions, and they use them to define object-recognizing routines of increasing power. Their sensitivity to computational issues leads them to ask not only *which* predicates are involved in a certain judgement, but *when* each predicate is applied in the judgemental process. (For example, the logically equivalent 'y over x' and 'x under y' are not psychologically equivalent: the first term in the relation should designate the thing whose location is to be determined, while the second should represent the immobile landmark that can be used to determine it.)

The perceptual routines they define as the meaning of words such as 'in', 'on', 'outside', and 'at' are surprisingly complex. Were a chimp to grasp the meaning of 'in' or 'on' in Ameslan, therefore, this would presuppose extremely complex perceptual computations on the chimp's part. And animals which, unlike chimps, have no great manipulative ability, would not be able to compute those perceptual discriminations requiring motor activities such as putting bananas inside boxes, so that their understanding of naive physics would be correspondingly impoverished.

General results in the theory of computation might throw light on animal perception, by showing that a given type of representation in principle could not express a certain type of information, or that it would be enormously less efficient than some other type. Abstract considerations show that computational mechanisms of a certain type (such as a nervous net with no significant prior structure) simply cannot achieve specific kinds of spatial pattern recognition (Minsky & Papert 1969). And certain mechanisms capable of performing some non-trivial computations are incapable of performing others which at first sight might appear to be within their range. For example, a system that can compute convexity may be in principle incapable of computing spatial connectedness (Rosenblatt 1958). So the *prima facie* plausible assumption that any creature able to perceive convexity would also be aware of connectedness is false.

Again, 'analogical' representations may be more computationally efficient than 'Fregean' ones (Sloman 1978a: 144–76). An analogical representation is one in which there is some significant correspondence between the structure of the representation and the structure of the thing represented. By contrast, a Fregean representation need have no such correspondence, since the structure of the representation reflects not the structure of the thing itself, but the structure of the procedure (thought process) by which that thing is identified. To understand a Fregean representation is to know how to interpret it so as to establish what it is referring to, basically by the method described by the logician Frege as applying *functions* to *arguments*. Analogical representations, however, are understood or interpreted by matching the two structures concerned (that is, of the representation itself and of the domain represented), and their associated inference-procedures, in a systematic way. Applying this distinction to our kingfisher cartoon, for example, the formula expressing Snell's law is a Fregean representation, whereas the diagram itself (with the lines representing the paths of light and constructing the relevant angles) is an analogical representation.

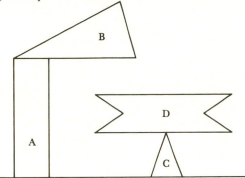

Figure 2

The use – and usefulness – of analogical representation has been exemplified in a program that can reason from visual diagrams (Funt 1980). The program's task, given a diagram like that of Figure 2, is to discover whether the arrangement of blocks depicted is stable, and – if it is not – to predict the movements (falling, sliding, motion ended by contact with another block) and the final state of the various blocks. The answers to these questions are discovered from the diagram (given certain simple diagrammatic transformations carried out by the system, which are structurally analogous to changes that would happen in the real world), rather than being computed in terms of abstract mathematical equations and specific numerical values. Much as it is 'obvious' to us from the diagram (though not from a verbal or mathematical description of the same state-of-affairs) that B will hit D, that D will then tilt with its left half moving downwards, and that B will end up touching both A and D but *not* the ground, so it is easily discoverable by the program that this is what will happen.

The program 'imagines' gradual changes in the position of the blocks. So for instance it imagines gradually moving an unstable block (such as B) downwards, pivoting on the relevant point of support. It studies 'snapshots' of the successive positions, and so discovers specific points of contact with coincidentally present blocks (such as D) which will interrupt the fall that would have been predicted by a theoretical physicist from equations and measurements describing A and B. As in this case, many detailed relations between blocks are implicit in the diagrammatic representation which could be explicitly stated only with the greatest difficulty. Also, what space is initially empty, and what would remain empty after stabilization of the blocks, can be directly discovered from the diagram and the imagined snapshots.

This work is relevant to the topic of naive physics discussed earlier, for the physical knowledge exploited by the program is comparable to that of the lay person rather than the physicist. Thus it has simple computational procedures, or 'perceptual primitives', which address the visual array in parallel so as to identify area, centre, point of contact, symmetry, and so on. These spatial notions are likely to be useful in many different problem domains. Also, the program has knowledge of *qualitative* physical principles relevant to its actual tasks, such as that if an object sticks out too far it will fall, and that it will pivot around the support point nearest to the centre of gravity. Moreover, since it is able to discover the empty space, and also those spaces that would remain empty throughout stabilization changes, it possesses a type of knowledge that would be crucial to an animal looking for a pathway or for a safe space through which to move. And leaping animals, at least those whose weight might cause significant changes in the terrain leapt upon, presumably have some understanding of support and can perceive potentially dangerous or unstable structures.

3

The *Punch* cartoonist recognized that, from the fact that *if* the kingfisher were consciously applying Snell's law its dives would be (as they are) appropriately placed, it does not follow that this is indeed the explanation of its diving ability. Analogously, if one had produced a computational model whose performance mapped onto the kingfisher's behaviour one could not thereby be certain of having captured the bird's psychology. For, as is often pointed out by critics of cognitive psychology (e.g. Heil 1981), there is always in principle more than one model capable of matching observed behaviour. However, this caveat is a special case of the general truth that *any* scientific theory is necessarily underdetermined by the evidence. That this underdetermination causes methodological problems is well known to every practising scientist. Someone offering computational theories of animal perception would be no worse off on this account than any other psychologist faced with the task of testing theory against data.

The special difficulty is not how to choose between several alternative computational accounts, once we have got them, but how to arrive even at *one* in the first place. Psychologists and philosophers unfamiliar with AI typically underestimate the procedural-representational complexity of human and animal minds, and may not even realize that there are unsolved computational problems related to everyday psychological descriptions. That is, descriptions of perception and action are assumed to be unproblematic which in fact are deeply puzzling. Thus most ethologists take the existence of various interpretative and representational capacities for granted, and concentrate on asking which of these capacities are shared by which species. Theorists sympathetic to AI, by contrast, are primarily interested in how such capacities are computationally possible.

For instance, the experimental psychologists Premack and Rumbaugh have asked *whether* chimps can perceive the world as humans can, and do things which we can do.[3] Can a chimp perceive a movie as representing a second individual trying to solve a problem, like reaching bananas or switching on a heater? Can a chimp plan ahead of time, either on its own behalf or on behalf of its fellow? Can two chimps cooperate in the solution of a task, perhaps using artificial symbols as publicly observable indicators of the tool that is required at a given stage of the problem? And so on ... Computationally-inclined psychologists or epistemologists, however, are more likely to be interested in *how* these things can be done, irrespective of which species manage to do them. How is it possible for a creature to form means–end plans for reaching a desired object, plans within which other objects are represented as instruments to the overall end?[4] How is it possible for an external symbol, as well as one in the internal representational medium of the creature's mind, to be employed by one animal and perceived by another as a request for a specific tool? How is it possible for a creature to perceive apparent movement, or to distinguish visually between replacement, motion, and change?

It is this difference in theoretical focus which has led one computationally-inclined philosopher to acknowledge the fascination of these recent studies of chimps, and yet to complain that such studies are premature:

In the long run we shall all learn more if we spend a little less time collecting new curiosities and a little more time pondering the deeper questions. The best method I know of is to explore attempts to design *working* systems [i.e., programs] that display the abilities we are trying to understand. Later, when we have a better idea of what the important theoretical problems are, we'll need to supplement this kind of research with more empirical studies. (Sloman 1978b)

[3] Premack and Woodruff 1978; see also Griffin 1978, and Savage-Rumbaugh *et al*, 1978.
[4] See Chapter 12 of Boden 1977, for a description of planning programs within which such questions arise.

Ethologists may reply that they wish to discover *which* achievements are within the grasp of chimps, beavers, and bees. This is indeed a legitimate question: natural history should include comparative psychology, an account of what different animal species can do. Many such questions have remained unasked by professional ethologists, because of the inhibitory influence of behaviourism – and even of the founding fathers of ethology, who were anxious to avoid sentimental anthropomorphism. But it remains true that a deeper understanding of animals' minds will require careful attention to the computational processes underlying their observed abilities.

However, perhaps there is a particular reason (over and above the *a priori* possibility of alternative theoretical models) for denying the relevance of AI ideas to animal psychology? Even in the human case, it may be said (Dreyfus 1972), it is doubtful whether computations like those used in AI go on (except possibly during conscious logical or mathematical calculation). And animal minds, *a fortiori*, do not engage in this sort of computation (which is why the *Punch* cartoon would have been less funny if it had shown a human fisherman). Introspection does not reveal complex sequences of step-by-step formal reasoning. If anything, it suggests that many unformulated ideas influence our experience simultaneously. Perception in particular seems relatively immediate, and the notion that a bird's perceptions are laboriously constructed by strings of formal computations is absurd. What is more, the vertebrate brain appears to be capable of parallel processing, so programs written for digital computers are of questionable relevance to human or animal psychology. In short, the complexity of thought may be less than is assumed by AI-workers – and, moreover, may be of a very different type.

This objection is, in part, an appeal to ignorance. From the fact that a mental process does not appear in introspection one cannot infer that it does not go on at non-conscious levels of the mind. What is more, there is a great deal of empirical evidence (amassed over many years) suggesting that human perception is the result of a non-introspectible process of construction, a process that takes a measurable amount of time and that can be interfered with in specific ways. One might, of course, argue that all talk of non-conscious mental processes is so philosophically problematic as to outlaw cognitive psychology in general (irrespective of whether it uses AI-ideas) (Malcolm 1971). This extreme viewpoint would deny to theoretical psychologists rights of extended language-use that other scientists enjoy (Martin 1973). Short of this position, one must admit the possibility of non-introspectible mental processes.

But what of the objection that, while such processes probably do exist, they may be very different from the processes posited by AI? The first thing to be said in reply is a familiar Popperian theme: a clearly articulated hypothesis, which fails to match the facts in certain specifiable ways, can be a crucial stage in the development of a more satisfactory scientific understanding. So even if AI were incapable of modelling actual thought-processes, it would not follow that nothing of theoretical interest could have been learned from it. The second point is related to the first: the scientific research-programme that is AI includes a number of significantly different approaches. As the reference above to 'parallel processing' suggests, the logical-sequential approach is not the only possible form of a computational model.

Some very early work in AI attempted to model parallel processing, but the machines available were so primitive that little was learnt from this exercise. Most research in the field has concentrated on modelling logical-sequential computation, which is well suited to general-purpose digital computers. As a corollary, AI-workers have tended to play down the importance of neurophysiological knowledge about the brain. This is partly due to the fact that many significant computational questions can be pursued quite independently of hardware-considerations, but is also due to the fact that a 'general-purpose' machine is precisely one whose hardware is capable of carrying out indefinitely many different types of computation. In recent years, however, neurophysiological and psychophysiological evidence has been taken more seriously by some AI researches – notably by David Marr's group at MIT. More recently still, hardware developments have made possible a radically new approach to computation, wherein parallel processing by dedicated (as opposed to general-purpose) hardware is used to compute properties previously assumed to require highly abstract sequential processing.

One such property is shape, and it is pertinent to our topic to note that the perception of shape is being modelled in this way (Hinton 1981). On this approach, a shape can be recognized as a whole without the constituent parts being recognized as such (a part is represented in a radically different way if it is seen as a Gestalt in its own right). We saw in Section II that shape-perception is not needed for the recognition of object-identity, so that if we were to attribute identity-perception to a creature (perhaps because of its ability to follow a moving target) we would not thereby be justified in attributing shape-perception also. But, if we were to attribute shape-perception to a perceiver, what computational powers would we be crediting the subject with? If shape-perception required the application of high-level concepts, it would be implausible to say, for example, that a kingfisher can see the shape of a stickleback (which I described earlier as 'a sort of narrow pointed ellipse with sharp projections on its upper surface', and which we could describe in many other ways). But this very recent AI work suggests that the bird might be able to perceive the shape of a stickleback despite being unable to represent it in terms of high-level concepts. Further, it implies that the kingfisher need not be able to articulate the image of the stickleback into independently recognized component parts: it could perceive a fish without being able to perceive a fin.

A computational model of this type that was initially developed for shape-perception is now being applied to the control of bodily movement.[5] The bodily skill of smoothly moving one's arm requires delicate compensatory movements in the various joints, as well as subtle control of velocities at different stages of movement. Earlier attempts to compute motor-control met with very limited success. For example, roboticists relying on sequential processing were unable to write programs capable of computing the subtly balanced flexions of shoulder, elbow, and wrist that would be necessary for smooth movement of the robot-arm. But these aspects of motor-control are now being modelled by these new AI techniques, with encouraging results. Many problems remain; for example, it is not yet known how to compute a path that will avoid an obstacle placed between the arm and the end-point of movement. But these new developments in AI should give pause to those philosophers who complain that AI can have nothing to say about bodily skills, and so is questionably relevant to human and animal forms of life.

But if simultaneous perceptual processing and bodily skills are not wholly intractable to a computational analysis, what of experience itself? Can AI have anything useful to say about consciousness?

I remarked above that von Uexkull's pictures fail to express the phenomenological quality of what it is like to be a sea-urchin, fly, or dog – or, one might add, a bat (Nagel 1974). Nor would different pictures have succeeded where these failed. As Nagel points out, the problem in understanding what it is like to be a bat rests on the difficulty of matching different subjectivities. Assuming (as we all do) that our experience is somehow intrinsically different from the bat's, how could we even conceive of what the bat's experience is really like – that is to say, what it is like for the bat? No mere subtraction or addition of conceptualizable features could transform our own experience into the bat's. Related points were made with respect to spatial perception, in the discussion of naive physics above. Since it is implausible to suppose that a creature's understanding of 'inside' is independent of its manipulative abilities, a kingfisher's perceptual experience of containment would differ from a chimp's. Similarly, no dog could perceive a bone to be *inside* a box in the way in which human adults can,

[5] G. E Hinton, in a talk given at Cognitive Studies Seminar, Sussex University, November 1981.

because a baby's sensorimotor understanding of spatial concepts is radically transformed (not merely added to) by learning of language.

This difficulty in understanding different subjectivities casts doubt on the possibility of a theoretical phenomenology, and *a fortiori* seems to dash any hopes of a systematic comparative psychology concerned with the experience of animals. But at the end of his paper Nagel hints at the possibility of an objective phenomenology. Its goal would be to describe (at least in part) the subjective character of experiences in a form comprehensible to beings incapable of having those particular experiences. Structural features of perception, he suggests, might be accessible to objective description even though qualitative aspects are not. Unfortunately, Nagel gives no examples of what might be meant by 'structural' features of phenomenology. Could AI ideas help to clarify these suggestive remarks?

Ullman's work is premised on the phenomenological fact that human beings can experience apparent movement in several different ways. From a subjective viewpoint, these differences do not seem to depend on linguistically-represented concepts, and moreover are of such a general character that it is implausible to ascribe them uniquely to human perceivers. That is, if a creature's phenomenology has any dimension comparable to visual experience as we know it, we can intelligibly ask whether (and when) distinctions such as these are perceived by it. We can ask, for instance, whether it enjoys any or all of the experiences, 'seeing the same thing moving', 'seeing one thing being replaced by another', 'seeing a thing of a particular shape', and 'seeing a thing being transformed into another'. Indeed, that such questions are intelligible is largely what is meant by saying that its phenomenology 'has a dimension comparable to visual experience as we know it'.

The relevance of Ullman's study is that he provides a theoretical account of differential (human) phenomenology that can be empirically investigated, and which if correct would explain how and why these distinct experiences arise when they do. This account is couched in computational terms, which are objective rather than subjective but which relate to what one might call the 'structure' of phenomenology. That is, phenomenological distinctions such as those just listed can be intelligibly related to hypothetical underlying computations (whether Ullman's hypotheses are correct is not of central interest here). Moreover, 'structural' relations between them can be clarified, by showing for instance that *this* computation is or is not a necessary prerequisite or accompaniment of *that* one. For example, Ullman's demonstration that computation of shape is not necessary for computation of identity gives theoretical support to the view that a creature might be able to experience identity without being able to recognize shape. So evidence (whether behavioural or biological) of a creature's ability or inability to perform certain computations could count as theoretical grounds for ascribing or denying experiences of certain types to it.

This is not to identify computation with consciousness. We know from the example of 'blindsight' that 'visual' computations can occur without any conscious phenomenology (Weiskrantz 1977). Nor can one escape the difficulty that Nagel ascribes to all 'reductive' theories of the mental, that their truth is logically compatible with the absence of any subjective aspect whatever. But Nagel himself is content to take for granted that other creatures do have experiences, and he does not require of an objective phenomenology that it provide a philosophical proof of this presupposition. Rather, he asks for what one might term a systematic study of the structural constraints of 'seeing-as', a study which would illuminate our own subjective life as well as enabling us to say something about the experiences of alien creatures.

Again, Nagel gives no examples to show what sort of study this might be. Possibly relevant are computationally-influenced investigations of visual imagery that have sought to explain introspectively obvious but intuitively mysterious facts about our visual experience. For example, it has been found that some striking perceptual differences in viewing a wire-frame cube (including, for example, the ease with which certain mental images can be formed of it) depend on which alternative structural description of the object is assigned to it by the perceiver (Hinton 1979). That is, an object seen as one sort of structure can be experienced (and imagined) in ways different from those made possible by seeing it as another sort of structure. This approach to visual perception illuminates the nature and generation of our own experiences, and could in principle provide theoretical grounds for saying that a bat, or a Martian, who applied a specific (objectively definable) structural description to an object would be more likely to experience a specific type of imagery accordingly.

In sum, computational ideas are in principle relevant to the psychology of animals, and to their phenomenology too. Counterintuitive though this may seem, AI might help us understand the perceptual experiences of kingfishers as well as kings.

REFERENCES

Boden, M.A. 1977. *Artificial Intelligence and Natural Man*. Hassocks and New York.

Collett, T.S. and Land, M.F. 1978. 'How Hoverflies Compute Interception Courses', *J. Comp. Physiology* 125, 191–204.

Dreyfus, H. L. 1972. *What Computers Can't Do: A Critique of Artificial Intelligence*. New York.

Funt, B. V. 1980. 'Problem Solving with Diagrammatic Representations', *Artificial Intelligence* 13, 201–30.

Gibson, J. J. 1950. *The Perception of the Visual World.* Boston.

Gibson, J. J. 1966. *The Senses Considered as Visual Systems.* Ithaca, NY.

Gibson, J. J. 1979. *The Ecological Approach to Visual Perception.* New York. Boston 281.

Griffin, D. R. 1978. 'Prospects for a Cognitive Ethology', *Behavioural and Brain Sciences* 1, 527–39.

Hayes, P. J. 1979. 'The Naive Physics Manifesto', in *Expert Systems in the Microelectonic Age* ed. D. Michie, 242–70. Edinburgh.

Heil, J. 1981. 'Does Cognitive Psychology Rest on a Mistake?, *Mind* 90, 321–42.

Hess, E. H. 1956. 'Space Perception in the Chick', *Scientific American* 195, 71–80.

Hinton, G. E. 1979. 'Some Demonstrations of the Effects of Structural Descriptions in Mental Imagery', *Cognitive Science* 3, 231–50.

Hinton, G. E. 1981. 'Shape Representation in Parallel Systems', in *Proceedings of the Seventh International Joint Conference on AI* 1088–96. Vancouver.

Kohler, I. 1962. 'Experiments with Goggles', *Scientific American* 206, 62.

McCarthy, J. and Hayes, P. J. 1969. 'Some Philosophical Problems from the Standpoint of Artificial Intelligence', in *Machine Intelligence* vol. 4, ed. B. Meltzer and D. Michie, 463–502. Edinburgh and New York.

Malcolm, N. 1971. 'The Myth of Cognitive Processes and Structures' in *Cognitive Development and Epistemology*, ed. T. Mischel, 385–92. New York.

Marr, D. 1976. 'Early Processing of Visual Information', *Phil. Trans. of the Royal Society* 275B, 483–524.

Marr, D. 1978. 'Representing Visual Information', in *Lectures on Mathematics in the Life Sciences* Vol. 10: *Some Mathematical Questions in Biology*, 101–80. Providence, RI.

Marr, D. 1979. 'Visual Information Processing: the Structure and Creation of Visual Representations', *Phil. Trans. of the Royal Society* 290B, 199–218.

Martin, M. 1973. 'Are Cognitive Processes and Structure a Myth?', *Analysis* 33, 83–8.

Miller, G. A. and Johnson-Laird, P. N. 1976. *Language and Perception.* Cambridge.

Minsky, M. L. and Papert, S. 1969. *Perceptrons: an Introduction to Computational Geometry.* Cambridge, Mass.

Nagel, T. 1974. 'What is it Like to be a Bat?' *Philosophical Review* 83, 435–51.

Premack, D. and Woodruff, G. 1978. 'Does the Chimpanzee have a Theory of Mind?', *Behavioural and Brain Sciences* 1, 515–27.

Rosenblatt, F. 1958. 'The Perceptron: A Probabilistic Model for Information Storage and Organization in the Brain', *Psych. Review* 65, 386–408.

Savage-Rumbaugh, E. S. *et al.* 1978. 'Linguistically Mediated Tool Use and Exchange by Chimpanzee', *Behavioural and Brain Sciences* 1, 539–54.

Sloman, A. 1978a. *The Computer Revolution in Philosophy.* Hassocks.

Sloman, A. 1978b. 'What about their Internal Languages?' in *Brain and Behavioural Sciences* 1, 602–3.

Sloman, A. 1979. 'The Primacy of Non-Communicative Language', in *The Analysis of Meaning*, ed. McCafferty and K. Gray, 1–15. London.

Sloman, A. 1980. 'What Kind of Indirect Process is Visual Perception', *Brain and Behavioural Sciences* 3, 401–40.

Stratton, G. M. 1896. 'Some Preliminary Experiments on Vision', *Psych. Review* 3, 611.

Stratton, G. M. 1897. 'Vision without Inversion of the Retinal Image', *Psych. Review* 4, 341.

von Uexkull, J. 1957 (Originally 1934). 'A Stroll Through the Worlds of Animals and Men', in *Instinctive Behaviour: the Development of a Modern Concept*, ed. C. H. Schiller, 5–82 New York.

Ullman, S. 1979a. *The Interpretation of Visual Motion*. New York.

Ullman, S. 1979b. 'The Interpretation of Structure', *Proc. Royal Society* B 203, 405–26.

Ullman, S. 1980. 'Against Direct Perception', *Brain and Behavioural Sciences* 3, 373–81.

Weiskrantz, L. 1979. 'Some Demonstrations of the Effects of Structural Descriptions in Mental Imagery', *Cognitive Science* 3, 231–50.

Index